Sister Wife

Sister Wife

A MEMOIR OF FAITH, FAMILY, AND FINDING FREEDOM

CHRISTINE BROWN WOOLLEY

G

Gallery Books

New York   Amsterdam/Antwerp   London
Toronto   Sydney/Melbourne   New Delhi

Gallery Books
An Imprint of Simon & Schuster, LLC
1230 Avenue of the Americas
New York, NY 10020

First Gallery Books hardcover edition September 2025

GALLERY BOOKS and colophon are registered trademarks of Simon & Schuster, LLC

Simon & Schuster strongly believes in freedom of expression and stands against censorship in all its forms. For more information, visit BooksBelong.com.

For information about special discounts for bulk purchases, please contact Simon & Schuster Special Sales at 1-866-506-1949 or business@simonandschuster.com.

The Simon & Schuster Speakers Bureau can bring authors to your live event. For more information or to book an event, contact the Simon & Schuster Speakers Bureau at 1-866-248-3049 or visit our website at www.simonspeakers.com.

Interior design by Jaime Putorti

Manufactured in the United States of America

10 9 8 7 6 5 4 3 2 1

Library of Congress Cataloging-in-Publication Data has been applied for.

ISBN 978-1-6680-7826-6
ISBN 978-1-6680-7828-0 (ebook)

To Dad, for being my hero: I'm still a daddy's girl.

To my mom, Annie, for helping me find my strength;

to my other mom, Susan, for the sagest advice I've ever heard.

For David, the love of my life. Gosh!! I love our life together so much.

You've helped me become stronger and recognize my value, and

you have brought so much fun and laughter into our lives while

helping me find a peaceful calm that I didn't know existed.

For the children I pushed out of my womb, as well as the children I've

gained through my family: my favorite thing is being your mom.

CONTENTS

Prologue xi

Daughter 1

Sister 31

Wife 85

Woman 209

Epilogue 289

Family Tree

KODY BROWN + MERI

Leon

KODY BROWN + JANELLE

Logan

Madison

Hunter

Garrison

Gabriel

Savanah

KODY BROWN + CHRISTINE

Aspyn

Mykelti

Paedon

Gwendlyn

Ysabel

Truely

KODY BROWN + ROBYN

Adopted by Kody from previous marriage:

Dayton

Aurora

Breanna

With Kody:

Solomon

Ariella

PROLOGUE

LOVE IS LOVE

*O*n sunny days like this one, it feels as if light touches every surface of the home I share with David and Truely. It's summer, so I've placed sunflowers and other bright bits of yellow throughout. Cheerful. Happy. It feels different from any place I've been before.

Truely bounds down the stairs, a towel wrapped around her shoulders, ready to head to the pool with a new friend. She's just made protein pancakes for the family, and spice fills the air. Cinnamon. Over breakfast, she and David grin and toss puns back and forth across the dining room table, with Truely whispering "Pray for me" when the dad jokes are too much.

It's perfect.

I'm gloriously happy, in a way that brings my shoulders to my ears in an involuntary self-hug and a satisfied smile to my face, which looks glowier even to me. Take that, menopause.

(Girl. We'll talk about that.)

David checks in throughout the day. *All good? Did you see this? I'm on my last job.* I had no idea a phone-alert chirp could leave me besotted.

I bustle through the house dealing with *Sister Wives* tasks—I honestly thought we were done with the show, but here's to season nineteen?—or hiding the breakables for a visit with the grandkids, or wrapping presents for another baby shower or wedding.

Sister Wives began just before Truely made her appearance in this life, and she was the first Baby Brown born to an audience. She's fifteen. That's a lot of years on camera, and yes, it changed us. It forced us to see, and confront, the ways we interacted with each other. We thought we were fine. We wanted the world to see what polygamy could look like, and I do believe we demonstrated that it wasn't what people envisioned. Our ethics were strong, and we raised our children with so much love.

And chaos. The children roamed through our homes depending on their snack needs or moods. Quiet time? Meri. Girl talk and makeup? Robyn. A place to relax without nagging? Janelle. One-on-one conversation, games, and hanging out? My house. No one got bored—someone was usually crafting or baking, and one of us always had time, even if it meant fewer moments to ourselves. We had seventy-five people at Thanksgiving one year, and untold hordes of people followed the kids home from school or practice for pool dates, movie nights, or homework. With twenty-three people in the household by the end, someone always had a birthday. Whenever I can, I invite it all back in.

I'm glad that love, down to all the sibling silliness, made it on film.

But the camera also shines a light. I saw the funny expression I make when I'm shocked. I decided my clothes were frumpy. And I realized I've spent years saying "It's fine" on repeat. It's fine because I'm angry and don't have the words for it. It's fine because it's not worth the effort to explain. It's fine, though I might be doing my best to hold the family together while feeling overwhelmed. It's fine because that's what I've been trained to be. Fine. Small. Not a bother.

I'm certain I come from a long line of women who have said "It's fine." The show forced me to see that it wasn't—and maybe recognize that my ancestors had figured it out, too. Strong women, all of them.

But was I in a cult?

Ahem. I can hear you.

If I was, I'm glad of it. I come from a family and a community filled with talent, nurturing, and love, and women who had the support and ability to make good decisions for themselves. I think of my grandfather as a hero because he pushed through his fear of outsiders after seeing his family torn apart to try to make our community safer. I'm glad I had the opportunity to do the same, even if I ultimately chose to leave that community.

I thought I had exactly what I wanted until I realized my husband had fallen in love. And then I realized I wanted some of that. I wanted to fall in love, to find my soulmate—an idea I hadn't believed possible until I saw it happen to Kody. But here's the funny thing about love: I couldn't find meaningful, deep, true, heart-skips-beats, secure love until I understood some of the wonderful things about myself.

You came here for a story, and I have a tale with every element, from an enchanted family cut off from the world, to four women trying to fit their toes into one glass slipper, to fathers disappearing in the night, to a perfectly ordinary man developing knighthood status after years of tending by his many wives, to a woman finally understanding that she deserved the fairy-tale ending she'd dreamed of before anyone taught her to believe any differently.

My favorite part of the story comes with a kiss so intense that every self-doubt I'd ever felt fled from my body, if only momentarily, and pulled me fully into a place where love *is* love.

DAUGHTER

Chapter One

IT FEELS BETTER

*U*ntil I was about five I was bald—I don't know why. So, I wore a towel as a wig as a little girl. I'd imagine my hair flowed down my back in the most brilliant shade of yellow. Sunny. Happy. Beautiful. My favorite was the lemon-colored one because I knew princesses had yellow hair, and my daddy called me princess. He still does.

I remember sitting in front of a mirror brushing my towel, and I remember it floating up and gently down behind me as I played on the swing set. It was hard to keep it on, especially on the swings, but I found ways to attach it to my head. Dad wondered why I was so into this towel, but that's just me. I chose, as a young girl, to be positive. Bald? Solution! Part of that was my upbringing: We didn't complain. That's typical of big families—you learn to deal because every boo-boo won't get a kiss, mom won't always see who pinched you, and siblings tease if you act like a baby. I could have moped and felt sorry for myself, or been a clown to get attention, or stewed and struck out in anger. Instead, I became a mediator, assessing everyone's emotions and working to keep things smooth.

I decided, and it was a decision, that I preferred to be cheerful and positive.

It feels better.

I remember being happy as a child and having fun. I played in the backyard all the time—playing, playing, playing. I loved makeup and dresses and dolls. That was my personality: having fun.

I would wait for my dad to come home from work every day, and he always made time for me, even after a full day. My normal looked an awful lot like most kids' normal spending their childhoods in the early 1970s, except for one thing.

By the time I was five, I'd gotten rid of the yellow towel and my hair was long enough for my mom to roll it in pink foam curlers when my dad married his second wife. I remember their wedding and the ringlets I wore with my pretty burgundy dress. I remember being excited because I liked her. My mom and I talked about whom I would marry—just being silly.

"Well, I'm going to marry my dad," I said.

"You can't marry your dad," she told me, smiling. That didn't make sense. My dad was my favorite person.

"Well, who am I gonna marry?" I asked, heartbroken.

She told me I would find a good man. I believed her. I knew so many good men. I was surrounded by adults who loved me and made me feel special, who held my hand, answered my questions, and showed me how to do what I wanted to do. I would find someone who would adore me just as they had, and whom I would adore back.

Everyone in my circle was kind, and I could go anywhere and feel safe. Someone's mom would inevitably include me with her kids for the day's activities, just as my mom did with my friends and cousins. We all believed the same things. We all knew the same people. We all worked toward the betterment of ourselves and our community. From the day I was born, I felt cocooned in love. That day, I weighed five pounds—I was premature. My grandpa Rulon delivered me—he was our midwife—and from that moment on, all I felt from him was love. I remember walking with him in the grass, holding his hand, and knowing that he was a kind, good, loving man.

I didn't yet know that Grandpa Rulon had to flee from the family when Dad was young, and that Dad didn't see him or many of his brothers and sisters for years. I didn't yet understand, at age five, that in our religion—a version of fundamentalist, polygamist Mormon—we had to be careful, that it was best to refer to children from another mother as cousins, to split up into smaller groups at the movie theater, and to not add Dad's name to school documents.

I didn't yet understand the darkness in our community, or in that of other communities like ours. I didn't yet know just how far apart we stood from everyone else, from presidential orders to attacks on compounds.

Grandpa Rulon was murdered when I was five. As usual, I sat on the porch one day waiting for my dad, and he got home early. I'm sure my first thought was that I would get to spend more time with him, but I remember that he looked so sad. I'm not sure I had ever seen him look like that before.

"Hey Dad," I said, "why are you home from work?"

"They killed your grandpa," he said, obviously in shock. Another fundamentalist church leader—a member of our family—had ordered his followers to kill my grandpa.

I don't remember a funeral or the days that followed, just that my dad was sad. I would hear the family's stories of trauma through the years, and they would become my own. But I would hold on to that feeling of being surrounded by love when I thought of Grandpa Rulon.

In a way, I would follow in his footsteps: he had tried to tell the world about our church to bring safety to our community.

But the threats to our group didn't always come from outside.

Chapter Two

THAT'S NOT US

*W*hen my parents decided to send us to public school, after years of homeschooling my older siblings and me, it felt like magic. More kids = more friends to play with. But instead of a new playground's worth of kids to bring out my inner extrovert, my personality shifted. I had been carefree. Nothing in my life was hard—everything had been good. But as the day grew closer, my parents sat all of us—my older brother, me, my sister, and my sister from my other mom—down in the living room. What followed was one of the most traumatizing conversations of my life. It didn't match up with anything I had learned to that point, and it terrified me.

"Look," they told us, "if the authorities find out your dad lives plural marriage, he's going to be thrown in jail, and you're never going to see him again."

Whoa. I was heading into third grade—I just wanted to play. My concept of jail was so vague: It didn't seem good, and I didn't understand what my dad had done wrong. I knew I didn't want to lose him.

Public school changed everything. I could no longer refer to Danielle as "my sister." I had to fudge relationships. Maybe my sister became my cousin when we were at school. I definitely couldn't say I had another mom, though today, I suppose if I said I had two moms, no one would think twice about it. But my other mom—my mom's sister wife—couldn't put my dad's name on her kids' birth certificates, so it looked as if the father was unknown. And my dad couldn't come to our school functions because it wasn't fair for him to come to my school plays but not attend Danielle's chorus concert because someone might figure out we had different mothers.

That's when I started to fear the outside world and everybody in it. Teachers would ask me questions, and I would freeze up. I developed a lisp. They brought me in for counseling for the lisp, but how could I speak properly if I couldn't speak my own truth?

At home, I focused on fun and youth activities at church. There, I was popular—I knew everybody. At public school, I didn't join any clubs. I didn't play sports. I had to live two lives. It was almost as if I had a split personality.

We learned a song in primary school: "My teacher told me I should never tell a lie, because a lie will bring you trouble by and by." And I'd think, *Except you do have to lie sometimes.*

People would ask what religion I was, and I was so afraid to answer that question. I was supposed to simply say I was Mormon, without mentioning the polygamist part, but what if they asked what ward I was in? The whole state of Utah is set up on a ward system. If you grew up anywhere else, it's bizarre, but in Utah, each neighborhood has its own ward, which is sort of a church. Wards are squat brick buildings, but there's no cross because Mormons don't understand why you would celebrate the vehicle by which Christ died. Mormons believe some of the same things about Christ that other Christians believe—that he performed miracles, that he's the son of God, that he died on the cross for our sins and was reborn. But they believe there was another prophet, Joseph Smith, and another holy book, *The Book of Mormon*. The LDS temple—the big white building with the angel on top—is for special occasions like weddings, but for everyday religious functions, Mormons go to their wards.

I just started telling people I was Christian but not Mormon. But then, when I was going into third grade, a kid asked me if I had been baptized. I was like, "What's baptized?" I didn't know how similar we were in our beliefs with mainstream Mormons, but I had no idea Mormons get baptized when they turn eight. Everything was a minefield, and I kept tripping myself up. This all meant I couldn't have friends because kids would ask questions. "How many brothers and sisters do you have?" Well, my mother had six children, and my other mother had five children—so ten, but five I can talk about.

I had a few friends through the years, but anytime we started to get close, I'd make sure they didn't find out anything real about me. I told two friends in high school about our beliefs, and we hung out at my house, so they met my family. But that was it—two friends in all of my school years.

I hated lying. I didn't like to act like I only had one mom when I had two and both meant so much to me. I couldn't bring attention to my dad. I wasn't allowed to talk about how wonderful he was.

None of it matched up with what I knew about my family and the people I loved, either.

But every family has stories.

I learned to balance and juggle. Being raised "with fear" rather than "in fear" seems like a small difference, but it means everything to a child. Being raised with fear meant that I knew who I was afraid of: the whole outside world. Being raised in fear meant that I was afraid of the people who took care of me, and I wasn't.

I know it sounds as if being sheltered was hard. I talk about it and people say, "That sounds like a cult." But it was the happiest, most cheerful thing I've ever experienced. I thought being in our church was awesome. We did everything together and had so much fun. There was no "hard." I didn't know any different.

At home, I felt secure, loved, and nurtured, but I was terrified of everything outside that bubble.

My dad had a seemingly perfect situation when he was a kid. His seven moms raised him with all his other siblings. It was like the *Andy Griffith Show* of polygamy—a small, idyllic community. But then the law figured out they lived plural marriage, and they threatened to arrest my grandpa Rulon. Grandpa's life story fascinates me: He grew up in Chihuahua, Mexico, in a polygamous family in the early 1900s. But when he was a teenager, he was part of the mainstream LDS church—I'll use "Mormon," "LDS," and sometimes "Saints" to refer to the Church of Jesus Christ of Latter-day Saints— and even married a woman in the temple in downtown Salt Lake City. He moved to California, where he worked as a chiropractor and naturopath. In the meantime, his dad, my great-grandpa, wrote a book defending polygamy—Grandpa wrote him letters begging him to stop practicing it and to come back to the mainstream fold. Apparently, Great-Grandpa won the argument because Grandpa Rulon then tried to convert his wife to polygamy. They divorced in 1935. The LDS church excommunicated Grandpa, which meant he was removed from the church rolls, and his temple marriage no longer held.

This isn't as unusual as it sounds, at least in Utah. I promise to make this quick: In about 1830, Joseph Smith founded the LDS church. By the time he died in 1844, he had as many as forty wives, according to the church. Our next LDS church leader, Brigham Young, married fifty-six women. We were taught it was a way to convert more people and grow the church through lots of children, though others have argued it was a way to build a patriarchal society and exalt virility.

Joseph Smith was killed by a mob while awaiting trial on charges of inciting a riot in Illinois after he ordered a printing press destroyed. Then, the Mormons headed to Utah. But Utah also wanted to be part of the growing United States—and things weren't getting any easier for the Church of Jesus Christ of Latter-day Saints. In 1858, President James Buchanan sent in federal troops to "quell the Mormon rebellion," by which he meant polygamy.

While polygamy wasn't unusual in Utah at the time, the rest of the world wasn't having it, and Utah wouldn't be allowed to join the Union until they stopped with the multiple-wives bit.

In 1890, church president and prophet Wilford Woodruff, who had ten wives himself, issued a manifesto denouncing polygamy after receiving a message from "the Lord."

Some polygamist Mormons thought that was all a bit too convenient: The United States makes polygamy illegal. Utah wants to become a state. The prophet receives a revelation that polygamy is wrong.

So, many Mormons continued the practice in secret because they had been taught, until that point, that God wanted them to be polygamists and that they couldn't earn their true place in heaven without the practice.

All of which brings us to today. There are several sects of fundamentalist polygamist Mormons. The fundamentalists you've undoubtedly heard of often live in extreme poverty—with the moms and their families getting government subsidies, wearing clothing straight out of *Little House on the Prairie*, and having a history of abuse and incest. The Kingstons made the news after a 1999 court case in which a teenage girl who didn't want to be her uncle's fifteenth spiritual wife went to the police because she wanted to finish high school. This led to David Ortell Kingston spending four years in jail after being found guilty of having sex with his sixteen-year-old niece. And Warren Jeffs is in jail for life for sexually assaulting a twelve-year-old girl and a fifteen-year-old girl he had claimed as spiritual brides.

That's not us. Grandpa Rulon led the Apostolic United Brethren beginning in 1954. We call it "The Work" or "The Group." We believe the Latter-day Saints generally have it right, with a few differences—the lack-of-polygamy part being the biggest.

Grandpa married sixteen women—many of my grandmas lived near us—and had forty-eight children, including my dad. Grandpa was well loved in our community and considered a great healer.

But every few years, the law would come after Grandpa for being a polygamist. When my dad was a kid in 1955, Grandpa learned from one of his patients that he was going to be arrested. Polygamy was a federal crime, and he could have gone to jail for a long time. Instead, in the middle of the night, Grandpa's wives disappeared with their children. My dad didn't see his father again for years, and they never again lived together as a family.

This story taught me that the outside world was a threat.

Grandpa Rulon saw a lot in his travels, and he's one of the reasons our sect is different. We're considered the "liberal polygamists" because we don't believe sex should be purely for procreation, but also because we engage with our local communities and tend to be more upfront with law enforcement in the hope that communication will bring understanding, which will bring safety.

My kids have always known they can be polygamous—or not— just as I did, growing up. It was also important to our group that people know we don't abuse children. Owen Allred, Grandpa's brother, even fought for Utah's legal marriage age to be raised from fourteen to sixteen, and he often spoke out against abuse.

But our family also encountered the dark sides of polygamy.

My mom's mom, Grandma Anna, married Floren LeBaron soon after meeting him. Floren founded, with two of his brothers, the Church of the Firstborn of the Fulness of Times, which was headquartered down in Chihuahua, Mexico, on property they called Colonia LeBarón. My grandpa Rulon spent some time down there, too, because the LeBarons had been associated with the Apostolic United Brethren, our group. Floren and Grandma Anna had two kids, Don and my mom, Annie, who was born in 1951.

It didn't last. Grandma Anna had moved to Mexico to try to make it work but ended up leaving Floren when my mom was two.

At some point, the LeBarons asked Grandpa Rulon to join their group, but he turned them down. Floren's brother Ervil eventually started his own group, the Church of the First Born of the Lamb of God, after a power struggle with his brothers. Then, Ervil "prophesized" that his brother Joel would be put to death. In 1972, one of Ervil's followers shot Joel in the head.

Ervil was also angry that Grandpa Rulon wouldn't bow down to him. Grandpa said he—Grandpa—was God's mouthpiece, but that's what my church believes about their leaders. This may feel familiar to some of you because that's what members of the mainstream Mormon Church believe about their leader, too. Russell Nelson isn't just the president of the LDS church; he's the prophet and is believed to receive revelations from God.

But Ervil's followers talked about "blood atonement"—which is basically the idea that some sins are so bad they can only be remedied through death. In Ervil's mind, Grandpa was a false prophet.

So Ervil sent his wives to kill my grandpa.

I still have a hard time comprehending this, especially when I think of all the sadness that came from that day.

In 1977, Ervil LeBaron ordered two of his wives, Rena Chynoweth and Ramona Marston, to shoot my grandpa. They killed him at his chiropractic clinic in Murray, just outside Salt Lake City. More than two thousand people went to Grandpa's funeral.

Rena, who pulled the trigger, was acquitted. No one cared much about the death of a polygamist, and that it had been a woman who had done the deed seemed unfathomable.

But Ervil was ultimately found guilty of ordering Grandpa's murder. He died in prison—killed by the other prisoners, I was always told. Officially, it was a suicide. According to *The New York Times*, he either overdosed or "punched himself in the throat." All the blood vessels in his neck had hemorrhaged. You'll also see that he died of heart failure or a seizure.

In any case, he's dead.

My mom doesn't talk about her childhood or past in general, so I only recently asked her about Colonia LeBarón. She told me she had never lived there, even as a toddler. I never met Ervil or his wives.

My mom didn't meet Floren, her birth dad, in a real sense until she was about thirty. Then my mom, me, and some of my siblings spent six weeks at Colonia LeBarón. We went down again a year later for a wedding. David—my future husband—was at that wedding, too, but I don't remember meeting him.

Grandpa Owen, who my grandmother married after she left Floren—yes, he was my great-uncle, too—took over our church when his brother was murdered, and he continued Grandpa Rulon's mission to tell the world about us. Grandpa Owen even invited state officials in to interview members of our group, without prior notice, to make sure child and domestic abuse were not part of our culture. For my grandpa Owen to go public was huge—and brave.

There are now a few thousand of us, mostly in Utah and Wyoming.

I say "us" as in, "That's how I grew up. That's who I was with Kody. That was my religion when I believed it was the best way to have a big family."

Now, I suppose I could say "them."

Chapter Three

I BELIEVED THE
WORLD WOULD END

I recently told my sister wife Janelle's daughter Savanah that I love the smell of Pine-Sol.

"Did you clean a lot as a kid?" she asked. "That's probably why you like the smell of Pine-Sol."

"What?" I said. "That's ridiculous."

We cleaned all the time. Both my moms are German. If I was sick, I preferred to not stay home because it wasn't restful. I couldn't just go to bed. Windows open! Fresh air will cure you! While you're here, you may as well dust the living room—a little bit of exercise will do you good! I remember faking that I was well so that I could go to school and get some rest.

We had no clutter—my friends say they remember me cleaning constantly. We woke up early to do chores before school. After school, I couldn't go play until we cleaned the house and did our homework, which meant I didn't have time most nights to play with my friends.

I don't know why our house was so messy.

We finally got our moms to let us clean extra on Friday nights so we could wake up early on Saturday and watch cartoons—and so we could spend time with Dad. He worked in sales at a car dealership and left the house before we woke in the morning. But on the weekends, he was ours. From sunup Saturday morning through Sunday night, we got to play with Dad.

But first, spotless. We're talking we cleaned between the slats in closet doors with a rag wrapped around a knife. Our moms were creative about their torture.

Despite the maniacal cleaning mandates, my mom was my best friend. Growing up, Mom often made bread, and when she opened the windows, that wonderfully yeasty smell would permeate the street. It was an invitation for the neighborhood, but it was also the smell of home for me, of conversations over countertops about whatever was inside my head. I had a lot of questions, but her chocolate chip cookies with the perfect amount of crispiness on the outside and gooeyness inside helped. And even with eleven kids running around, Mom exuded a cool vibe, so my house was the "party house." We could hang out there without constantly worrying about the rules.

In fact, Mom loved to bend the rules, especially to accommodate joy. Our fundamentalist church opposed everything from pierced ears to Christmas—some people didn't even celebrate birthdays.

"That's ridiculous," Mom would say.

My grandpa's wives, many of whom lived within sight, followed the rules about holidays more strictly than my mom. We grew up in Taylorsville, which is a suburb of Salt Lake City. It's parks, shopping centers, and highways, just like any other metropolitan area. But it's also a Mormon metropolitan area. In Utah, the Saints have developed their own culture—from green Jell-O to red punch to saying "Oh my heck!" to celebrating Pioneer Day—and Halloween is considered good family fun, so people go all out. Monsters, cobwebs, and pumpkins line every sidewalk, and hordes of children (Mormons have a lot of children) trick-or-treat in the Latter-day Saint wards, where everybody knows everybody, and there's no fear of razor-blade-laced apples. Or apples, because handing out apples for Halloween is rubbish. Unless they have caramel on them. In any case, we felt like we were missing out by not celebrating all the holidays.

But one Halloween morning, when we came down for breakfast, we found both our moms sporting green faces and pitch-black hats. They served our orange juice with dry ice in a cauldron, they made us green pancakes, and they cackled and laughed all the way through it. It's one of my favorite memories as a kid.

I adored having two moms. If I felt frustrated by my mom, I could go to my other mom, and she would listen to me gripe while encouraging me to think about something from a different angle. Because she wasn't the mom I was miffed at, I could usually hear what she had to say. When I was fifteen, I even traveled to Europe for six weeks with my other mom, spending time in Belgium, France, Switzerland, and Austria, as well as four weeks in Germany with family.

For a bit, my other mom lived in the other half of our duplex, so only a wall stood between us. At some point, my mom moved across the lawn into another house, and my grandpa lived in another little house in the same area with a couple of his wives. I had aunts and uncles all over the place. We used to call it "the compound," but only among ourselves. I don't think outsiders would have appreciated that bit of dark humor, but my family was fun—and funny.

While I questioned the things that scared me, I didn't question plural marriage or our faith. Mom believed we needed to be good people—that's all. She probably wouldn't say it this way, but don't be a jackass. She believed no one religion was better in God's eyes than any other, which went against our church's—and most churches'—teachings. As far as I could tell, she believed in our faith, but she was also a bit of a feminist. I think my grandma may have been, too, which is not unusual in polygamy. I come from a long line of divorces, which to me says more about freedom and strong women than it does about dysfunction, though we certainly had our share of that. They would have been surrounded by other strong women growing up.

In our church, we marry whom we want, and there are no underage marriages. We don't marry our relatives, though distant cousins sometimes come into the mix. No one forces us to marry old men or widowers with ten children.

My mom took that freedom a step further: she didn't automatically take church leaders at their word.

"Why don't we look at them as individual men?" she asked. "How do they run their families? What kind of dads are they?" We looked at families that ran well and talked about why.

I knew it also angered her that women couldn't hold the priesthood—just as they can't in the mainstream LDS church. Only men—well, and boys—can act in God's name, according to our faith.

While Mom worked to teach me the critical thinking skills that might help should I ever leave the confines of our conservative culture, she couldn't always protect me from the lessons of our church.

I believed the world was going to end when I turned fifteen.

This went far beyond the typical concerns of a kid growing up in the 1980s: the wall still stood in Berlin, a mysterious virus was killing young men, Russia was gonna nuke us, and Sting hoped they loved their children too—but none of this concerned me.

Three ladies in our church led our Sunday school and youth classes, and they filled us with terrifying lessons about the end of the world.

It would end during the fifteenth year of my life. They were specific about it. We were told we didn't need to worry about college because who needs an education for the end-times. Somehow, it was still important that we planned on marriage and babies. Good girls were pious and none of us wanted to be left behind. It sounded terrible: wars, plagues, locusts. We all knew that Mormon crickets don't mess around. We needed to purify ourselves—there was no time for AP History.

They taught us that we needed to meet Christ before we died. It made no sense to me. *You know what this is? Rubbish. I'm not even going to think about this. Life is stressful enough without worrying about locusts.* But it added another fear factor to my life. Even as I tried to reason my way out of it, I worried I would be found lacking and that I would burn in hell, and that it would all happen before my first kiss.

I felt like I was a bad person—and I wasn't. I was so wholesome, looking back. Even if I hadn't been wholesome, I was just a kid. What God sends children to hell? End days felt pretty judgmental, which Mom and Dad taught me was wrong. If I did make it to heaven—or the Celestial Kingdom—in the first wave, what would happen to everybody else? Is that love? Good luck with the plague!

"Dad," I said one evening, "I think the world's going to end when I'm fifteen."

"What are you talking about?" he asked.

"Well, that's what I'm learning at church."

I told him I didn't want him to pay for my college. It would be an awful waste of the money he wasn't going to be able to use, anyway.

"For goodness' sake!" I cried. "There's no point if the world's going to end!"

I'm sure he stared at me as if the angel Moroni were making chocolate chip cookies on my forehead.

"Oh honey," he said. "That's not true. The world isn't ending."

That wasn't all.

"You can't live your life in fear, and you're going to college," he said.

While my friends planned for the future by avoiding it or planning their weddings, my sisters all earned an education.

I trusted my dad. His advice has always been good: He believes you should never burn a bridge. You should always maintain good relationships with people. When you get a wedding invitation, you go. When there's a funeral, you go. He speaks softly, has no ego, and loves people.

And, like the rest of my childhood, he's a walking dichotomy. Dad reads Revelation, which is terrifying, and he believes it, but he didn't want me to worry about the world ending amid trumpet blasts and fouled rivers and robes dipped in blood for my fifteenth birthday.

"Look, you just gotta prepare yourself, live your best life," he told me. "You just have to believe in Jesus. You need to treat people like you would want them to treat you—like Jesus treated people— and then you're gonna be fine."

I had so much to learn.

In the meantime, the church ladies didn't stop preaching that I should prepare for the eternal flames of hell.

Finally, I told my mom. She freaked out. She made a couple of phone calls, and the ladies disappeared from our Sunday school classes. Polygamy PTA.

The church leaders themselves continued to teach end-times from the pulpit.

I didn't know what was real.

Chapter Four

NO GIRL WANTS
A STORY LIKE THAT

*S*poiler alert: The world didn't end on my fifteenth birthday.

But in my mind, it ended soon after I turned eighteen.

Kody Brown, who is four years older than I, entered our church like a storm. He converted to our faith; his parents became involved with my church while Kody served his two-year Mormon mission in San Antonio. The more he talked with his parents and spent time with the leaders of our church, the more he felt called to leave the mainstream LDS church and join ours. Soon after, he married Meri, who grew up in a polygamous family.

On our end, everybody in our church liked him immediately. He led our youth-group activities, such as hiking and camping, and he could speak about the teachings of our religion in a compelling way. And he was cute, with electric-blue eyes and perfect blond eighties hair.

My sister went on a survival trek with the church, and she said her group referred to Meri and Kody as "Ma" and "Pa."

"You have to meet Kody!" my sister enthused.

She was right: When I met him at church, we hit it off instantly. I had never met anyone like him, and I loved that he was outgoing, adventurous, and funny. Dynamic. I don't toss that word around often, but it suited him.

At around the same time, I struck out on my own. At age eighteen, I started community college and moved into an apartment with two roommates. That didn't work out as well as I had hoped. We were all church girls, with one being a cousin and the other probably also being a cousin because the family tree in a polygamous church is more of a weeping willow than an oak—everybody's related through a mom or a second mom. The new apartment was close to home, so I could hang out with my family, but I still felt independent.

Almost.

One of my roommates insisted on knowing where I was at all times. "You need to check in," she said. "Let us know where you are."

Nope.

"I won't be doing that," I remember saying. "I don't want to check in."

We spent most of our time together, anyway. When I wasn't with them, I was with people from my church or my parents. It's not like I was meeting strange men on the internet.

(That would come much later.)

Within a few months, it became too controlling, so I moved out. I moved back in with my family for a bit, and then I moved into an apartment with a girlfriend from our church, which I loved. We were in choir, and we were in plays together, and it seemed like we headed to the church building for an activity almost every night. She was much more popular than I was, so she always had something going. Sometimes, I told her I needed to stay home to study just to have time to be on my own—even though I loved hanging out with her.

While I was in college, I took a public speaking class, and it changed my personality completely. I loved telling stories or explaining how things worked, and I enjoyed the challenge of engaging people through a joke or a shocking statement.

I became outgoing, built friendships, even went to parties. I still didn't get close to anybody, but I had a blast, and that year of self-esteem led directly to *Sister Wives*.

My roommate knew Kody and liked him. My mom knew Meri because she had been in kindergarten with my brother Phil and had been to the house. I was close with both Kody and Meri because of our youth-group activities.

They moved to Wyoming, where Kody's family lived, but I kept in touch, often talking with Kody on the phone, especially after my world crashed in a way that hadn't been predicted by church leadership.

My mom left my dad when I was nineteen. That shook me hard because I didn't know she wasn't happy. She was done with religion, and she didn't love my dad. I hadn't seen anything but an adorable, loving relationship, but if I had been paying attention to the lessons she taught us as children, I would have understood the signs had been there for much of my life.

When she left my dad, she also left the church.

Before she left, she taught us the Book of Mormon was an incredible book, and Captain Moroni served as an example of everything I wanted in a husband: He was brave, strong, and a leader. He held a banner of liberty and motivated his army to serve for justice. I loved that guy.

While Mom taught us that ours wasn't the only religion, she also said it was the only right religion for us.

"This is what you were born into, so this is what God meant for you," she would say.

This was the rock my life had been built on. When she left, I realized it must all have been lies.

And I still lived with her. In our religion, it's hard to know what to do with people who leave—maybe it's like that with every religion. If I sought to live in the Celestial Kingdom, would she be there? She started dating a man named Wayne, and I felt angry at her for dating right away—and I didn't know what to do with her in a relationship with someone besides my dad. I didn't trust her, and I didn't like her, this woman who had taught me to love everyone and who had ensured my childhood had been safe and fun. I moved back in with my dad, and I tried to figure myself out.

I rebelled by becoming more religious. My other mom, Aunt Susan, is more proper, and I emulated that. I trusted her. I became more involved with the church, and I developed strong ideas about chastity. That would play out awkwardly on my wedding day.

I called Kody and told him about the divorce. "What are you going to do?" he asked. I told him I was struggling. I was devastated, just spinning and wondering about my religion and why I hadn't seen any sign of trouble.

He was supportive and kind.

"I think you need to spend some time figuring out what you want for your future," he told me. "Whether you want to stay in the church, whether you want to go with your mom—you need to make that decision."

I knew Kody was a good person and a good man. I loved his charisma and his maverick attitude—this idea that he didn't have to do things the same way everyone else did them. He wasn't afraid of anything, and he did what he thought was right, rather than what the priesthood leaders thought he should do. He tried to think things through on his own, rather than taking someone else's word as gospel. As he helped me through my parents' divorce, I watched his relationship with Meri, and I thought he would be a good husband.

When I thought about how he had been with our youth group, I knew he would be a great dad. He was easy to fall in love with.

But one day, Kody called me and said, "I'm getting married again. It's Janelle."

"Wait. Who?"

Janelle and I had been at some of the same parties, but we had never met.

The news bummed me out, both because I thought Kody, Meri, and I were friends, and they hadn't told me—though it's not unusual for these things to happen quickly in our community—and because I was crushing on Kody.

But it didn't break my heart. If he took a third, it could be me. I didn't want to be a second wife because then I'd put a wedge in an established relationship. I'd known since I was seventeen that I wanted to be a third wife, because the family would have worked through all the kinks as they brought in the second wife.

What could go wrong?

I thought I would have two sister wives who would become my best friends or at least would help me become a better person.

In church, we learned we could be monogamous, but that it would be so much better to live plural marriage. And, because we had been born into that church, we had an opportunity that most people didn't get: we would be exalted in heaven for living by God's true intentions our whole lives.

When you live plural marriage, you get to live in the Celestial Kingdom and be with God and Jesus for eternity. Who wouldn't want that?

I would also live with my husband and sister wives for all eternity—them and my ten siblings and my dad and my two moms.

That hadn't worked out, with Mom leaving Dad, but everything else would surely fall in line with my version of God's plan.

As it turns out, falling in love with someone who already has two wives is complicated.

We couldn't date. In polygamy, it's not cool to date a married man . . . because he's married. From the outside, I'm sure it doesn't make sense, but we saw marriage as sacred, and you don't want to disrespect that sacred relationship by flirting with another woman. It's inappropriate—just as it would be in a monogamous relationship. Not only would Meri and Janelle need to approve of our courtship, Kody would have to get permission from my father and the church. He couldn't do any of that until I instigated it. Typically, a woman lets her dad know she's interested, and then he makes inquiries. But Kody and I had been hanging out as friends for about three years.

When I was twenty-one and Kody was twenty-five, I said, "Of all the guys I know, I would just as soon marry you." Subtle, huh?

He took it as a proposal.

He talked with my dad, who adored Kody. If my dad would have arranged my marriage, he would have picked Kody, he told me. I thought my mom was excited, too—Kody could be so charming.

I, of course, knew Meri, but I didn't meet Janelle until just before we went to talk with the church leaders, aka my grandpa and his brethren. She was so sweet about the whole thing. The church leaders approved, and we moved forward with our three-month courtship, which was an awful lot like it had been hanging out for three years. I wanted to remain chaste, and for me, that meant no kissing until we were married.

One evening, Kody asked me to sit on my mom's couch. My sisters ran amok as he came in with the romantic proposal.

"I guess I should ask if you'd marry me," he said.

Be still my heart.

"Yes," I said. "I'll marry you."

At the time, it was all I thought I needed. There's no point wishing for anything different because I did what I felt was right.

Still. Even though he'd proposed to two other women, I expected something—moonlight? Snow? A ring? Something.

"No girl wants a story like that," I told him.

Soon after, on a pretty night, Kody looked at the moon.

"This is a better setting," he said, before asking me again if I would marry him. I smiled and said yes.

He had a claddagh ring for me.

And I had a better story.

SISTER

Chapter Five

WHY ARE YOU HERE?

*P*iety can lead to bad choices. I'll bet no one told you that growing up. I had one opportunity to feel like a bride: the dress. But it had about as much flair as a sack—and covered more skin. Mom sewed it beautifully, and it was exactly what I wanted: I knew I couldn't appear anything other than modest or I might upset the other wives, who undoubtedly didn't want any hint of what would happen when the dress came off.

(We'll get to the polygamy PJs. They make special Mormon underpants seem sexy.)

Though Mom made the dress, and lovingly so, she and I still felt uncomfortable together. That I had so thoroughly embraced our faith and intended to marry a man who lived plural marriage so soon after she had said she didn't believe any of it made it especially awkward. Still, Mom seemed excited for me to marry Kody because she knew I loved him.

I wish I had felt comfortable enough to ask her for advice—to ask her about her wedding. Had my second mom's wedding, with its pretty burgundy dresses, been awkward? Had they worked together to plan it? How did she make sure my mom was okay? Or did she? Did my mom work to make it less awkward for my second mom?

Like most brides, I was so eager and excited and full of my own ideas that I probably didn't think to ask how I could make it lovely and inclusive. I also believed feeling like a bride would be inappropriate. I got so caught up in my piety that I couldn't relax and let the day be special for anyone.

I couldn't do anything romantic because Kody's wives would be at the wedding. I couldn't be sexy. I couldn't make eyes at my fiancé. I couldn't hold Kody's hand or whisper in his ear over cake.

My piety may even have ruined my chances of finding true love.

I worked at an auto dealership at the time, and I remember telling my coworkers that I refused to kiss Kody until our wedding had been blessed at the altar. I believed there was romance in that. But that belief came from old-fashioned, puritanical control that had been written into Victorian novels and embedded into my brain. Somehow, I had diminished the importance of intimacy and passion while embracing a burlap dress and a chaste first kiss in front of witnesses, my dad, and my sister wives. My coworkers detected a problem.

"Wait?" they said. "You're gonna go from a kiss to sex on the same day?"

"Yeah!" I said, grinning. "It's fine!"

Fine.

That was a difficult moment. My coworkers' response gnawed at me, but I figured that, like all other good women living plural marriage, Kody and I would build our love over time, beginning with a friendship based in trust.

I trusted that he wanted to marry me.

But as my sister and I planned the wedding, Kody wasn't interested. After looking at venues and tasting cakes and picking dress patterns, I was super excited about having a low-key dinner on a riverboat after our tiny ceremony.

"Just do whatever you want to do," Kody told me. "I'm too busy."

I wish I had included Meri and Janelle in my wedding. It might have been fun, and it could have been a good way to build a strong relationship before I suddenly showed up in the third bedroom of their small house in Wyoming. I could have asked them about their own weddings and what had been fun for them, but I worried about upsetting them—even though they had also chosen me to come into their family.

I didn't do anything to let them know how thrilled I was to have them as sister wives, and that set the tone for an awkward day, and problems to come.

We are taught to believe that being strong enough to watch your husband marry another woman is why polygamy makes us better people. Anyone who can push down the jealousy that inevitably arises has done some work on herself.

But damn.

The big day arrived—but not quite as the five-year-old in the yellow towel imagined. We got married in my dad's living room. It made the most sense for religious reasons.

I would be marrying Kody for eternity. I would be joined with Meri and Janelle. I would be the third wife, just as I had always dreamed, and I would be living God's principle.

When I thought about kissing Kody, I felt all the butterflies a young woman who had never been kissed should feel. I felt nervous and in love.

I remember Kody opening the door and looking at me in my shroud-like dress. I remember realizing he was stressed out on our wedding day. I remember understanding he wasn't as excited to marry me as I was to marry him.

Kody had a thousand-yard stare.

My God, I thought. *What are we doing?*

I won't go into the ceremony. It's sacred for those who practice polygamy. But I will tell you my grandpa married us, and that my grandpa was the one who said, "You may now kiss the bride."

In spite of what I had seen on Kody's face, I still imagined the kiss would be magical and it would seal us. It would be our first spark of intimacy.

Kody gave me a peck, barely brushing my lips.

You know how people like to clap after that kiss at the altar?

Silence.

"Wow," my grandpa said. "That was the quickest first kiss I've ever seen."

After that, I lost count of the awkward moments. I don't even understand why—I wasn't the first woman to marry into polygamy. Shouldn't there be a playbook? Someone to say, "Listen. Let's set you up for success cuz this is gonna be rough."

We did pictures after the ceremony. How do you pose one man with three women? And of course, I wanted pictures of my new husband and me, but would that be offensive? Would Meri and Janelle be angry? I didn't know them well enough to know, and I didn't know anything well enough to ask. We did do the traditional photos, but I felt uncomfortable—not flirty. Not beautiful. Certainly not sexy.

I didn't feel like a bride.

Things just got worse after we arrived at our riverboat reception. My sister made me a beautiful bouquet, but I understood that if I tossed it, it would cause friction, so I didn't. It didn't matter. Meri and Janelle did not seem happy. Dinner was quiet. We all sat at one table—no separate bride-and-groom table—because I wanted Meri and Janelle to be there. But yeah, awkward.

They know, I thought. *They know what we'll be doing later tonight.*

At the time, I couldn't imagine what that would feel like. I knew the basics of what would happen, but even though Kody and I had been friends for a few years, we exchanged no excited, silly banter on our wedding night.

I still figured things would get better.

When we got in the car to head off on our honeymoon, Kody still seemed morose.

"Where are we going to go?" I asked. I figured this would be the moment when he could show me he'd put some thought into it—that he wanted to make me feel special.

"Well," he said, "I don't know. What do you want to do?"

"You didn't plan anything?" I asked, flabbergasted. I thought the groom was supposed to plan the honeymoon.

No.

"So, where are we going to stay tonight?"

"I don't know," he said. "I figured we'd just take it as it comes."

I felt as if he'd punched me in the gut. *Have you not thought about marrying me at all?*

He told me he had been too busy. He had two wives at home, and Janelle was expecting a baby. The evening remained awkward.

In my original draft, I skipped from "The evening remained awkward" to "The day after the wedding . . ." without going into the in-between. I had a couple of women who are close to me read this, including one who lives polygamy, and they both said, "You have to tell it."

But it's so painful. Looking back, I thought it would be the best night of my life—magic. We stayed in a motel shaped like a castle near Ogden, Utah.

"You like fairy tales, right?" I remember Kody saying. I still had high hopes.

I knew Kody already had some experience, so I thought I would be safe with him, that he would be careful not to hurt me. I wasn't completely clueless, and I trusted him. I also thought, because he had some experience, that it would be, you know.

Good.

Oh my gosh my cheeks are burning.

It hurt like crazy, and I cried.

"I'm so sorry," he said, as I recall. But it hurt because there was no foreplay. There was no anything. It was my very first time after having my very first kiss at the altar, and he was experienced so he should have known.

"I've been looking forward to this for so long," I said, crying from the pain.

I envisioned handholding, moonlight, gentle touches. I imagined feeling beautiful and adored. I imagined a loving acknowledgment of our eternal life together.

For the rest of our honeymoon, I was too sore for us to try again.

The day after the wedding, Kody needed to return his rented tux, and then we went to my mom's house so she could wash and store my dress. My sister was there.

"What are you doing here?" she asked.

"We're on our honeymoon," I said.

"But why are you here? You're on your honeymoon. Go. Just leave."

We dropped everything off, and then we started to drive. We hit random hotels and saw some neat things. It was a great car trip.

I didn't know anything else, and it was romantic enough for me.

I figured things would get better.

Chapter Six

I ASSOCIATED THEM WITH PAIN

$\mathcal{S}$ ister wives aren't supposed to have any special privileges based on order of marriage, but some things are automatic, and those things can cause friction. Because Meri was the first wife, she'd had the easiest wedding. Big dress, big cake, dancing, photos that don't include extra wives. Legally, Meri and Kody were a couple. She could talk about him at work and take him to work events as her husband, and he could do the same.

They had established themselves as a couple. They dated as monogamists, and during that time, they could openly kiss and laugh and snuggle. Meri could even get crazy with a tight sweater when it was just the two of them. I had known them in those early days, and I had no doubt they were in love: he looked at her like he adored her. We all saw them as a perfect, fun couple.

I can't imagine what it was like for Meri when Janelle married Kody three years later—or what it was like for Janelle to move into that situation. In our first book, *Becoming Sister Wives*, Janelle wrote about how she would sit in a chair in the living room while Kody and Meri sat together on the couch holding hands under a blanket.

Janelle wrote that she felt like an imposter.

And then, about a year after Janelle married Kody, I showed up in their three-bedroom trailer in Wyoming.

That was never going to end well.

I believed Meri and Janelle would be settled in, so I would simply have two new women in my life and we would all support each other. Janelle and Meri both worked—Janelle for the state government and Meri at an engraving shop—and I planned to look for a job immediately. In my mind, we would basically be roommates, especially since Kody traveled much of the time for his job selling religious products and there weren't any children yet.

Right, so I didn't know, when I married Kody, that Janelle and Meri didn't get along.

Almost immediately, I felt like the middle woman between them, trying to keep the peace and bouncing around. That's probably how Kody felt, too—like he was a ping-pong ball that got whacked as he tried to figure out how to be married to three women, two of whom didn't like to be in the same room together.

I think both Meri and Janelle hoped I could relieve some pressure, and while the wedding wasn't the best start, I do think I helped. Meri and I were already friends, and I got along with Janelle as well. Kody used to say I added equilibrium. We were young, and a lot of it was just nonsense, so it wasn't hard to choose to be positive—to keep trying to add fun.

But Meri was so judgmental of everything Janelle did, I thought. I remember thinking, *What does it matter what kind of pancakes she likes? Who cares?* And Janelle was so independent that she'd just be like, "I'm done," and she'd disappear, which wasn't easy in a three-bedroom trailer. I thought Janelle could be controlling, too—especially when she had a project she wanted help with. Some of our behavior in those early days was personality, some of it situation, and some of it youth.

I got along with Meri better, but only because Janelle tends to be quiet and shy, and we didn't have as much in common. We did things together, like gardening, but it was more out of necessity for the family. We didn't have a ton of money, so we canned food together. I would help with whatever projects Janelle took on. Don't get me wrong: Janelle is lovely and easy to get along with. She's the nicest out of all of us—she's truly kind.

I wish I had understood earlier how close we could be.

Kody and Meri fought all the time, even if we were hanging out, just chatting. Meri remembers it differently from how I do, but I remember it being volcanic.

I think they were in love, just rocky. She got mad about everything, and I didn't understand why. I think she always doubted where she stood with Kody—and I don't think bringing in two more wives helped. It was the weirdest dynamic because Kody loved how Meri managed things—from keeping house to raising children—so that gave her more clout in the day-to-day running of the household, but then they always fought. Jealousy was tough for all of us, but I think it was especially hard for Meri at first because she'd been the only wife for a while.

While I could manage my relationships with Meri and Janelle, I felt like I didn't know Kody at all. I missed the fun-loving friend I'd spent so much time with before we married, and his seriousness shocked me. I started to notice a major personality change. For the first few years of hanging out with him, I believed he was an independent thinker. After we got married, I was stunned to see how much he relied on other people's opinions. Before, when I thought about our future, I looked most forward to how much fun we would have together because I'm me and I like fun. But everything changed, in part because he was overwhelmed. We didn't have enough money, he fought with Meri, Meri and Janelle fought with each other, and Kody had to appear to outsiders as a monogamist.

He remained distant from me, and while he had resumed his rotating schedule—he stayed a night with Meri, then Janelle, then me—I didn't feel as if he and I grew any closer. I knew how close he could be with Meri and Janelle. The walls were thin. It's one thing to know your roommate is having sex in the next bedroom over. It's another when it's your husband and you can hear everything.

Yes, we were all married to him. Yes, I knew what he was up to on the nights when he wasn't with me. And yes, it shocked me how much it hurt to hear it, especially when it sounded as if they had actual relationships where they talked and played and enjoyed each other physically. We were all careful not to demonstrate affection in front of the other sister wives—no handholding or terms of endearment—but at night, I could hear the affection.

It was different in my bedroom.

When I got married, like most polygamists, I began wearing "garments." We're not talking about the mainstream-Mormon garments Utahns know and love: the long white boxers and T-shirts with the telltale smiley-face neckline for men and cap-sleeved blouses for women.

In our church, the garments—polygamy PJs—go to the ankles and wrists, so they look more like long johns. They're meant to remind us of our covenant, protect us from evil (because it's hard to feel evil while channeling Colonel Sanders?), and proclaim our faith to the world. They have been blessed and are considered sacred.

I loved them. I did! They were perfect for my "pious" stage, and I loved that they connected me to our faith and that they were symbolic of my becoming a woman, at least in the eyes of our church.

But as time went on, I associated them with pain.

We were supposed to wear them all the time—yeah, even then.

But sometimes Kody and I wore them during sex, and it didn't seem to be for religious reasons, because if it were, wouldn't we always wear them during sex? According to the church, we were supposed to wear them under wet suits when we swam, even if we were at the public pool.

Nobody's going to wear a wet suit to the public pool. That's just dumb.

The garments are about as practical for sex as they are for swimming. It's messy, and hot, and you end up with garment wedgies . . . and you get the picture.

Actually, try not to think about that.

Anyway, sometimes Kody wanted me to wear them. If I wasn't wearing the garments, he wanted me to wear lingerie—but it never felt like it was for sexy reasons. It felt like it was so I would be covered. So he wouldn't have to see me. So it wouldn't be skin on skin.

I was always covered. It would take me years to figure out why. It would take years for me to feel good in my own body. I had been so confident when I got married, but that part of my personality started to erode.

That first year, I lost myself.

Chapter Seven

SHE WAS HURT, I WAS HURT

Janelle gave birth to Logan, the Brown family's first baby, two months after Kody and I got married in 1994. At the time, I thought Kody and I didn't have a honeymoon phase because Janelle's baby came so quickly after our wedding.

I loved being there for Logan's birth and supporting Janelle afterward. There's nothing better than the smell and the tiny feet and the burbles of a new baby. The kids—that's where I found true love. Every one of them.

I had Aspyn within the first year of our marriage, and her birth brought me a gift I never could have imagined: the ability to forgive.

When I was pregnant with Aspyn, I was chill. I was newly married, and I was excited about being pregnant, but I was also oddly reasonable.

Not like myself exactly.

And very much like Aspyn is today.

With Aspyn, I even lost thirty pounds—but she was growing well, and it was never a concern because I had been heavy when I got pregnant.

It would take me years to realize that I took on my children's personalities when I was pregnant with them.

After I got pregnant, Kody went wedding ring shopping because he wanted to make sure I had his ring before my first prenatal appointment with Aspyn. He'd given me the claddagh for our engagement, but no gold band on our wedding day. I was a bit bummed that I didn't get to pick the new ring out with him. Not like pouty, but I like the story—the having-a-good-day-and-choosing-something-special-together piece of the story. He picked a beautiful ring with a diamond in it, and I was thrilled and thought it was sweet that he made sure I had it before that appointment. He wanted everyone to know I was married.

I planned to have Aspyn in my grandma's house in Utah. In our culture, women have babies at home with a midwife so we don't have to deal with weird questions at the hospital, like, "Weren't you just here a couple of months ago with your other wife?" Polygamists have always feared putting the father's name down on a birth certificate because it could serve as proof of bigamy in a lawsuit, but Kody would sign his name on each and every one of our kids' birth certificates. It was important to him to be the dad.

Because Kody traveled so often for his job, I often handled my prenatal appointments on my own. Independence was hardwired into us because Kody couldn't, even if he had worked nine-to-five in town, attend to all three of us at once. So, every month, I would drive down from Wyoming to Utah for a prenatal appointment. As I headed back to Wyoming by myself one day, baby bumping against the steering wheel, I realized I needed tire chains to go up the mountain pass. I still don't know how to put on tire chains, but I definitely wasn't going to learn in the snow with a baby basketball. I walked into a gas station and asked if someone could help me.

"You'll be fine," they told me. "Just get behind a diesel."

You know what they say about chivalry.

I drove behind a diesel through a blizzard in the terrifying South Pass, scared out of my head. But I made it.

When it was time, Kody joined me in Utah at my grandma's house.

Our usual midwife couldn't make it because her sister was in labor, so she sent her assistant. It was my first baby, and Kody's first home birth. As it turned out, it was our midwife's first home birth, too. My grandma had assisted with a few births, but my mom had helped with dozens of births.

I didn't want my mom there.

She had made my wedding dress, but she wasn't allowed to come to the ceremony because she wasn't a church member. We were okay together, but uncomfortable. I still felt so angry, and I didn't see her as part of my community because she'd left the church—and my dad.

But the birth didn't go well.

"Your hips just aren't lining up," the midwife said.

I walked and walked, but my hips wouldn't cooperate, which hurt and could have made it harder for me to have the baby.

Kody was incredible—there's no one I'd rather have in the room with me when I'm giving birth. As I walked around trying to get my hips straight, I would stop when I felt a contraction, put my arms around Kody's neck, and drop. He would move my hips, just swaying me from side to side to help my hips spread.

I knew my grandma was making calls, but I didn't know to whom.

She was calling my mom.

"I don't know what to do for her. Can you help?"

As I struggled through Aspyn's birth—for eleven hours—Mom told Grandma how to help ease my pain and realign my hips. I can't imagine what that was like for her. She quietly assisted, knowing that I couldn't be close with her yet—knowing that I didn't want her there for the birth of her grandchild.

After the baby was born, I called my mom. She showed up the next day. When I saw her, I realized how much I needed her. That day, my heart could have broken from need—as I'm sure hers did the day before.

As soon as she arrived, I relaxed. She took Aspyn, and I slept. You don't sleep until someone you trust holds that baby.

Chapter Eight

MY MOST MAGICAL MOMENTS

When we got married, we moved around a lot. It seemed like every few years Kody would need to look for something new. We lived poor for so long, and he wanted to better support the family. That first year, Janelle had Logan, and I had Aspyn.

The trailer in Wyoming couldn't accommodate all of us, so about a year later, we moved first to West Jordan, Utah, then, a year later, nearby to Sandy, and then, a year later, we moved to another house in Sandy. In the meantime, Meri had Leon, Janelle had Madison, I had Mykelti, and Janelle had Hunter and then Garrison, so we had four adults and seven kids to care for and feed.

So many babies, too. It seemed as if someone was pregnant at all times.

When I was pregnant with Mykelti, I felt decisive and beautiful—the most beautiful I've ever been in my life.

When it was time, we called the midwife, a man who usually worked with his first wife, but she couldn't make it, so he brought another wife I'd never worked with. I did know her through our church.

"Do you know what you're doing?" I asked when she arrived.

"Yeah," she said. "I've been delivering babies for far longer than my sister wife."

She brought her Bible, and during contractions, she read verses.

Once again, Kody was fantastic. He got right into my face and stared at me the whole time. He took every breath with me and was completely present.

That was my fastest labor, which describes Mykelti to a T. If she's going to do something, she just does it. That's all there is to it.

Afterward, I passed out immediately.

Meri and Janelle, in their own bedrooms, slept through it. My labor lasted only four hours, then Kody and I both fell asleep, so no one in the house knew I had given birth.

And oh, she was beautiful. Mykelti was the prettiest newborn. But we constantly needed more space, and each move involved babies and pregnancies and three households—along with an abundance of food. In addition to canning and freezing, we bought everything in bulk because there were so many of us. But Mormons were preppers before prepping was a thing. During the Cold War, we were taught—all of us, not just polygamists—to store food in case of a nuclear war. Now it's so we can be self-reliant, as well as help others in need. You can even buy bulk food items, like canned flour and oxygen-absorption packets, at the LDS online store. It's a lot to move.

But while the moves caused chaos, we had also come to rely on each other for childcare, cooking, and financial stability. Kody and I also started to even out, and I believed we were building a deeper relationship that would continue to grow. About four years into our marriage, Kody and I had a moment that made me believe I could be with him for eternity.

Kody sold educational and entertainment DVDs and other products about the Book of Mormon, the Bible, and religious history. We had them for our kids, too. Kody won a competition, and he got to go to the LDS historical site of Nauvoo to sell the DVDs, which would likely be a windfall for our family. He chose me to go with him.

In 1830, Joseph Smith, our original prophet, founded the LDS church in New York state, but he and his followers had to flee several times because people didn't take kindly to his new religion. After fleeing Missouri, the Mormons landed in Illinois, where the church bought land and called their new city "Nauvoo." People didn't much like the Mormons in Nauvoo, either, and a mob killed Smith and his brother. Mormons go back to see the Joseph Smith homestead, the Smith Family Cemetery, the site where Smith and his brother were killed, the original temple site, and the Joseph Smith Mansion House, where temple ceremonies were performed.

Kody and I got to spend two weeks together, with Aspyn, who was three, and Mykelti, who was two. We stayed in a tiny hotel room, and it was so much fun—I spent the whole time finding things for Mykelti to do because she was curious about everything. Cutest and busiest little kid. Aspyn was a little calmer as a toddler.

On our last day in Nauvoo, Kody introduced me to a coworker as his wife.

"Has he met Meri?" I asked.

He hadn't. Meri had gone to Kody's work parties back home, but the Nauvoo guys hadn't met her. I remember thinking it was so cool that he'd introduced me to them as his wife—it didn't happen often.

Kody later told me he looked at me as we drove home from that trip and realized he was in love with me. That was hard to hear. I had fallen in love with Kody long before, and now we were four years into our marriage. I thought maybe that's just how love works. Maybe love is slow. Maybe you fall in love over your shared story, over your experiences.

I remember telling my brother I thought *Titanic*—the movie—was dumb because that's not how love happens. I told him, "There's no such thing as instant love or love at first sight. No one falls in love like that." Romantic, huh?

I'm sure the little girl with the yellow towel would have rebelled against the notion that true, deep, soulmate love didn't exist. How could I have my fairy tale without it? But I believed Kody and I had something rich and emotional because we had been friends first and then had worked to develop our love. That was my experience—my only experience—with love. I told my kids that's how it works: build a strong friendship, and love will come over time. In the meantime, Kody talked to the kids about the need for a contract, like love is a business agreement you enter, rather than a romantic, loving partnership.

I understood that fairy tales were for monogamists, but they didn't have the special relationship with God that we did. And Kody and I had great dates. We went on trips together, we sang together in the car. We loved *Phantom of the Opera*—I, of course, sang the Christine parts, and he has a great voice. We loved to dance together.

We even got into a rhythm with sex, and there were a few years where it was kind of good. About two years into our marriage, I had my first orgasm.

Oh, that's what everyone's been so excited about . . .

It was entirely accidental, but still.

Knowing Kody loved me helped me feel like I had a solid role in the family.

As crazy as it sounds, considering how difficult it had been for the four of us to get along, as well as our limited financial situation, we were all open to the idea of Kody bringing in a fourth wife in those early years. We were all close in age with children who were close in age, so it made sense to us to add a fourth while we were young. I'm sure we were thinking she could also get a job, and we'd make it work. And we probably figured she could help change the family dynamic to something more positive yet again.

A young woman, maybe nineteen, from our church expressed her interest. I liked her a lot, and she had gone about it properly. Kody asked the head of our church, who was my grandpa, if he could court the girl—respectfully, just as he had done before dating Meri, Janelle, and me.

I can picture my grandpa nodding as he listened, then taking a slow breath.

"You know, Kody," my grandpa said, "I don't think you're taking care of the wives you have."

Whoa.

My mom had told my grandpa that we didn't have any money. I asked her how she could say such a thing.

"Well, because it's true," she said.

Fair.

But it caused a problem between my mom and the Kody Brown family for a while.

Life continued as before, with little break. In 1998, I gave birth to Paedon while we lived in Sandy.

With Paedon, I had awful morning sickness. I worked at a car dealership while I was pregnant with him, and my personality completely changed: I felt so easygoing. I could talk to anyone—and I did. I was more talkative than I've ever been in my life. People would come in, and I would chat forever. That's Paedon. He can talk to anybody about anything, and there's never a barrier.

Paedon was my hardest labor. He kept yo-yoing up and down and up—which is still what he does. He vacillates and has a rough time making decisions.

Like whether he should come into the world: Kody and the midwife had to press my belly to help push Paedon out.

Immediately after he was born, Janelle came in and held him, and he opened his eyes and looked right at her. They have had the closest bond since the first moment, and it was such a cool thing to witness—especially since her sons became his brothers. At our house, he had only sisters.

From Sandy, we moved back to Wyoming in 1998, and that's where I had my most magical moments with the Kody Brown family. We lived in a three-bedroom ranch-style house, which meant the kids, who were toddlers, lived in the bedrooms with their mothers. Kody rotated from room to room. We would wait until the kids were asleep and then try to keep quiet.

The house was small: Janelle and I each had a bedroom off the living room by the only bathroom. Meri's bedroom was on the other side of the living room, and while she had one child, hers was the biggest. Neither Janelle nor I wanted the other to have to share a wall with Meri because she could be difficult, so we volunteered to take the small bedrooms. That meant I shared a wall with Janelle, which was ridiculously awkward because we also shared a husband. But everything was hard, including having to share a tiny kitchen while trying to feed an enormous family.

In the tiny space, Meri's rules grew even stricter. I don't care how towels are folded: They go in the drawer and they're folded. In fact, I don't care if they get folded at all, as long as they end up in a drawer. We went through towels so quickly we barely had time to fold them. I don't care if kids play in the Tupperware cupboard or make a mess. I don't care if they eat all the food on their plates or take three bites.

You should have consequences for your actions, but I'm more casual with my parenting style. When we all lived together, Janelle and I, as well as our kids, followed stricter rules to keep the peace with Meri, but also because when you have so many people living with you, the kids can't be making messes all the time.

Chaos. I'm sure the kids felt as if they always had someone yelling at them. My bedroom had a queen bed and a bunk bed shoved together in that tiny space. I walked past one day and saw the kids jumping from the top of the bunk bed onto my bed. I didn't want to ruin their fun, but I knew that if they saw me, I would have to put an end to it.

I walked away.

That memory still makes me smile.

Soon after we got to northern Wyoming, I applied for a job at the Powell museum. The interviewer asked me about my children. When I talked about Meri's and Janelle's children, I called them my nieces and nephews—but really, they were my kids. And I described my sister wives as my sisters. "Yes, I have childcare because my sisters are nearby."

The interview went well, but when I got to my car, I sat there feeling awful about it. I went back inside.

"I lied to you," I said. I'm sure she was in shock, figuring I was going to tell her I was a felon or didn't have a visa or something. "I'm really sorry. I'm a polygamist. There are three wives. We raise our children together. If we're going to be working together, you need to know the truth."

I apologized and told her it's common in our culture because we've had so much to fear from the outside world, but she was great. We got on so well, and I loved working there more than anywhere else I've worked. I gave tours through the Homesteader Museum in Powell, Wyoming, and sometimes I got to work at the Buffalo Bill Historical Center, which I loved.

During the five years I worked part-time there, my boss never told a soul. The real magic began about a year after we moved into the ranch house, when we built Meri a house on the same property and she moved out. Then Janelle moved to a house closer to town.

In Wyoming, we added to our family: Janelle had Gabriel a few days before I had Gwendlyn. That's ten kids, if you're keeping count.

I hadn't planned to name the baby Gwendlyn, but she gave me no choice.

As I was driving home from work, I heard clear out of the blue, "Mom. My name is Gwendlyn."

I went home and told Kody, "Her name is Gwendlyn."

"Huh?" he said. "I don't know how I feel about that."

I explained.

"She told me her name's Gwendlyn," and that was that.

When I was pregnant with Gwendlyn, strangers would rub my belly. I don't know why people don't ask if they can do that, but it was almost like Gwendlyn pulled them in. She would move for them—usually when someone touches your stomach, the baby freezes. Gwendlyn would press up against their hand, wanting to be seen—just like today. She loved it.

I loved being pregnant with her. I worried about things being fair and just, and I would bring things up with Kody I never would have talked about before. That's what Gwendlyn's like. She needs things to be balanced. Even as a kid, if she got two cookies, then Gabe should get two cookies, too. There's no drama in it, she just wants the justice with the blindfold and the scales.

Her birth was my absolute favorite. The pain never got that bad. My hips, as usual, weren't aligned.

"Turn on ABBA," I said. "I got this."

They turned on "Mamma Mia," and I started lip syncing. I went into transition during the song, crouched down on the floor on all fours, worked through the transition, got up, finished the song, and had her in fifteen minutes. It was amazing.

Also, I recently found out, through DNA testing, that I'm related to Meryl Streep.

Years later, when Gwendlyn started saying things like, "I don't think that's fair," or "I don't think that's right," I understood.

I remembered.

Oh, I was like that when I was pregnant with you. That's when I started to piece things together—that I take on the traits of my kids when I'm pregnant.

After Gwendlyn was born in 2001, Janelle worked full-time during the day, so I watched her kids and was the main caregiver in our family. This saved me. Polygamy appealed to me most because of the kids. I wanted my kids to experience having other moms. But I also wanted the friendship with those sister wives—and didn't understand how much work would go into that. When you think about it, fifty percent of marriages end in divorce, so what are the chances of building permanent, loving relationships with three adults you barely know? It was work, but I was committed.

They were too. We had a lot of good days.

As I was figuring out my spot in the family, I realized that I like get-togethers, and I love holidays. I love to play. Party wife!

Thanksgiving was a production. One time, we had seventy-two people for dinner. Crazy. But it's a lovely holiday because it's just about gathering and gratitude—not so much about consumerism. Pumpkin everything! I talked with Meri and Janelle about their favorite traditions and foods. Meri liked to cook the turkey—and Kody liked her turkey—and she liked to make her mom's dressing. Her potatoes are so good.

Holiday foods are important to all of us, but maybe more so to Meri than anybody else. She had things she made for specific holidays—and that was the only time they could be eaten. We couldn't make crab dip for Valentine's Day because it was for New Year's only. Fondue was for another holiday.

Why? I thought. *Why can't we have fondue anytime?*

Tradition.

Even now, I make some of those foods for specific holidays because my kids love those traditions so much.

For Thanksgiving, I make beautiful rolls. One of my favorite memories will always be Kody's mom teaching me how to make those rolls. She swore by certain brands and used a wooden spoon to beat in every cup of flour by hand—I use an electric mixer.

Then we figured out the pies.

Mmm, pie.

Janelle and I started making pies together in Wyoming. We perfected a recipe we called "Chocolate Pie Heaven." I'm salivating at the thought of it. It's just perfectly rich enough. Whipping cream. I'm not talking about frozen "whipped topping"—that's an abomination. My German mothers would have my neck. And Janelle made the crust. That woman excels at homemade pie crust. (I cheat and use Pillsbury!)

In that first house in Wyoming, we had to figure out the oven and what to make ahead of time. We started preparing months before. Meri's pretzel salad (Jell-O, cream cheese, pretzel crust—my kids loved it) could be handled the day before. Pies could be done the day before. But if we were having dinner at two p.m. Thursday, we'd track back to figure out what went in the oven when. The turkey needed to be warm, but it would take time to make the gravy, and that would give me a chance to put the rolls in the oven, and that was key because we needed to smell them as we sat down for dinner.

As the kids got older, they helped in the kitchen. They still love making those rolls. One year, I had everyone write what they were grateful for on a slip of paper, and I baked them inside the rolls. No one could eat the rolls until everyone read their slip of paper.

My kids say that was the most rubbish year ever.

The meal itself? I rarely got a chance to sit down for it, with all the ups and downs of platters and courses and second helpings. So much work always goes into Thanksgiving, and then it's over in an instant.

But I loved every bit of it, from planning it together to preparing the meal together. I'm sure it was more stressful than I remember, but I loved Meri's and Janelle's company as we cooked together. Always. I always loved that.

I love holidays. I loved honoring everyone's family history and traditions. I loved thinking about what everyone brought to the family.

On December 6, because of my German ancestry, we celebrated Saint Nicholas Day by putting candy in the kids' shoes. But then they would have too much candy, so we made and decorated gingerbread houses. Eventually, we used graham crackers because the gingerbread never held together. One year, Garrison decided to make an elaborate graham cracker train, and he couldn't get it to hold together with frosting. Finally, I pulled out a glue gun.

"But then you can't eat it!" he said, so worried about missing out. So cute.

"It's okay," I told him. "We'll set some graham crackers aside for eating."

He made a massive train, and as the other kids looked at their own leaning cottages, they wondered at and admired Garrison's project.

"Whoa! Garrison's is the best!"

From then on, everyone used the hot-glue gun, and I let them eat all the crackers they wanted afterward.

For a while, Kody didn't want to do Christmas. His best friend had decided to do only the Jewish holidays because he felt that was most pleasing to God. He figured these were the holidays Jesus had.

"Absolutely!" I said. "Whatever you want to do, I'll do it. Of course I'll do Shabbat. I'll do Hannukah." I would braid the challah bread, and my kids loved that, but more than anything, it was about having everyone together once a week. I hosted Shabbat often.

We stopped doing Easter, too. Kody and Janelle researched it and determined it was more pagan than Christian. That broke my heart. My moms, with their witch hats and cauldron of orange juice on the Halloween mornings of my childhood, didn't approve—my other mom, Aunt Susan, worried that the kids would be sad and said we should replace it with something equally fun. Kody went with Passover, which somehow wasn't the same.

I continued to live in the small ranch house, where I cooked for, cleaned up after, disciplined, and homeschooled our ten kids. They were a rowdy bunch, but as they got older, they started to look after each other—when they weren't wrestling or yelling. I did everything I could to keep them focused on their lessons. At one point, we built an Incan Empire in the backyard—complete with canals and homes. Then we created this intricate communication system with quipu, or strings with knots tied in different numbers and distances to relay messages. The kids would use a quipu to show how much corn or wheat they had, and then they would run it over to another "tribe."

I did my best, but I didn't have much money, and I had ten kids under the age of thirteen, so while I have fond memories of teaching them, I knew they weren't getting the education they needed. We played games to teach them math and Latin roots, but Mykelti struggled with reading, and I could see that Garrison and Paedon were falling behind, too.

It wasn't always ideal, because of my work situation—I worked at the museum, spent one evening a week at Walmart, and had a paper route—but it helped me find my place in the family. I felt like, as women, we started to figure out how we could live togetherish, but also help each other. If you think about it, most of us have friends we love to spend small amounts of time with but who would drive us crazy if they lived in the spare bedroom. We started to settle into something more realistic.

Another woman started to show interest in Kody, but this time, none of us were interested. She and Kody worked in the same town, so she would get a ride to our house and then have Kody take her to work. She flirted with him constantly—and Kody can be ridiculously flirty, too. But her flirting with a married guy was not super cool. She was extra. Her mom and dad started hinting at possibilities, but nobody talked about a potential courtship. Her dad had two wives! They should have known better. And she didn't work on a relationship with Meri, Janelle, and me. She called constantly, and Kody spent a lot of time on the phone with her.

I got sick of it—I thought she disrespected our marriages to Kody. I remember I was tired all the time because I was pregnant, so I took a nap. "Look, if she calls again, you need to let me intervene," I told Meri and Janelle. "This is ridiculous." She called. Janelle knocked on my door.

"Where's the phone?" I asked.

"We gave it to Kody," she said.

Seriously?

Kody was in the garage working with his brothers. I opened the door and could see he was on the phone, so I roared her name.

Picture Samuel L. Jackson in *Pulp Fiction*.

Well, or maybe Ursula in *The Little Mermaid*. (I love Ursula.)

"Are you talking to her right now?" I said to Kody.

"Yeah," he said.

"Give me the phone," I said as I grabbed it.

"You have made a wrong decision here," I said to the woman. "You should have been brown-nosing me. In a plural family, you have to build a relationship with the wives, too. And you chose to ignore us, and that is your problem, and you will never get further than this. It is over. You will get your own rides to work. You will not call him anymore. You will not get through me."

And then I hung up the phone. When I looked up, Kody's brothers were all standing with their mouths open because they had never seen that side of me. I'm the fun, happy-go-lucky, everything's-always-peachy wife.

But don't cross me. That's not going to work out well for you.

I've talked with the woman since, and she said, "Yeah, I behaved badly." And I said, "Yeah, I may have too." She's happily married now.

We focused on raising our kids together as siblings. In our culture, "aunt" is synonymous with "other mom." My other mom was Aunt Susan, and as a kid, I didn't understand why until I realized it was a protection against the outside world. Even before we went public, we decided we didn't want to do that. We also didn't like "Mother Meri" or "Mother Christine." It felt old-fashioned. Mother Goose. Mother Teresa. Old Mother Hubbard.

Ew.

We had the kids call us by our first names—so I was "Mom" to my kids, and "Christine" to Meri's and Janelle's kids. Then we raised them as siblings. Gwen learned to speak before Gabe, and because she called me "Mom," he started to, too. I stopped it immediately, of course, but it was so cute. I loved taking care of all those kids.

I also liked having a set community of women I trusted and could count on to help raise my kids. We had the same morals and values, and I knew the kids' other moms could help sculpt them into good people, especially because the three moms had different personalities. There was always someone each kid could identify with. During their teenage years, we knew that would be especially important—I had lived through it with my own moms. Our kids would also learn how to be around different kinds of people, with all the kids and all the moms, which I thought would help them in the future. We created our own village to raise our children.

I'd also seen beautiful relationships among sister wives. When my grandpa died, my grandmas became close. They'd always been best friends, but that friendship grew after he died. I wanted that sisterhood. Grandpa was brilliant at plural marriage: each of his wives believed she was his favorite. I asked some of them: they each said they knew the other wives also believed they were grandpa's favorite. He made them all feel special and like he loved them as individuals. That's why it was so devastating when the law found out about them, and they were separated for years. When they found each other again, they built a tight bond.

For a while, it felt like Meri, Janelle, and I might be headed that way, especially if we kept working on ourselves.

Even the kissing got better in Wyoming. As a young woman, I was all about practicing.

"What do you want to do for your birthday?" Kody would ask.

"Can we go for a drive and make out?" I'd ask.

"C'mon," he'd say. "Let's do something different."

He was never into the idea. But he was attentive in other ways.

When I was pregnant with Ysabel in 2003, the diamond fell out of my wedding ring. We were on a drive, and I had my hand out the window, and when I pulled it back in, the diamond was gone. Have you ever seen a ring without its stone? It gapes, like a black hole. I was devastated,

"That's okay," Kody said. "Why don't we go and pick out a new ring together? I think you need a story for this one."

We drove to Billings, Montana, where he often worked, for a weekend, and we picked out a second ring. I loved that ring. Those were happy times.

I found out a week before Ysabel was born in June that it was only my midwife's tenth birth. That freaked me out completely, and I talked to Kody about the need to focus during her birth.

"Kody, you cannot talk to the midwife during contractions," I said.

As always, he was fully engaged. He rubbed my back through the whole thing.

But Ysabel? She was an awkward-looking baby.

Ooof, I remember thinking. *What have I given birth to? She looks nothing like me. She looks nothing like Kody. I don't know who she looks like.*

She knows that's what I thought, and she also knows that if she weren't absolutely gorgeous, I would never make fun of what a, yeah, silly-looking baby she was for the first several months of her life.

I've heard people say that moms don't know when their kids aren't attractive. I know this to be untrue.

When my dad first saw her, she was about six months old. "She looks just like you," he said.

What? Rubbish!

I dug up the old baby pictures. She looked just like me. And I was a homely baby. I wasn't cute at all.

After a few months, she became adorable—and the cutest little sass you've ever seen—and we figured we'd go ahead and keep her.

She was such a daddy's girl. She just wanted her dad, always.

Kody was a good dad. Janelle had Savanah in December 2004, so we were up to twelve kids while we were in Wyoming. Kody was usually gone during the week for work, but on the weekends, he'd always do something with the kids. That usually meant yard work, but they also helped Meri build her house. The kids loved being around him. They all had little tool belts, just like Dad. He was fun, and I loved to watch him with them.

We would pull up all the weeds in the garden, then bundle them together for bonfires. We always had one for Garrison's birthday because he was a bit of a pyromaniac, and Kody would let him light the fire.

"You can light only three matches," Janelle would tell Garrison, "and you have to do it with an adult."

As we gathered wood for the bonfire, six-year-old Garrison would stare at the cupboard where we kept the matches. Finally, I would get the matchbox for him, and he would take it to Kody. Kody would let him hold the box and light the fire. It was adorable. He loved to light the fire.

On the weekends, we played. If it snowed, we had snowball fights and went sledding. We'd go for drives and to Kody's dad's ranch.

We tried to set up piñatas a few times, but our kids were just too happily aggressive to be waving sticks around. They're crazy with Red Rover, too. They're all built tough and fierce—little forces of nature.

This is what I wanted, I often thought.

My mom and I continued to work on our relationship, too. She tried to work out her religious beliefs, and it was hard on me when she gave up on religion completely—at least in the organized sense. It felt like she was forever changing her identity, which I wouldn't understand at all until much later.

But she was the best grandma ever. I realized I wanted her in my life in a big, meaningful way, and things got so much better. We stopped trying to reconcile her not being in my church anymore and decided to be mother and daughter. I don't know how I would have made it through any of it without her.

Just before I married Kody, she married Wayne, the man I'd been so angry about her dating after she left my dad, and he was an incredible grandpa to my kids. I saw them both differently through my children's eyes.

I'll never forget when my sister called and said, "Wayne's in the hospital. You have to get here."

None of us had known he was sick.

"We don't know what's going on, but you have to say goodbye," my sister said.

Kody and I packed up—Kody didn't hesitate—and within an hour, we were on the way to Utah to see him at the hospital. Wayne died a couple of days later of undiagnosed cancer.

He helped me heal my relationship with my mom.

I loved Wyoming. I think we all did, and we'd found our rhythm there. Things could be tight, but we had a flock of kids, and we did everything together. But just after Gwendlyn was born in 2001, after another argument in the family, Janelle moved in with her mom for about eight months. That's Janelle's story to tell, but it would never be easy for all of us, including Kody, to manage personalities and jealousy, and sometimes, it felt hard to get away from the conflicts.

Soon after, Kody announced he had gotten a job in Utah.

"Are you kidding me?" I remember saying. "There are fourteen people in this family, and you're only concerned with one."

I thought we would stay in Wyoming for the rest of our lives, but it would only be five years. We were close to his family, and we were close with members of our church. I was homeschooling the kids. Sure, we were poor, but we had a big magical garden, and we canned and bottled, and we bought food in bulk. We made it work.

And I had moved around so much as a child that moving still stresses me out. It causes so many disruptions—school, friends, kids, housing, proximity. Everything's a struggle.

"I'm just trying to create a better life for my family," he said.

"How is that a better life?" I asked. "It's not going to be a better life."

Chapter Nine

IT WAS A BUMMER

*A*fter Kody said we would be moving back to Utah, I said I would go under one condition: that our kids could go to the school our fundamentalist church ran there. I called the school to ask about it, and they countered with, "Do you have anyone who can teach?"

Why yes. Yes, we do.

I told them I had been homeschooling our kids for five years in Wyoming, and they asked me to teach at the church school, which was essentially an organized homeschooling operation that ran classes three days a week. They put me in second grade with the team teacher, who was brilliant and taught me a lot about teaching second graders. I taught seven- and eight-year-old kids. So much fun.

I took our kids with me for teacher setup day, and they hung out with some kids at the school.

The car ride home was oddly quiet.

"I've got something I've got to tell you," said Janelle's son Logan, sounding like he was about to get in trouble.

"Okay?" I asked.

"I told someone today that I have three moms," he said, sounding confused, "but then he said he has two moms."

"Oh," I said, relieved. "Everybody who goes to this school is from a polygamist family, just like you."

Every child in that car breathed "Oooooh" at the same moment. Apparently, I had failed to mention that the "church school" was our church.

"I didn't know how I was going to explain Mykelti," Logan said.

We had always told them to be honest if people asked questions but not to blurt out information about our family. Still, it was always a touchy subject, and it was hard for them because they didn't always know how to answer. They were relieved that they wouldn't have to worry anymore. That school cemented their relationship with one another: they entered as a pack of brothers and sisters.

Because I taught at the school, I was right there if the kids needed anything.

As I started teaching second grade, we found a house in West Jordan and I loved it. It was five stories—really—and for the first four months, it was just Kody, me, and the kids. While we were in Wyoming, Janelle lived in her own place near town, and she had a steady job working for the state. For Janelle, the move to Utah was disconcerting: She likes stability. She knew her paycheck helped keep the family afloat, and she worried about finding another job with the same benefits. When we moved to Utah, she moved into Meri's house on our property, which we still owned, and kept her job for another year before moving down. We had a few of Janelle's kids with us so they could go to the church school and Janelle wouldn't have to worry about childcare. Meri stayed with her sister's family in Utah for the first few months, but I still watched Leon often while Meri worked.

I love so many memories from that time, especially of the time Kody spent with me and our kids.

After a few months, Meri moved into our house in West Jordan, while Janelle remained in Wyoming. While I was teaching, I found out I hadn't taught Mykelti to read well, and she caught up with the rest of her class within three months.

After about a year in West Jordan, I think 2003, we bought a big house in Lehi. Janelle decided to move down after seeing the house—it seemed like the perfect place for us. In the new home, we had our own apartments with separate entrances. I had the basement, Meri's apartment was above mine, and Janelle had the east side of the house, so the top and bottom floors. Janelle's kitchen was about eight hundred square feet, so we could have massive family gatherings there. I had five kids. Meri had one. And Janelle had six. That put us at sixteen people.

At that point, I felt necessary both in the community and in my family because I helped educate the kids. I had moved from teaching second grade to teaching middle school. Gosh, I loved those kids—especially the rebel kids or the struggling kids. We'd be in these meetings where everyone would try to figure out the problems. Blah, blah, blah. The kids just need to be heard, and they need to be loved. That's all.

Those were golden years. I had a purpose.

That would soon change.

Meri and I were friends for a while—we even worked as counselors at a girls' camp together through our church for several years. The two of us won all the skit contests and came up with great things for the girls to do. After a while, she became a camp director—because she was that much fun.

But none of us would have chosen to be best friends. And if we had, the little things that drove us nuts about each other wouldn't have mattered if we didn't spend so much time together. We talked, as sister wives, about the constant self-improvement we did to ensure our relationships with each other remained solid, but in the real world, if you have a personality conflict with someone, you probably don't share a house—or a husband—daily and to eternity and beyond.

I've also learned over the years that you have to make time for and develop a friendship, just as you do a marriage, and while we talked often about improving ourselves, maybe we didn't talk often enough about the commitment, trust, and time a friendship takes. Janelle and I had a squadron of children between us, and all the sister wives worked. I felt overwhelmed by teaching, volunteering with Sunday school, helping the kids with homework, fitting me and five kids into our small apartment, and my marriage to Kody. I didn't have time for a walking club with my sister wives, or to go sip wine and paint ceramics, or to create a mini book club.

Would it have mattered? Who knows.

I sometimes missed the comradery we'd had in Wyoming, even when we were fussing. Realizing I didn't have to time out the rolls for our one oven and that I would have to cook my own things by myself before we all headed over to Janelle's big kitchen for Thanksgiving felt lonely. Soon enough, I told Janelle I would be cooking in her kitchen on Thanksgiving so we could hang out and celebrate the day. Meri would show up later, and it would feel like old times.

Even that was short-lived.

Meri has said in an interview that she and I did fine as housemates for a while, but our relationship never went deep. I think that's true, and that's not a dig at either of us. It's hard to find people we click with enough to spend significant time with, and it makes sense that I wasn't automatically going to bond with someone Kody picked—and that Meri and Janelle wouldn't necessarily bond with me, either.

Meri's place on the floor above me was pristine and had a lot of breakables, and I felt like she reacted harshly when the kids roughhoused—so much so that I didn't want my kids around her. At her place, they could count on doing something wrong. And even as she had an abundance of rules for us to follow about folding towels or whatever, she played her country music so loud that we could hear it throughout the house—it didn't matter if a baby was napping, or if Janelle or I were trying to catch up on sleep or spending quiet time with a kid.

About ten years after I married Kody, Meri and I fell out. I didn't trust that she would be kind to me, particularly in front of other people. She said demeaning things about me when she was with her family—in front of me. My weight. My intelligence. My parenting skills. We could be laughing and telling stories, but then she'd throw a painful dart and I would feel myself deflate.

I debated whether to tell this part, particularly because I know we've all changed so much since those early years, but the dynamics of polygamist parenting can feel like a seesaw, and Meri, even with one child to care for, was the top wife in our polygamy pyramid. We followed her rules when she was around to keep the peace, but her rules felt punitive and unfair. I had to make a decision about what was best for me and my family within a family, and it changed our relationship forever.

One day, the kids went to the store. Mykelti, who was about eight, went up to the cash register, and she was maybe ten cents short. It was little-kid stuff—she was probably buying candy. The cashier, who knew us, spotted her the dime. No big deal. But Meri's Leon, who was also just a little kid—maybe nine—told Meri about it.

Meri lost her mind.

She was mad that Mykelti had embarrassed her in front of the cashier, and that she had embarrassed Leon. She yelled at Mykelti, who couldn't understand what she had done wrong. I couldn't either.

That was the day, after a series of too many similar experiences, I ended my friendship with Meri. I'd had enough, and my mama bear came roaring.

"Don't talk to my kids," I yelled. "I don't want you near them. I don't want you to come downstairs anymore. Our relationship is done!"

I may have been the mediator between Meri and Janelle, and I know her relationship with Kody was hard, but it wasn't fair for her to take her mess out on my kids—or on me. It wasn't safe for us.

It was a bummer—I had always had fun with Meri, and I loved hanging out with her, but ultimately, I never knew what to expect. We'd made so many good memories together, but I needed my kids to feel strong, supported, and safe, and not like the rules were always changing on them. It was the right thing for my children.

Meri and I continued to get along to take care of the kids and the family, and we still hung out on trips together as sister wives. We were always cordial, and we often had a good time and laughed together. But it was superficial. As far as a heart-to-heart conversation, we only had a few of those through the years because I didn't feel like I could trust her not to hurt me. I never knew when she would belittle me or simply be mean.

Janelle worked, and then she went back to school, so I didn't spend much time with her. When I did, it was often because she had a new project she expected me to help with—but then I'd be angry at her because she hadn't checked with me to make sure I had the time, which added to how overwhelmed I felt. We didn't have a tight bond, either.

With Kody, things weren't exactly inspiring. I always had to initiate. In return for meh sex, Kody required a back massage, which would turn into a full-body massage. He never offered to return the favor.

I did ask. I told him I would love to have my shoulders rubbed, that it would be a big deal for me.

"It's not a turn-on for me," he'd say.

Or "I'm already tired."

Or "I had a hard day at work."

The foreplay was for Kody.

I don't know if my sister wives gave Kody massages—we never talked about what happened, or didn't, in the bedroom. But I felt like I had to give him massages so he would have sex with me. I qualified it as "the special thing I did."

I spent so many nights in that house crying, and yes, jealous, and, worse, feeling like it was my fault. If I just tried harder, our relationship might improve. One night I told him I felt neglected.

"I move away from pain and toward pleasure," he told me.

Am I pain?

Does my pleasure matter at all?

"You're an idiot," I said, because I couldn't even imagine saying something so hurtful to another person.

"I'm not smart," he said, "but I'm honest."

Speaking off the cuff is not honesty. You think about the truth, you figure out the truth. You don't spit out truth.

Everything hurt, but we had children together, and Wyoming had been so beautiful, and my grandpa had joined us for all eternity in our wedding ceremony.

We were taught to continue to work on ourselves, to make ourselves better so we could earn our award in heaven.

But it's hard to work on yourself when you feel like you're worth nothing at all.

Chapter Ten

THE LDS CHURCH'S BASTARD CHILDREN

*B*oth of my grandpas were precinct heads of our church and well known within our community, as well as the non-polygamist community. But people didn't know about me or my family's situation. The Kody Brown family lived as openly as possible while trying not to get fired or arrested. Because I worked for the church, I was less worried about getting fired, so I could be outspoken about our situation.

Eventually, someone from Principle Voices, a pro-polygamy group, said, "We need Christine," and I became part of a coalition of people from each of the groups that live plural marriage. We worked to educate the outside world about what polygamy is like.

A representative from each of the polygamous churches, except for the Fundamentalist Church of Jesus Christ of Latter-day Saints, or the FLDS, would talk to hospitals, universities, and police organizations—first responders. They need to understand our culture so there aren't misunderstandings in emergencies. In a way, I was following in my grandpa's footsteps by speaking up to keep our communities safe. I talked about what it was like to be a polygamist before we ever went public as a family.

I loved it.

I used only my first name. I'd make a joke to break the ice. I'd talk about how hard it sounded to be monogamous—like I couldn't imagine having a guy around all the time. I said I'd rather be independent, do what I want to do, live how I want to live, and decide what I want to do with my home. Having a monogamous relationship sounded like a ball and chain.

People always responded the same way: "Wait, what?"

I'd bring in the crowd by telling stories. Usually, on a panel, they wanted to open it up to questions, so I learned how to handle the unexpected, the rude, and the ignorant. Before then, I couldn't stand questions. Questions signaled danger.

It was scary for any of us to go public because polygamy was a felony in Utah. If you went public, you could lose your job. There's fear on the other side, too. Confrontations between the police and polygamous groups in the 1970s and '80s had resulted in deaths for both polygamists and police. In 1988, a police officer was killed and a polygamous leader seriously wounded after a thirteen-day standoff.

So, we educated people. We had panel discussions, and I usually went first because they knew I could work the crowd. People! I loved it! I love public speaking. Isn't that funny? I went from a kid so terrified to speak at school that I developed a lisp to loving public speaking. It makes sense—it's safer to speak to a group of people and be able to control my message. Intimate, one-on-one conversations still scared me because I was used to lying about who I was.

We had a forum with some lawmakers, the attorney general, and the governor. We argued that America was built on religious freedom and that we deserved it, too. The women deserved to be recognized as wives because they would be safer. Women have essentially no rights in polygamous divorces—and polygamous wives will never report abuse if their marriage is a federal crime. The men deserved to be recognized as husbands who provide for large families rather than guys having illicit love affairs.

The ones who did make the paper? The FLDS? We heard things. I've met people who have left that church, and it seems difficult and wrong. Warren Jeffs, I believe, is evil. But there's probably goodness in some of the people in that group. Besides, what happens if you say they're all horrible, but someone's trying to get out, and they can't because they can't get past our judgment? What if that proves to them they should be afraid of the outside world? We must make it easy for them, to treat them kindly so they feel comfortable asking for help.

During our discussions, I would talk about what it was like having two moms, and what it was like having to lie to keep my family safe. I had to protect myself and protect my dad. Unfortunately, child abuse in the polygamous communities often goes unreported because no one will ever call the police. If you talk to the police, they can come and take away your dad and you may never see your other moms or siblings again. And some kids and women are so secluded that they don't know what's abusive and what's normal.

If you decriminalize polygamy, the actual crimes of abuse can come to light. As for the adults in a polygamous relationship—the grown, consenting adults—why on earth does anyone else care?

In early 2009, we went to New York City to appear on a pilot for a talk show with Carlos Watson, an MSNBC news anchor, that didn't end up airing. His producers had contacted us through Principle Voices after hearing about our family. They flew us out and put us up in a hotel, and then they pampered us with tourist attractions and gift certificates. We went to TGI Friday's in Times Square one day and had just the older kids—Logan, Aspyn, Leon, Maddie, Mykelti, and Hunter—with us, along with the four adults. Tiny tables filled the restaurant, and we wondered how we were going to fit. Polygamy problems, but we sorted it, and no one seemed to notice that we had one dad and three moms.

When you're raised as a polygamist, you learn that restaurants don't accommodate big groups of people. We always felt like we stuck out—like everybody knew. In some cases, you do know because some polygamists, like the FLDS, dress as if they arrived in Utah with Brigham Young in 1847. For us, it was this weird mix of wanting to be proud of our family and faith, but also not wanting to be stared at. If we went to the movies, one wife sat next to Kody and the rest of us would sit somewhere else. At restaurants, we'd put Kody at a table with the kids.

I realized in New York that we'd always been careful at restaurants and movies, and no one cared. In New York, no one noticed us walking in a group down the street. It had always been us being paranoid about the outside world. I had put limitations on myself based on fear of a thing that didn't exist.

When people see a large group, their last assumption is that the members must be polygamists.

On the show, Carlos introduced the topic of polygamy, and then he asked the audience if they wanted to meet Kody. It was so surreal. Everyone was like, "Oh, yeah!" The wives all went out first, and then Kody came out, and it felt like we belonged there. It was the most bizarre thing, and a little bit scary. Carlos invited the audience to interact with us. The people in the audience had great questions, we enjoyed explaining, and the whole thing felt so good.

Safe.

I'd been public with Principle Voices, but never with the family. I realized that none of the people in the audience cared that we lived plural marriage. They were curious, but they didn't seem to be judging, and they were never rude.

After we appeared on Carlos's show, when we felt safe and heard, we scooped up the kids and made them do everything you ever saw in a movie about New York City. We took a couple extra days and hit the Museum of Natural History, the Met, the Museum of Modern Art, and the library with the giant lions. We did everything the kids had seen in *Night at the Museum*. We also went to Ground Zero, which felt raw only a few years after the attack. It felt good to pay tribute and take a moment to explain to the kids. I thought about the unity we had felt as a country, and it was a good reminder that my family members and I are also Americans, mostly average, who love this nation as hard as anybody else.

The crowded bustle of New York scared us, at first. We didn't know what we were doing, and we spent half the time lost. But we were well versed in chaos, and we ended up loving New York.

Back home, after several appearances and news interviews, some reporters asked me to work on a documentary with them. I said no for all the reasons polygamists always say no: it's not safe. Eventually, I told Kody.

"Why didn't you talk to me about it?" he asked.

"I didn't figure you'd be interested," I said.

The next time someone asked, I told Kody, who then met with a producer named Tim Gibbons. Tim saw our situation as a civil rights issue. None of us but Meri and Kody were legally married, and we were essentially the LDS church's bastard children. Local media represented us unfairly because of all the stereotypes. When you think about it, it's perfectly fine for a married guy to cheat on his wife with several women and have several babies. In Maryland, one of the sixteen states where adultery is considered a crime at all, it's a $10 fine. Adultery is a felony in three states but rarely prosecuted. People openly have open marriages, where both partners sleep with whomever they like. I recently learned that if one person is in a committed relationship with a couple, it's a throuple. Who knew? Here we were, raising our children together, paying our taxes, going to church, and causing no problems—but at risk of having our family torn apart because we were . . . immoral?

After talking with Tim, we realized this would be a great opportunity for us to show that a polygamous family isn't all about control, patriarchy, teen marriages, and abuse—in other words, what people saw in the newspapers and on the evening news.

But there was still one problem: We could lose our jobs. We'd seen it happen again and again. We told Tim the project would need to be more than just a documentary.

Tim decided to pitch a series. He tried HBO, because they had started a series *Big Love*, a few years before, and they said no.

Then he went to TLC, and they loved the idea.

Chapter Eleven

YOU HAVE TO MEET HER

*M*eri and Janelle were always more open to another wife. Maybe they were hoping for a sister wife who was more of a soulmate, like my grandpa's wives? I felt like our situation was tenuous, that we all worked hard to maintain our balance, and that adding another person could tip us.

Things were always tight financially, even with the canning, extra jobs, and bulk shopping. But there were sentimental reasons, too. We'd made it through sixteen years together—years in which, for all our squabbles, we had grown from young women into young mothers. We each had been among the first faces every child in our family had seen. We'd offered each other wisdom and childcare. We knew families, backgrounds, habits, and needs. I thought that was special.

What would it be like to bring in someone who hadn't experienced it all with us? Someone who hadn't been in those early family scrapbooks?

Meri and Janelle were open to a fourth. Now that I no longer filled the role of mediator between Meri and Janelle after my falling out with Meri, perhaps they wanted someone who could bring back some equilibrium. Or perhaps, like me, they felt lonely in that house.

After a wedding or a morning at church, the conversation felt inevitable.

"What do you think about her? How about her?"

"I think we're fine," I'd say. "I think our family is just fine."

In December 2009, after we were in talks for a reality show with TLC, Kody and Meri went on a date to a church event. After meeting Robyn there and talking with her, Meri was ready for Robyn to join the family.

"You have to meet her," she said on repeat, all the while talking Robyn up to Kody.

Kody initially said he had some concerns. Robyn, who was thirty to Kody's forty, had been married before and had three children when she met Kody: Dayton, nine, Aurora, seven, and Breanna, five. She had grown up in a polygamous family, but her marriage had been monogamous. The divorce had been acrimonious—and recent. It had been finalized that year.

But pretty quickly, Kody started talking about how he wanted her to join the family.

I hadn't met her yet. I felt left out—FOMO—because I hadn't been included. Once again, he needed sister wives' approval before making any decisions about bringing someone into the family. He started talking about his testimony—essentially a revelation that Robyn was supposed to join us.

Testimony this, pal. I need to meet this person.

Meri was full in, too. Janelle was reserved. I was panicking. For all our troubles, Kody was my best friend. He parented my children with me, checked in with me during the day, and was the person I debriefed my life to. All of us felt that way. But because I hadn't met Robyn or been included in the decision, I felt like I was losing him.

Two weeks after the church event, I met her. One day, Kody invited Robyn and her kids to our big Lehi house, so Meri, Janelle, and I spent the day making sure our kids were spit-shined and dressed to the nines. I knew she was special to Kody and might join our family.

I got to see how she was with her kids, and see how she fit with Kody. She was sweet to me—like she understood what it would be like to watch your husband fall in love. And she also understood that she was falling in love with Kody, and that we had helped create this man.

Kody had told Robyn about the show—that TLC would undoubtedly want to film their courtship, and that her life would be on full display. She didn't run. Every weekend, he drove down to see her. That meant he didn't spend any time with our family. That hurt. On an intellectual level, I knew he needed to get to know her, but I felt like our family needed him, too.

Then Kody and I drove down to St. George, where Robyn lived, together. On the way home, I received the strongest testimony I've ever had that Robyn should join our family.

Oh my gosh, I thought. *Robyn needs to be a part of our family, and I fully believe that she would be a perfect fit with her kids and how compassionate she is and how open she has been with her whole story.*

A testimony, in our faith, is a belief stronger than you can comprehend. It just hits you in the gut. It's like this burning feeling inside that's an absolute confirmation—a tingly feeling everywhere. It was stronger than anything I had when I was checking into marrying Kody, though I'd had a pretty strong testimony about polygamy itself—and about being a third wife.

I'll tell you about the next strongest testimony I had later. But the one about Robyn was powerful.

That doesn't mean it didn't hurt.

Kody and I were hanging out at the house, and as he rushed around getting ready for another trip to St. George, I realized he was giddy.

"I can't think straight," he said, and he jabbered on about nothing and everything.

"You're in love," I said.

He paused, did the Kody head cock.

"I am," he said, near tears. He was so excited. "I'm in love with Robyn."

God, it hurts to watch him fall in love.

Robyn came up the next weekend, and we had a family gathering at Janelle's place in our Lehi house, where we usually went for larger gatherings. I'd taken food over. I was pregnant with Truely, and emotional with the pregnancy. I felt overcome by all of it. *I just can't do this*, I thought, and I went to my room and started to cry. As I sat sobbing, Kody came in and sat on the edge of the bed.

"What's wrong?" he asked.

"This sucks," I said. "It's so hard watching you fall in love again." He held me as I cried.

"It's heartbreaking," I told him. "I feel my heart being broken."

He was so sweet and kind.

"I appreciate you being open with me and talking with me about it," he told me. "I'm sorry. I know it's hard."

I'm sure he just wanted to feel excited and to spend time with Robyn, but he took the time to make sure I was okay.

I did say "fall in love again."

I thought that he was in love with me, too.

I tried to be upbeat, to make the best of it. Everything would be fine. I think we all hoped that, as had happened when I first joined the family, Robyn would help even things out. I thought—I hoped—we would become best friends. I desperately needed a best friend.

I think we all fell in love with her, at first. Her kids were similar ages to ours, and they were kind, so I figured their mother must be as well. Because she had been raised in polygamy, she knew how to treat us and what to ask. She understood that she needed the sister wives' approval to be a part of the family, and she worked hard to get it.

And honestly, she was adorable: funny, cute, and young. She seemed to need us.

As we invited her into the family, all our lives were about to change in ways we couldn't begin to understand. A fourth wife. Three new children. Another baby on the way. That would bring us to twenty-one people.

And a new reality TV show.

You know I like a party.

WIFE

Chapter Twelve

YOU'LL HAVE SOME
GREAT HOME VIDEOS

*E*verything we thought we understood about ourselves would be placed under a brilliant white bulb and dissected like a frog in a sixth-grade science class. At times, the social media posts (must not read the comments . . .) would also feel like middle school.

We were so excited.

Tim put together a pilot in 2009, and it was cute: We went on a camping trip, and the kids were adorable. I told the family I was pregnant with a girl—Truely—and we were fun together. Giddy. It's easy to overlook differences when something so exciting was happening, and, after sixteen years together, we played well off one another. It was so wholesome, too, like *Leave It to Beaver*, except Mr. Cleaver was sleeping with three women and about to sleep with a fourth. The network loved it.

We all figured the pilot would be the end of it, and that we would find ourselves exposed and jobless. But it felt like a hopeful decision, like it was time to move into the modern world, even if the show fell flat. So many other civil rights issues dealing with different lifestyles were coming to the fore, so we figured it was time.

If we couldn't get acceptance, maybe we could get open minds. We wanted people to see us as a big, loving family made up of generally good humans.

Our church, on the other hand, wasn't happy about it, which cemented our decision to downplay the religious aspect. We also wanted to protect other members of the church. We didn't say the name of our group, though it wouldn't be hard to figure out. We also refused to talk about our personal, intimate relationships with Kody—though that happened spontaneously on set. We hadn't talked about what we would say before, but when Tim asked us about the bedroom during filming, it felt obvious to say we weren't going to get into it. We didn't talk about each other's personal relationships with Kody at home, so we certainly weren't going to do it in front of a camera. TLC was great about it. We decided some things were off-limits, and they partnered well with us.

Ironically, some people who supported our work with Principle Voices and thought we should engage more with our local communities were reserved about us doing the series. There was always the fear aspect—the threat of exposing other families. But polygamists also believe there's something sacred and special about living polygamy, something that shouldn't be put out into the world for public entertainment. And what if people began living polygamy without the religious aspect? That, in the church's view, would be an abomination.

We saw going public differently: We believed our family was a beautiful thing we wanted to share. And we didn't want to live in fear anymore.

"We don't know how well the show is going to go," the TLC executives told us at the beginning, "but we have enough for a season, so at worst, you'll have some great home videos."

But nobody sits down and analyzes home videos. We had big changes coming, and we would be forced to think and talk about them. My coping mechanisms—"It's fine" and "I'll just focus on the next birthday party"—couldn't save me from breaking down on set. That first season, oh my gosh that first episode, I broke down a lot.

Kody and Robyn dated for about six months before they got married. As a viewer, it probably felt more like two months, but she came along just after we'd agreed to do the show. Even though I felt jealous sometimes, that was more about Kody than Robyn. I thought everything she was bringing to the family was good, and I thought we'd be close.

We wanted to be authentic, open, and honest, and we never wanted to be scripted.

None of us wore much makeup in everyday life, so that's how we were filmed. We didn't even know how to apply "TV makeup" in the beginning. Someone would do our faces and hair when we made appearances, were on talk shows, or did the end-of-season tell-all, but I think we usually came across as typical suburban moms with busy lives. Even though we were polygamists, every soccer mom across America could identify with having no time for eyeliner. Robyn was usually camera-ready, but she and Kody were in the early stages of their relationship, and Kody always liked a full face of makeup. That, for her, felt authentic, too.

I just remembered this: Before the show started, the sister wives and Robyn got together to do a photo shoot for Kody as a gift. Janelle didn't wear any makeup. When we gave the framed photo to Kody, the first thing he said was, "Why didn't you have any makeup on?"

Janelle with the big blues and perfect coloring.

Oh my god, I remember thinking. *You're welcome for this.*

Looking back, image was authentic to Kody. The car, the curls, the heavily embroidered jeans. He was true to himself.

Tim was great—I loved working with him. He kept his crew as small as possible, and he made sure we worked with the same people over the season, and ultimately through the years, so we knew we could trust them. If we didn't like to work with someone, we could talk with Tim and he would, no drama, bring in someone else.

Early on, a soundman helped put on what they call a "vampire clip" for my mic. Well, he stabbed me—not deep, but I bled a bit.

"Ow!" I said. "That stabbed me!"

"Yeah, you'll have to get used to that in your line of work," he said.

I told Tim, and I never saw that guy again. They simply swapped him out to another show. As it turned out, he's the sweetest man, and he has a dry sense of humor. The crew still teases me about it: "You got that guy fired."

Here's the gist: The crew would film us having an event—a party, camping, sledding—and then they'd arrange an episode around that event. The season timeline would be based on a big thing we knew was coming, so Robyn's wedding for season one. They might film things we did as part of the "big thing," like shopping for dresses or a gift for Robyn. And then, for every episode, we'd sit down on a couch in the studio and the producer would ask us questions about what they had filmed. At the end of each season, we would sit down with a host who would ask us questions about what had happened throughout the season or, eventually, seasons past.

We filmed every other week, and at first, we could work only on nights and weekends because our set was in the basement of a dentist's office. Our sessions would go until eleven or even midnight. They got us out of there as quickly as possible, but it was rough at first, especially with the adults all having to be on the set at once. The older children took care of the younger ones while we worked, and the set was close enough that we could walk, so we were nearby if there was an emergency.

The crew didn't follow us around or dig into our daily lives. We always knew where they were, so there were no sneaky shots from a distance or during private conversations. We had a rule against coming into bedrooms unless it was to film a conversation.

The kids could choose not to participate, and we never did the adult couch conversations in front of them. And they never had a mic on during an event—only the adults did. At first, they were excited—giddy and trying not to play for the cameras. They were so young. But some of them were less comfortable, and they stood back. We told them that was okay.

It started to get hard when the crew wanted to put the kids on the couch to ask them questions, but we were all careful to make sure they were never on the couch by themselves, only as a group, and our producers were good about the questions they asked. "What do you think about Robyn?" won't get much more from an eight-year-old than "I like her. I think she's nice." We kept them away from the adult drama, and if my kids were on set, I was hovering in the background.

We talked about everything on the couch: What we thought of Robyn. How we felt about Kody bringing someone else into the family. How the kids got along.

In those early days, we were careful to keep the hard stuff off-camera and to provide a united front. We wanted to work toward our ideal as a family but also to present this lifestyle to Americans. While we wanted it to be realistic, we didn't want to hurt each other, especially publicly. I'm sure that made what came later seem all the more surprising.

But that didn't mean we could always control our emotions. In the first episode, as we sat on the couch, Kody talked about how hard he had fallen for Robyn. And then they asked me about the day when I'd cried as Kody acted all infatuated.

I cried again.

Red nose, pregnant, husband giddy over another woman, and a camera.

At the beginning, they interviewed us all together, so the whole adult family witnessed my tears. My family was used to just living life without addressing the difficult things, but now we had someone saying, "Tell me why you're upset." Sometimes the producer would ask a question, and it didn't feel safe to answer. If I said how I felt, it might cause hurt feelings or a fight later. I know the others worried about the same thing.

About six months after we finished filming the season, the show aired. It can be as long as a year from the time something happens to the time it airs, which often meant we had to relive something we'd already put behind us.

Intellectually, we understood we were filming a TV show, but it was such a vague concept—especially for the kids. We figured our friends and family would watch it, and that Utahns might be interested, but we simply didn't know what it would mean for us.

Even before it aired, our lives changed in several big ways.

For one, our budget loosened up: the show provided a financial cushion—though we didn't know how long it would last—so we could do some things our kids had always wanted to do, like go to Lagoon, the local amusement park. We also knew we could relax a little about food and basics. Kody bought a Lexus convertible, which appeared so often that first season it seemed like its own character.

I loved that, with the show, I got to be an official wife. Before, when we went out as a group, Meri was the wife, and Janelle and I were just friends or sisters-in-law. But when we started doing media interviews and publicity, I was recognized as a wife for the first time in public. I loved that because I loved all the kids so much, and I got to claim them, too. Our kids, all of them. I felt accepted.

I also realized I wanted to be better spoken and better informed, both for myself and my community. After watching some of the footage, I felt like I sounded uneducated. I came from a closed community, and when you live in fear, you don't necessarily seek out people and ideas that are different. As we met more people, I became more curious. I started to pay attention to the news and reading business guides and self-help books. I love novels, but I understood if I wanted to improve myself, I would have to actively seek knowledge. I learned how to phrase things differently and to clearly say what I meant. I started reading travel books, suddenly fascinated by faraway places. This all made life so much more interesting, and I was able to better connect with the people we met—and my kids.

It was almost as if I had aimed a hair dryer at a foggy mirror and begun to see bits as they were slowly revealed—things I'd missed subscribing to the tenets of our faith, tending to the madness of a flock of children, and believing the story of my life had been set for eternity.

We were so naively optimistic that everything would turn out great. Kody had a good relationship with most of the kids, he divided his time among us evenly, and we got along well enough to function as a family. We weren't best friends, but we enjoyed doing things together. We believed the family was more important than anything else, and we believed our kids were cool, good people, so we were willing to adjust. The show seemed like an incredible opportunity for us, both in our ability to care for everyone, as well as for our message about polygamy. We were excited and hopeful.

But Kody didn't have a favorite wife back then.

Chapter Thirteen

JUST BE PRESENT

I worked—we all worked—hard to be kind and inviting to Robyn and her children. Not only were they all joining a new family, but they were about to be on a reality show. Nothing about their lives would ever be the same. I loved Robyn's children immediately and loved the instant connection her girls had with ours. I loved how compassionate Robyn was with her kids and ours, and how Robyn and Mykelti immediately bonded.

I remembered how important it had been for me to have my second mom when my mom and I struggled—or even just as another adult I knew I could trust. Robyn loved to talk through things, and I hoped that would bring a deep friendship between her and myself, as well as help our family grow.

Without a camera and a producer asking hard questions, I would have focused in harder on my kids and limited my meltdowns about my jealousy to just Kody. With a producer asking me about my deepest feelings, I needed to be authentic, but "authentic" me probably wouldn't have let on to Robyn how much it all hurt.

Kody traveled to see Robyn every weekend in St. George, or she would come up. That meant Kody's family time with the big group stopped. Before, we had done everything together. Now even the weekly Shabbat meals, where the whole family gathered and grounded, ended. He said he spent more time getting to know Robyn than each of his other wives because he needed to integrate Robyn and her kids into the family, but that meant just Kody. He spent less time with our kids. We had kids the same ages as Robyn's, as well as older kids who needed attention and time to adjust to a new mom and a new TV show, too.

Paedon, who was in sixth grade, had some concerns.

"Why does Dad go to KFC with Robyn and her kids?" he asked. "I thought KFC was a treat."

I tried to explain that we didn't go often because we didn't eat fast food.

"But they get it all the time," he said.

Paedon's a sensitive kid, and I think he noticed the difference in how Kody treated Robyn and her family before anyone else did. That was hard for him.

Even when Robyn moved a mile and a half from the Lehi house—we filmed the whole family helping her unload in episode three—we didn't see much of Kody unless Robyn was with him. I think we all felt deserted.

Sister Wives covered all of that from a friendly distance: our first episode aired in September 2010, and it ended with a date with Robyn while she lived in St. George. Those initial episodes aired about six months behind real life.

And in real life, I was pregnant. Truely was due in April 2010, or "Episode Four."

I'm sure it's not possible to be more pregnant with one child than another, but oof. I was so pregnant with Truely. My emotions were all over the place, and so was my belly.

Again, my personality changed with True, but this time in a more obvious way. I didn't like crowds of people—including our own family. During parties or functions, I would go to my room. That's Truely—she's introspective and needs her own space. Me? Parties are my love language. This time, the rest of the family noticed my personality change.

"We're just gonna leave Christine alone," Janelle would say. "Leave her be."

I became an introvert—exactly what was not needed at the beginning of a reality show or as we brought more people into the family.

As we began filming *Sister Wives*, my time with Principle Voices also ended. It was time, but it was also bittersweet. I had learned how to speak in public through Principle Voices, as well as to reason. I developed strong opinions and learned how to argue them, but I had also made friends and created an outlet and an identity outside my family. But the church needed to control its message, and the Brown family was a wild card. No one knew how the public would receive us.

The church was also dealing with a public relations disaster—one that I had no desire to be associated with: At about the same time as we started filming, news broke of accusations that members of my church had molested children—exactly what I had always decried about the FLDS. That shook me. Even the thought of something like that happening to one of our kids could bring me to tears, and this was the group that provided the morality rules for how we should behave. I thought back to Mom and how she had always said we should judge church leaders individually, rather than assume they were righteous or good.

As the church admonished us for going public, they continued to live in secrecy, and nothing could convince me that being afraid of the outside world justified a system where true evil could exist. It's like a petri dish: bacteria grow and grow because nothing is coming in from outside to stop it. Both my grandfathers had pushed for change for years for exactly this reason. I would continue that fight.

I had told the church school I would work right up until my due date and then I'd be done: no more teaching. I knew I'd be busy with the baby and filming. We also wanted to put the kids in public school—we felt it was important for them to not live in fear, either.

But it was more than that. As we began to film, went on our first media tours, and got to know people from the outside world, I realized my values didn't match with the people I knew from church. Isn't that funny? After so much time spent angry at my mom for leaving the church, the values that felt most true to me were the ones she taught me: Nobody's better than anyone else. Love everybody.

In the meantime, things were tough at home for Meri, Janelle, and me as the Lehi house became too small for our still-growing family.

And the camera crew.

Even with all those people in one tiny space, I felt loneliest in that house. In my basement apartment, there wasn't a lot of light or room—but there was a ton of traffic because Janelle's kids and Leon spent much of their time at my place. To get to Janelle's, I had to go outside because Meri didn't like seventeen people using her home as a hallway to get between Janelle's and my apartments, but it always felt weird to have to put on shoes and a coat to gather with the rest of the family in our house or send the kids to play with their brothers and sisters. Janelle worked full-time, so I didn't see her much. My relationship with Meri was strained after the candy incident with Mykelti. Kody was otherwise occupied. I didn't spend a lot of time with grown-ups, and no matter how much I love our kids, our interactions were always more about them than about me because I was the adult.

Even as we filmed every other week, I started working a couple of nights a week because I wanted to pay off all my debt before I had Truely so I wouldn't have to work after she was born. I asked Kody to help put the kids to bed at night because I wouldn't be there. We had Aspyn, Mykelti, Paedon, Gwendlyn, and Ysabel.

Just tuck them in, please.

"I don't have time to do that every night," he said.

"We live in the same house," I said.

"You need to ask your sister wives for help."

Really? Janelle had six kids of her own and she and Meri both worked.

"I can't help you."

I have given you everything, I thought. *These are our children.*

Aspyn read stories to the children. Aspyn tucked them into bed. Aspyn was fifteen.

I paid off my debt. I quit my job.

And I stopped giving Kody massages.

I'm not going to take care of you at the end of a hard day so you can chill while I continue my long day. I'm done.

But I was also devastated. The intimacy in our marriage would never be the same, not in any consistent way.

I thought about my relationship with Kody, my partner. My helpmate. I realized I didn't have a functioning marriage.

It's over, I thought. *I can't respect him if he won't help me with our children.*

Funny thing about eternal marriages, though. And piety. There's a narcissism to piety: God will reward me if I suffer through this marriage. God will see me as deserving above others. If I was suffering, and

God loved me more for it, how did he feel about happy people? Isn't that what I had questioned as a child? The idea that God was judgmental? Hadn't my parents taught me he was a loving entity?

But I had also made a promise to that same God, Kody, and my sister wives, and relationship promises can also feel like narcissism. Yes, don't cheat on me with women you aren't married to. Yes, parent our children with me. Yes, work with me hard to make this eternal. But also, if you don't dig me, let me go find someone who does. Don't take away my opportunity to be loved. I'm sure you think I'll fall apart without you, but your rejection won't kill me, and I don't believe God wants us to be miserable.

I wasn't able to recognize that Kody's inability to be a partner was a violation of that eternal contract. Nobody teaches you that. My mother had left my father, but I didn't know why, and I saw it as a failure. Besides, I had other things on my mind—and many of them erupted on-screen.

For example, I was livid when I found out Kody had kissed Robyn when they had gotten engaged. Kody found that confusing.

Remember how mortified I was by our awkward kiss at the altar?

"Kiss the next one before you marry her, because our first kiss was awkward and that was terrible," I had told him, long before another bride had appeared on the horizon. "Also, no wives should witness your first kiss. That needs to be special."

Kody agreed.

And then I found out he had been kissing Robyn.

"You're married and you're kissing another woman?"

"We talked about this," he said, as the cameras rolled. "You said you regretted having your first kiss at the altar. Don't you remember that?"

"I do," I said, because I did remember—remembered vividly how unromantic every bit of it had been. "But this hurts."

Because it was all so terribly romantic.

Because he was in love with her.

Looking back, I don't think the kiss bothered me as much as the intimacy. It didn't feel fair, but it also felt like something he couldn't control—like a different kind of love from what we shared. I was excited to have her join us, but I worried about how their relationship would affect our family.

TLC filmed a session of us all taking engagement photos with Robyn and Kody—the joining of the two families. It was a fun, happy day, but it showed our differences and warned of days to come.

"That's pretty sexy," one or all of us said about Robyn's outfit. I'm sure we all worked to control our faces. Awe. Judgment. Jealousy.

As a practical matter, it took some finagling to cover our garments. Some of our online fans made fun of our fashion choices—the long-sleeved T-shirt under a short-sleeved T-shirt? We did that to try to look hip while covering up yet another layer.

But our garments didn't limit our clothing options as much as our sister wives did. If we dressed sexy, it sparked jealousy, so we didn't do it—ever. Our church requires modesty as well, but we shied away from even high heels and form-fitting clothing.

Kody had his typical routine of spending dinner and the night with each of us in rotation, but he also planned date nights with each of us. Rather than us making dinner and serving it with the kids, Kody might take us out for dinner and a movie or on a road trip. He planned fun things for us depending on each wife's personality and preferences. Still, we all feared running into another wife while we were out for dinner or heading to the movies. What might one wife think if another wife looked hot? It wouldn't be kind. I look back on photos from the time, and it's all frump girl. Baggy clothes—I have curves and they were hidden. No style. Colors that didn't suit me. Awful.

While Robyn's clothes covered most of her skin, she had a different mindset than we did: She looked cute. And sexy. Very sexy.

Wait. Wait. What? I remember thinking. *We can do that?*

As Meri, Janelle, and I struggled to hide the collars of our special fundamentalist garments under our clothes for both the TV camera and the engagement-photo camera, Robyn, who was as of yet garmentless, wore tight jeans, tight T-shirts, and—gasp!—sexy shoes. Heels. It wasn't that we thought Robyn was doing something wrong, like she wasn't modest enough. We realized we could have been dressing like her all along, instead of so shapelessly. Robyn had style, even if it was Stephenie Meyer's Bella style. (The camisole-layered-over-T was *the* style at the time.)

And then, as is often done in our church, Kody and Robyn took engagement photos on their own. Their photographer posted one of those pictures on social media, not realizing no one was supposed to see them. In it, Kody leans back against the hood of his little white sports car, and Robyn leans into him. Their foreheads touch, with the setting sun glowing behind them. Robyn has one foot lifted behind her, showing off an incredibly high stiletto heel. Her hips press into his as he wraps his arms around her waist. They're cemented together, and there's no hint of shyness.

Robyn confided in me when she learned the photo had been leaked, and it felt like damage control—like she knew the picture would upset Meri, Janelle, and me. They're awfully suggestive for a chaste polygamist couple in the courtship stage—and for a guy who has three wives. Keep in mind that I hadn't even kissed Kody until our wedding ceremony. When our viewers later saw the leaked photo, they had plenty to say about it. The Sister Wives were feeling it, too—just not for the cameras.

We were polygamists, and we knew jealousy and its ups and downs came with our eternal agreement. We would bide our time and wait to see if things would settle after Robyn became a part of the family.

About a month before Robyn's wedding, Kody and I went to see my obstetrician, Dr. Bean, for a checkup. I was a week overdue.

"You're not really progressing," Dr. Bean said. "There's no real signs at all."

"Well, what does that mean?" I asked. "Do we just wait another week?"

Dr. Bean worried that the baby would be put under extra stress if I waited.

"Why don't we just do it now?" I asked.

Dr. Bean induced me right away, but I didn't have my go bag. It was packed and ready at home, as was Truely's. And Aspyn planned to be there for the birth. So, Kody left to collect Aspyn and the bags.

He was gone for what seemed like a long time, but my bag was right there. Run home, grab it, come back. But maybe he had to wait for Aspyn. Or maybe he'd hit traffic. Or maybe he was buying me flowers.

I didn't have a book, so I was in labor and bored, and grumpy because my husband was taking so long. When you go into labor, you expect Dad to rush around. It's a big deal. But maybe he didn't think he needed to rush because this was our sixth child. Or because I was in the hospital. He'd been incredible for the home births.

Grumpy. Or maybe lonely. Unimportant.

That's my memory of the time before Kody arrived.

The camera crew followed Kody that day, too. He rushed home, to Robyn. He needed to check in on . . . I don't know. The kids? Her feelings about my labor?

The crew filmed him kissing her. I was in labor, and he let them film him kissing his girlfriend. I found out only after I watched the episode, and it gutted me. Their premarital kissing was still hard for me, but the timing felt particularly inappropriate.

I was scared about a hospital birth because I'd only had home births, but I was thirty-eight, and I worried that something might go wrong. I knew I loved Dr. Bean. He had already helped me through so much.

Truely's birth was great. Kody was less present, but he didn't need to be so engaged because I had no pain because of the epidural—he didn't need to guide me through breathing to ease it. When it was time to push, he held my hand, gazed into my eyes, and two minutes later, Truely arrived. Easy-peasy.

Still, it was childbirth, and in my mind, that means it's all about me. All moms everywhere, you've got my back here, right? All about Truely and me.

Well, and the camera. Fortunately, I was so caught up in the "Truely and me" bit that I barely noticed, and the production team did everything they could to keep it that way. There were rules in place about where they could be and when.

My hips, of course, did their usual thing of not doing anything, so Dr. Bean put me on a bouncy ball. Then he put me in a chair to try to line up my hips.

And that's when Kody decided to talk with Dr. Bean, on camera, about how Meri had struggled to have a child. When Meri saw the episode, she lost it. We all know the deal about focusing in on the wife in labor, and also, please don't talk about my fertility issues without me.

And I was trying not to flip out while on camera having a baby. Wait a minute. I'm here in labor having your child—I don't think it's the right time to bring up Meri's infertility issues. Why don't you and Meri schedule an appointment with Dr. Bean and come in later to have that chat? Focus, Kody. Focus.

Just to be clear: We all hoped Meri would be able to have more kids. We'd had that conversation for years, so it was never a problem to talk about it in the proper setting.

But maybe not when I'm trying not to bear down. Just be present.

Truely proved to be magic. She was our smallest baby, at seven pounds, eleven ounces—the smallest of all our kids.

Everyone came to the hospital to meet her. Kody had given the kids a lecture about being quiet because it was a hospital, so they all silently trooped through the hallways to come see her.

Somehow, that teeny-tiny baby bonded with everybody. We couldn't let everybody hold her, because that's an awful lot of people with an awful lot of germs.

Kody held her first, then Aspyn, then each of the adults held her briefly. But with each person, she had these moments of connection in this cool, focused bubble of time.

And then everyone trooped back out again, and I started my first hospital recovery. Anyone who has stayed in the hospital knows that it's not a great place to rest and recover. After two days, I said, "I can't stay here anymore," and the doctor sent me home.

When we got home, Robyn took Truely for hours, and I finally got some great sleep. I was so grateful. I asked Kody to stay with me for an extra night, because I was exhausted. I still needed to take care of the kids, but he said he didn't have the time. Two weeks later, I had to start taking them back and forth to school.

My milk never came in for Truely—she just wasn't getting anything, so I had to go with formula. I was devastated: It's the only thing she needed that I couldn't give to her. I had nothing. I think it was because I was too busy. The show had just started earlier that year, so I went back to work without giving myself some time. We were new to it, and it felt like we were just sitting on a couch, so I didn't think it would be hard.

I didn't consider the stress of those conversations.

I felt as if I had crazy PMS after Truely's birth. I didn't feel logical. I look back now, and I think my feelings were legitimate. I wonder how often that is the case for postpartum depression? I'm not saying it's not real. It is. I mean, there's the normal turmoil caused by hormones and chemical imbalances during pregnancy. Then we expect that our spouses will step up when the baby is born—that they will offer help, love, and kindness. But if help, love, and kindness from your spouse wasn't the norm before, it's not going to change when you give birth. In other words, nothing changes. And then maybe— when we're expected to believe that our new gorgeous baby, with the midnight feedings and poopy diapers, should fill us with so much love that our own needs and desires don't matter—we break down.

Our culture put an extra bit of spin on it. When we sister wives talked together about hard times, it was always about how to smooth away the rough edges of our own personalities and be better. It was never about Kody's behavior; it was about our responses to Kody's behavior. Therefore, I needed to control my feelings of jealousy and rage, and if I couldn't, something was wrong.

Kody reinforced these conversations by telling me he would only spend time with me if I was "lovable," which meant on my best behavior, not comparing his behavior with Meri and Janelle to his behavior with me, and catering to his needs—like those massages, a clean house, and meals cooked to his preferences. "Lovable" meant swallowing down things that hurt. "Lovable" meant everything's fine.

But it wasn't.

"Could we put a diamond in my claddagh ring?" I'd asked as our tenth anniversary approached about five and a half years before he met Robyn. All of us had claddagh rings from Kody, but Meri and Janelle each had a diamond in theirs. "That would be really cool."

Our family loved the significance of the Irish symbol of two hands holding a heart with a crown above it: love, loyalty, and friendship. My sister wives' rings had a diamond in the heart.

"No, we don't have the money for it," Kody said.

It was a tiny diamond—a chip.

After Truely was born, we all sat together in church. Robyn had a beautiful ring, and I told her so.

"Oh, it's an old ring that Kody put a diamond in for me," she said.

"He did what?" I asked.

"Yeah, I didn't even ask. He just asked if he could borrow it, and then he brought it back with a diamond."

I blinked back angry, shocked, heartbroken tears. I had justified things to myself—the convertible, for example—but this was so specifically close to what I had asked for that it felt as if my heart had been pierced.

Do I mean so little?

"What's the deal?" I asked Kody. "I've been asking you for years for a diamond in my claddagh ring."

"We never had the money," he said.

"But you put a diamond in Robyn's ring," I said.

He was irate. It wasn't his fault; it was mine.

"You're comparing again," I remember him saying, blaming my jealousy for his behavior. "I will treat you like you are lovable when you make an effort to be lovable."

Later, humiliated and hurt, I hucked that ring into a field. I couldn't look at it anymore—I realized it didn't mean anything.

I wish I would have kept it, but I was heartbroken that he didn't believe I was special enough to warrant a diamond chip. Right away, without being asked, he'd done it for Robyn.

Who are you? I remember thinking after I threw the ring. *What is going on with you?*

I had an appointment with Dr. Bean, and he prescribed vitamins and antidepressants.

Everyone was wonderful about my postpartum depression. The kids understood, and they pitched in. Aspyn was fifteen, and she'd been excited about me having a baby. She just took over, but all the kids were helpful.

I was on the antidepressants for about a year.

"I think I'm done," I said at an appointment. "I don't think I need them anymore."

Dr. Bean knocked me down to a half dose to wean me off. While my situation hadn't gotten any better, my mind had.

Chapter Fourteen

WE'VE CHOSEN YOU

*N*ot long before Kody married Robyn, he and Meri went to Mexico for their twentieth anniversary. While we were all excited about the upcoming nuptials, there was some tension. Meri told Kody she felt a little jealous, and then said something like, "How would you feel if I were courting another guy?" That offended Kody—he said it was against God and an abomination. Meri wasn't asking him to let her marry a second husband. She just needed him to walk in her flats for a minute.

During the trip, he asked Meri if she'd like to try IVF because they'd had a hard time getting pregnant. Meri's Leon had twelve brothers and sisters with my six and Janelle's six—and more coming with Robyn's kids—but Meri had always said she wanted more children. It was a conversation we'd had as a family for years—but she knew she would either carry her own child or not do it at all. She had bonded with Robyn's kids—and Robyn—especially well.

It seemed as if their trip ended on a good note. We know because TLC filmed it: handholding on the beach, cozy over drinks, swimming with dolphins. Kody apologized for being impatient when she said she felt jealous of Robyn, and while he seemed sad about her need to try to have a baby naturally, he told her he loved her.

When they got back, we had a big discussion about whether Kody should spend more or less time with Robyn. Janelle and Kody thought he should spend more time with Robyn because he was courting her and integrating her into the family. Robyn, of course, felt she should get equal time—especially since she had moved her family to a new town. Meri and I felt like he already spent so much time with her that it was detrimental to the rest of his family—but our issue was still not with Robyn.

In fact, we liked her well enough that we wanted to get her something special to welcome her into the family: a claddagh ring. Kody had gotten her an engagement ring, but it wasn't a claddagh. Meri, Janelle, and I wanted her to feel that we loved her and were happy to have her as part of the family.

The sister wives and TLC went ring shopping. It's another of my favorite days, and it almost felt as if Robyn would bring all of us closer. I still couldn't trust Meri with my kids, but when it was just the three of us, we did okay. Though we tried to keep things real, I'm sure having the camera crew there kept us all on our best behavior, and we were excited about finding just the right ring.

"Is it for a birthday?" the jeweler asked. "Or just because?"

"Yeah, just because," Meri answered. We were still getting used to this whole "being public" thing, and it can slow down a day when you have to explain it all to every person you meet—or ruin a mood if you encounter prejudice.

"It's easier now to just say 'sisters,'" Janelle explained during that episode. "That usually shuts down the conversation."

Afterward we talked on the couch about how much we loved the detail in the ring we found for Robyn.

Robyn was amazing about the wedding. "It would be fun to include everyone," she said, especially in light of the moments of jealousy she had seen. She taught us some lessons about how to be a good sister wife. I asked Meri and Janelle if they had felt I had included them in my wedding, and yeah. No. There aren't many things in my life I wish I could change, because I wouldn't be where I am if I had, but I would change that. I would change that first kiss, too.

Robyn asked our opinions about everything. She had us pick our own flowers for the wedding, as long as they were color coordinated. I chose a wrist corsage so I could carry Truely. She invited us to the cake tasting, which was so much fun. Robyn asked us to close our eyes to vote on our favorites, and Kody took that moment to stand up and dance. Silly. None of the wives liked the same cake, which was basically how we moved through life—we were all so different. We teased Robyn for picking the same cake that Kody did.

We went with them to pick the venue, which felt odd. Meri had a big reception. Janelle didn't have one at all. And mine was small and awkward. We joked about living vicariously through Robyn's reception. She included all of the kids, which made it feel like a party and gave us so much more to focus on as a family. Robyn asked our opinions about colors for our dresses, which would all be part of her theme. She went with brown and purple, but we all picked outfits that suited us.

"I want you guys to have whatever you want and to feel beautiful that day," she told us.

She took it one step further by getting a second, brown dress for herself so we could have family photos that were about all of us, rather than about their wedding. It was all so thoughtful. It was a great example of what a sister wife could be.

There were some rough spots, too. We went shopping with her, believing we were helping choose her wedding dress. We tried on different styles for ourselves, and, standing around in our bare feet, laughed about how they fit—or didn't. Each of us had had short engagements, and the buildup for Robyn's wedding seemed never-ending. Laughing felt like a release. Then Robyn tried on so many incredible dresses, and yeah, we laughed and debated, but there's nothing quite like watching your husband's fiancée wrapped in white lace. She looked amazing in all of them, but we all liked different dresses, of course, and Robyn decided to make the decision on her own and have it be a surprise. That made sense.

"It's a secret," she said. "You'll see."

Months later, we talked about the wedding dress on the set, sitting side by side on the couch.

"I've got a bomb I'm dropping today," Kody said proudly. "You'll love this one."

Robyn looked as if she'd swallowed a frog, while the rest of us looked confused. "Bomb" could mean a lot of things, and we never knew what Kody might say.

"I picked the dress," he said.

"Did you really?" I asked.

Robyn looked as if the frog had gotten stuck in her throat. The rest of us went silent.

Kody said they had gone shopping together, and then he'd seen the one true dress.

"I was like, 'Holy cow!'" Kody said. "It was like I'd seen it in my dreams."

So many thoughts. His ten-thousand-yard stare when I'd walked into the room in my wedding dress. The special day I thought we'd had with Robyn. The intimacy involved in watching a woman trying on dresses. It felt like a betrayal. We believed she cared about our opinions, but in reality, she cared about Kody's.

"I think it's important," he said. "I don't think it's fair that I not be involved in it."

He had not been involved in our wedding at all, by choice.

"When is the groom ever involved with the wedding dress?" I asked. "Like you cared what I wore at our wedding at all?"

"It's kind of a slap in the face," Meri said.

She saw it. Janelle saw it. Robyn saw it. Vague smiles, just as we had been taught.

I took off my mic and stood up.

"You don't have to do this this way," Kody said. "It's not very . . ."

Lovable. My behavior. My rough edges.

"I need a couple of minutes to myself."

"Let her take some time, if she needs it," Meri said.

I walked away.

After we regrouped, Robyn said she had asked Kody not to say anything. Kody apologized. I explained that Kody, as a polygamist, could be a different kind of an idiot to each of his wives.

Kody said he felt numb. I apologized. For his feelings.

"You can step it up," I said. "You've chosen this. We've chosen you. We expect more."

As I got ready to go on the morning of the wedding, I hadn't seen Kody for hours. Then he stopped by.

"Hey, is everybody ready?" he called.

He was obviously excited, but we had a few moments to connect.

"You doing okay?" he asked me.

"Yeah," I said. "I'm doing okay."

We had each chosen a song for a dance with Kody, and we each had chosen flowers. I had worried so much about my bouquet at my wedding, but Robyn found a solution that ensured she could be the bride but make everyone else feel special.

We didn't film the ceremony because it's sacred to polygamists, but we had our families there, as well as mutual friends. We laughed a lot—the invitations had the wrong address, so Robyn and Kody placed a jar with balloons at the random address so people could grab the correct one. Celebration not here! And then we went crazy with family photos: Each wife with Kody and their kids. Everybody. Kody and the girls. Kody and the boys. They were beautiful family pictures. We danced.

We wore heels.

Robyn was incredible that day. I still remember it as an awesome family day.

Chapter Fifteen

MOJITOS ARE DELICIOUS

As the honeymoon began for Kody and Robyn, it ended for me.

Eleven days. Eleven days and they knew exactly where they were going. To be fair, TLC wanted to film it, so they needed to have a schedule, and they spent time with them in San Diego. Kody and Robyn then took some extra time without the crew. We had more money, which we didn't have when Kody and I got married. But it felt like a gut punch. Who leaves for eleven days when they have a hockey team of children back home? It hurt that he had planned so many activities—surfing!—and that romance had been built into the trip. Kody often accused me of comparing his treatment of each of us, but ouch. He hadn't been involved in the planning of any part of our wedding, and he'd looked miserable when we took off on our honeymoon. Even when I tried not to see, I felt like his love for her shone as if under a spotlight.

He compared her to a Diesel jeans model. I mean, c'mon. How am I going to compete with that? It was just another giddy note of his infatuation. While they surfed, I dreaded the moment he would come home and return to my bedroom, now on every fourth night rather than every third. I didn't feel wanted.

I felt miserable, like he would do his duty so he could get back to his soulmate.

While they were on their honeymoon, I took my kids on a vacation. There are always choices, and I think choosing to be positive helped me be resilient. You can't let other people steal your joy—fun can be a choice, too.

But I've never watched the honeymoon episode.

When Kody and Robyn returned, we moved forward in a swirl of kids, activities, and filming. Our schedule was so insane that we barely had time to interact, besides on the couch.

We flew to Los Angeles for our first major media trip. Once a year, all the networks announce their shows for the year, so TLC had us out. We weren't exactly city people with big-name connections, but we found ourselves sitting at a table with the TLC executives. They showed the pilot of *Sister Wives*.

When it ended, everything went dead quiet.

And then the applause began. People laughed and started talking—they loved it.

We had filmed just a few episodes, and only the crew knew about us, so we didn't know how people would react.

So far, so good.

Next up: a panel discussion with a bunch of reporters.

"Isn't polygamy a felony in Utah?" someone asked. "Are you worried that you're going to be arrested?"

A felony. Up there with murder. Yes, we are worried we will be arrested, but thanks for making a national headline of it.

"Polygamy is a felony in Utah," I said. "And it's something we're concerned about. I hope that, living in America, people can see that we're a family based on love." And so on. We're just like you, except my husband has four wives. And no, we're not swingers.

(People were all about our sex lives.)

Then we spent two days in meeting after meeting.

The press tours stressed me out more than anything I'd done in my life. We had to be "on" all the time. Oh my gosh, the media stuff is so hard. The *Today* show? Come on. I spent my days trying to sort socks for a dozen or more kids, not prepping for prime time.

TLC would take us out for dinner after our events. One night, a woman said, "Have you ever had a mojito?"

Mojitos are delicious.

I'd had beer before, and we had wine in our house for Shabbat. It wasn't Manischewitz—my sister was, at the time, a sommelier, and she found us a lovely kosher wine and said, "You can have this for Shabbat." It's still my favorite wine today: Bartenura Moscato. It's like dessert in my mouth.

I started drinking mojitos after stressful press days, and then I realized I like Moscow mules as well. It took the edge off those tough days. Yes, Mormons, fundamentalist and otherwise, don't drink alcohol. Except when we're stressed to the point of eye twitching— or realize a beer would be awesome on a hot day.

Or when we're slowly moving away from our faith.

Things changed yet again when Robyn entered the family as a wife. Before that, Kody had seemed intent on integrating Robyn into the family, but he left us out. It was more like Kody integrated himself into their family. We had some interactions together, but Kody traveled to St. George alone or with one of us, or spent time with Robyn at her house after she moved to Lehi.

After the wedding, we did more together, especially for the cameras. Parties, dinners, holidays. There were good days when

I thought our bonds would increase and we would all grow old together. There were days when I wasn't sure I could be any happier, days surrounded by happy, healthy children. We'd been blessed with our babies, and at that point, Kody made time for them.

When I was a kid, my family went "ice blocking," which is like sledding in the summer. We would get large blocks of ice, put a towel or sweatshirt over them, and then ride the blocks down a hill. On a hot day, it's even better because the blocks get all slippery. Ice blocking goes way back for Utah families—to pioneer days—and I had been encouraging Kody to do it for years. For a large family, it's cheap entertainment, but it also gets everyone outside and active.

This probably provided our viewers the first glimpse of how rough-and-tumble our kids could be: in one shot, as an older kid shoots down the hill, one of our little girls launched herself on her and they rolled off the block in a bundle, giggling hysterically.

It was a good day.

But the nights changed after Robyn married Kody, too.

When Robyn joined the family, Kody would come to my house for his normal visit, but then he would go to Robyn's house—she had remained in her own house after she married Kody—to tuck in her kids every night.

You caught that, right? This was the man who refused to tuck in our kids when I'd begged for his help when I was working nights. "Ask your sister wives," he'd said.

I didn't understand why he couldn't have done the same for me. Acts of service is my love language (well, and parties). I did things for him to show him I loved him. For him to not do back meant, to me, that he didn't love me—especially when he was willing to do for Robyn. When I understood that he was over at her house all the time to help her, I also understood that he loved her in a different way from how he loved me.

To stay in this family I had to make a decision. Do I pretend I'm helpless to try to get more help? Do I throw a fit when he does come over? Do we talk about it?

Or do I shove it under the rug because he's going to be at my place only one of every three or four nights, and if I try to talk about what's going on, he'll simply go to another wife's house?

Some guys do great in polygamous families—and they would find what I'm saying offensive. But some avoid their responsibilities by leaving it to the wife to take care of everything, or by leaving if the wife tries to address an issue. It wasn't a partnership, even—as Kody showed when I needed help when I was working—in parenting our children. I often felt like a single mom. I'm sure you're reading this and thinking, "Why didn't you leave when . . . ?" If you've been through a breakup, there are a million places where you know you should go, but you keep waiting for a sign anyway—usually a sign that you're wrong or that he's changed. Or you worry you can't afford it. Or that people will judge you for your failure. Or that you'll lose the father of your children.

And just because Kody didn't love me, just because I knew he wasn't a partner, just because I knew he was in love with Robyn, didn't mean that I wasn't still in love with him.

It'll get better, I told myself. *Relationships tend to cool after those first infatuated months, and things will go back to normal.*

As a polygamist, I had a hard time understanding what "love someone more" meant. It hadn't been my experience. I love my kids the same. I'd never felt like Kody loved me more or less than he loved Meri and Janelle, even if I had moments of jealousy or frustration. Kody was different with Robyn.

I wonder what we would have done if he'd torn off the Band-Aid? If he'd said, "Listen, I know this isn't what you signed up for, but I'm in love with Robyn, and I think we need a change of plan." What if he'd said, "I can't stand to spend my days away from her"? It would have felt like the most terrible thing in the world, but would it have been better for all of us in the long run?

Chapter Sixteen

IT FELT SO REAL

As soon as we went national-TV-show public, Utah state authorities had to decide what to do with us. Do they allow us to flaunt our felony offense? Do they hope interest dies out after season one and we disappear? Do they decide it's not a big deal after all and change the law?

The answer seemed predetermined.

A beehive symbol represents Utah and the LDS church. About one-third of the people who live in Utah are actively involved in the church. Think about that: All the busy little bees go to work, go to church, and then they report back to the mother hive. Everyone stays in line. If you drink coffee, it's a religious offense and you can't go to the temple. Alcohol? Forget it. The phone chain for school emergencies operates along the neighborhood ward lines. (Even now, I can see the neighborhood ward from my front door.) If you're new to the state, everybody knows and the local missionaries will show up at your doorstep to "talk about our savior, Jesus Christ." The LDS church owns a TV station, a newspaper, and a part of the main street in downtown Salt Lake. In fact, locals believe the IRS is based in Ogden because the U.S. government knows Utahns will dot their i's and cross their t's—and everybody else's, too.

If they don't, their bishop will counsel them. If they don't, they can't go to temple. If they don't, everyone will know.

The church has spent the past several years trying to modernize their image, but people still associate Mormons with polygamy, even though the church banned it more than a century ago. They don't much like that we exist as a reminder.

They weren't going to give us a fine for a felony offense and let us live happily ever after. We assumed they would arrest Kody with the local TV stations alerted and the talking points determined ahead of time. And frankly, we knew we took a risk when we agreed to the show, but we hoped to shine a light on the civil rights argument for leaving polygamists alone.

People don't have to like it. People don't have to engage in it. But why are they worried about what other consenting adults are doing if it's not hurting anyone?

I believed that then, and I believe it now that our children, as consenting adults not involved in behavior that's hurting anyone, are making their own decisions about their relationships, religion, and even sexuality.

In any case, our demonstration of a kinder, gentler polygamy seemed likely to rile up the locals.

Our own church didn't support us, either. When we decided to do the show, it upset many of our leaders. One leader, who had always been a friend, deserted us entirely. Church leaders didn't like the idea of the show generally, and then we talked about sex on the first episode. We felt everybody needed to know it was three separate marriages, that there was no weirdness going on in the bedroom. Seriously, there was barely anything going on in my bedroom at all, but our point on that first show was that our sex lives were monogamous and nobody else's business beyond that.

"We each have sex only with Kody."

Clutch my pearls.

The church leaders pulled us in and yelled at us.

They believe polygamy is a secret, special lifestyle that should be kept private. Even the phrase "sister wife" is considered private and important, so it angered them that we called the show *Sister Wives*. How do you argue back? We were raised in so much secrecy that it's hard to know what is because of sacred teachings and what is because of fear.

Just after Robyn's wedding, TLC showed us in an absolute panic trying to get out of Utah because the police planned to arrest Kody and, possibly, the rest of us. It may have seemed dramatic, but for us, it was real. It felt so, so real.

We got a veiled threat from the Utah County Attorney's Office. It sounded as if people called in and complained, so the police felt they had to do something. After that, every sighting of a police cruiser brought visions of cops bursting through the front door and dragging Kody off into the night.

I kept thinking about my dad and how the police had separated his family. I had been raised to fear the law, anyway, but when we learned they planned to arrest Kody, we realized we had to go. Meri had already lost her job working with troubled youth after we went public, and there didn't seem to be any good reason to stay—not only might we lose Kody, but anyone who associated with us could be at risk. We worried that, ultimately, Kody would be able to have a relationship with only Meri and Leon.

We had planned to leave Utah when we went public, but we needed some time to sell the house and find a new place to live, not to mention herd all the adults, children, and their possessions in some reasonable manner so we could pack.

We knew that in Nevada our family legally looks like cohabitation with several partners, rather than bigamy, as long as Kody was legally married to only one wife. Las Vegas was the closest-to-home city that would allow us to live our lifestyle. We figured we'd be the least of Vegas's problems.

We told the kids just after Christmas, and I think that's when the first visible cracks in our family appeared. The kids were old enough to have opinions, and they did not want to go. They did not feel as if they had any input, and some of the older kids had planned to graduate soon with their friends. In their eyes, I think, it felt like a betrayal. Not only were their whole lives suddenly in the public eye because of the show, but they were about to lose the support system they'd built in Utah. I know it didn't feel fair to them.

Some of them started packing, and some rebelled by slow rolling it. But when the cops began to slowly patrol our street, our kids understood the threat. It terrified them. We packed so fast, just taking necessities, and then basically fled in the middle of the night. We didn't know if the government hoped we'd go and solve their problem—so they'd just let us drive away—or if they'd show up suddenly and make an issue of us. We finally got out of there, but we created an unwieldy caravan of cars and moving trailers and trucks, so we could have been stopped anywhere along the way.

When we arrived in Las Vegas, we felt like fugitives—from the law, and each other.

Chapter Seventeen

WE'RE JUST DOING
THE BEST WE CAN IN
A HOUSE FULL OF LOVE

*T*elevision is an ego trip, or it can be. We learned that 2.26 million people tuned in to the first episode, and it was impossible to make that make sense. I used to rib Kody that the show was called *Sister Wives*, not *Kody and the Sister Wives*. And he'd say, "But it's really about me." He was right, to some extent. He'd say that he was the most dynamic of all of us.

"I would agree that you're the most dramatic of us," I would tease.

He had always been like that. When we went to his high school reunion, that was his reputation in school—that he always had an ego. Wrestling champ, popular, and bigger-than-life dance moves.

We worried that the kids would be bullied in public school, but that was never a problem. They had wonderful teachers, particularly at the high school. The kids outed themselves as being part of the polygamist Brown family, but the funny thing about being a kid is you're a bit self-involved by default. Zits. Clothes. Crushes. The other kids had their own stuff to worry about. And, in Vegas, kids expressed themselves in big, weird, wonderful ways. Purple hair or combat boots. Gender fluidity. Drama Club. Football. They could see past the polygamy to our kids' individual personalities. Usually, they were just curious, and our kids happily answered questions—explaining that they weren't polygamists themselves, they simply had polygamist parents. They talked about the things they liked about it—lots of siblings and close adults—and the things they didn't—strict rules and limited one-on-one time. The Brown children also traveled in a pack, and there was never a shortage of older siblings to come to a younger kid's defense or to defuse a situation.

At first, being recognized was fun for them. They were mini celebrities. Then it became exhausting. These weren't kids who had ever sought the spotlight. They'd gone to a small church school and spent most of their time with their brothers and sisters. Suddenly, strangers wanted selfies or to tell them they loved them on the show. Usually people were great, but sometimes someone would ask the kids an inappropriate question or offer up opinions about them as humans. As kids, they needed the freedom to figure out who they were outside the spotlight.

Their feelings about it all came in waves: One kid might be shy one season and outgoing the next. Another might feel bitter about spending their life on TV. They could choose how much they wanted to participate, but their family still showed up in homes across America once a week or for a weekend of binge-watching.

As a family, we were careful about our outings. People got used to us in the grocery store and the neighborhood. There might be initial excitement or concern, but the novelty quickly wore off. We avoided the Strip, with the casinos and scantily clad humans. It was too crowded, and people recognized us every time we went. They'd make a big, awkward, drunken fuss about seeing us, which could be fun but was mostly just weird.

We had a few *Sister Wives* events for our fans in Vegas, so we'd get to interact with people, which I loved. One time, I hit the bathroom during an event. While I was in a stall, I heard a lady say, "I think Kody and the sister wives are out there."

"Oh yeah," I said from my stall. "I saw them, too!"

"No way!" I heard some other woman say.

"I'm sure it's them," the first lady said.

"Yeah, it's definitely them," I said.

Then I walked out of the stall.

"Hey," I said.

Heh. They were lovely.

Generally, the adults felt pretty comfortable with the cameras and the publicity. We knew who we were, and we often talked about our ethics, principles, and beliefs. Still, the show affected each of us differently.

I found myself making more choices. I think that happened for all of us: When I saw myself on camera, when I had that mirror held up for me, I realized I can be pretty selfish (though now I wonder if I was being selfish in a self-care way because my needs weren't being met, rather than a self-involved way). And I saw that I asked my kids questions but didn't wait for the answers—I just answered for them. I wasn't great at conversations.

Ouch.

Everything felt hard, but there were things I could control. I decided to use that mirror to make some changes, to listen better to my kids and improve my mom skills. I had always been a good mom, but good moms want to be better.

Kody's an internet comment reader, and comments can make you feel like an awful human. (Which is why I avoid them.) Because of social media, Kody believed the show made him look bad. The comments about Robyn? The love of his life? Those upset him. It's funny how that stuff can affect you. At the beginning, the comments were more positive than negative, but the negative ones could dig in like fishhooks and then drag you down.

Being married to Robyn changed him, too, and I could see that clearly as the new episodes came out. Kody and Robyn became similar—he started to use her expressions: "I'm just sitting here thinking," "You got to understand," and "Bull crap." He dressed differently, his shirts tighter. They began to look like a couple. I'm sure some of that came from never having to hide their relationship—they had, after all, had their wedding broadcast to an audience of two million people—but some of it came from falling in love.

Robyn liked to say that she could "speak Kody," as if the wives who had been with him for as long as two decades needed a translator. In reality, it often seemed as if he repeated on camera what he'd heard in a discussion they'd already had at home.

Unlike the Brown family tradition of simply moving forward, Robyn liked to think about everyone's perspective, and to talk through conflicts, which made for great TV. She tried to help Kody see how his words or actions might affect his other wives. I think she wanted to make sure Kody treated everyone well. But that also meant Kody talked about his other relationships with her. I hadn't agreed to that, and I was often hurt by how much she knew, as well as irritated by how she influenced Kody's behavior toward me, even if it was in a good way. She wasn't my counselor. I wasn't married to Kody and Robyn—just Kody. And I'd known Kody for long enough to know when he parroted Robyn's words as reasons for his own behavior.

I think, as I met more people, I saw them as members of my expanding community. It felt safe to me. But in my mind, Kody's outlook seemed to become fear-based, as if everyone were judging him and his family even as he seemed to enjoy the celebrity. It's possible that's why he started to worry about loyalty and which of his wives supported him, and whether he was doing enough to control outcomes in his family as the "patriarch." He started to use the word *covenant*, which wasn't something we did in the early days of our relationships with Kody, as well as *agreement*, as if we had all entered a contract with him where we agreed his word was law.

We wanted to present a positive image on the show, but we also had to be careful not to upset the balance, precarious as it was. If I complained about our marriage on the show, Kody spent less time with me and my kids. If we didn't do things his way, he'd punish us by withholding his attention—Vegas was all about that. If I raised a concern, he would say, "Well, we can choose to fight, or we can choose not to, and I'll stay." Husbands don't go to the doghouse in polygamy. They go to the next wife in the chain.

I stopped telling him when something bothered me.

It was exhausting. I felt like we always had to be on, but in the background, everything felt hard. I never knew what we would dissect on the set. My face shows everything.

Ev.

Ry.

Thing.

If someone says something dumb? Side-eye. Shocking? Eyebrows all the way up. Funny-but-not-meant-to-be-funny? Lips pursed to hold back inappropriate laughter. Angry? Oh. I will stand up and walk away.

So I tried to rein that in. But they'd ask a question I didn't expect, and I'd think, *Crap. Now what do I say?* Best face forward. We needed people to believe we still functioned as a family, even though I rarely saw anyone but the kids off the set.

"We're just doing the best we can and raising our kids in a house full of love," I would say to the camera.

Before that point, our relationships with Kody had been a bit more push and pull. Kody had always withdrawn his attention when he was angry with one of us, but when Janelle left town in a huff or I headed off to spend time with my parents, he'd pull us back in. A big date. A lovely gift. A visit where he engaged with us.

Love bombing.

Through it all, the sister wives returned to our core principle of working to improve ourselves, but sometimes it seemed only to apply to the women.

Soon after we moved to Vegas, Meri counseled me as I struggled through my relationship with Kody. He'd skipped both my birthday and our anniversary that year. We all used to talk about how when he looked at you, you felt as if you were the only woman in the world. But that stopped. Feeling seen? That's a form of intimacy.

"I have to block it out, and make pretend everything is okay," I told her.

Meri told me, on camera, that I was in charge of my own choices, and that only I could make myself happy.

"You have to do it without putting it all on him," she told me. "You're the only person you can change. You can't change anyone else."

I do believe that. But in a relationship, there has to be some give-and-take, and our rule was always, "Make Kody happy." I could change myself and try to look at things more positively, but if the other person doesn't change too, then it's not really a relationship.

After my conversation with Meri, Kody and I went on an on-camera date. He took me to play paintball, and then up in a helicopter, which I had always wanted to do, and it was amazing. He even threw me a birthday party to make up for the one he'd missed. I felt incredible, as if I had found my best friend again.

Afterward, I apologized to him for what I had been feeling. Like, *Oh you're wonderful. I'll just go back to being a good wife now.*

But nothing had changed. We'd had one good day.

Chapter Eighteen

I PUT ON MY BIG-GIRL PANTS

*I*nitially, we couldn't find homes near each other in Las Vegas, let alone a place big enough to accommodate Kody, his four wives, and their sixteen children. The mansion-sized houses had only five massive bedrooms.

We moved into four separate small rental houses. None of us had room to have everyone over. In Lehi, we had to work through our differences each day because everybody but Robyn and her kids lived in the same house. In Vegas, we would have to make an effort to see each other.

I had some hope, though: I lived about six doors away from Robyn, so I thought, *Oh my gosh. We can get closer, and our kids can hang out together.* It would be an opportunity to develop our relationship. I'd been lonely in Lehi, and Kody had been on my case about getting along better with my sister wives—even though he didn't get along with Meri, either—so I hoped Robyn and I would be tight.

When I first met Robyn, I noticed that she cried often. I saw it as sincere—she's an emotional person who's in tune with her feelings. I thought she was altruistic and kind, and I believed she wanted what was best for everyone.

The friendship dream wouldn't pan out. Robyn was always busy, so she needed to know if we planned to come over ahead of time. I never felt invited to her house, and we couldn't just drop by, as had been our habit in the big house with the kids scrounging for other moms' leftovers. The kids couldn't just walk down the street to play. And I felt like I couldn't pop in because Kody was always there.

I could see his car in her driveway.

Our kids could too.

They had noticed Kody spent more time with Robyn and her kids in Lehi, but I told them what I told myself: "He's just spending time getting to know them. It's going to be fine—it'll all balance out." I kept thinking back to what it had been like in Wyoming. If we could get back to that place, I would stay for eternity, even with the ups and downs. The kids were, for the most part, not thrilled about the move, so I figured we'd pull together as a family to make the transition easier. I thought things would even out.

But it felt like Robyn ended up needing more. Kody wanted to give her more.

That meant Kody didn't hang out with our kids, either. He came over at five or six in the evening on every third or fourth night, and never during the day on the weekends. We all had the same work schedule, and we didn't work full days. He'd come for dinner, spend a little bit of time with our kids (Truely, one; Ysabel, eight; Gwendlyn, ten; Paedon, thirteen; Mykelti, fifteen; and Aspyn, sixteen), and then when they left for school in the morning, he'd leave. My kids have told me that, starting in Las Vegas, Kody was an absent dad.

I was caught in this bizarre love pentagon/Catch 22: I wanted a better relationship with Kody. Kody was angry with me for not having a better relationship with my sister wives. I wanted to improve my relationship with Robyn, but Kody was always at her house.

Meri and Janelle didn't believe me that Kody still spent the majority of his time with Robyn.

"Can you not see it?" I'd say. "Don't you listen to your kids?" Both Janelle's and my kids talked to me about it—about how Kody didn't have time for them because he was always with Robyn. I felt like I was yelling into the wind. But Janelle and Meri couldn't see Kody's car in Robyn's driveway.

Janelle didn't need to see it—she and Kody were fine. She was living her best life and liked the independence. Meri had a stronger friendship with Robyn and a strained relationship with Kody, so it would have been harder for her to see.

After I had Truely when we lived in Lehi in April 2010, Kody stayed with me for two days.

"Can you stay longer?" I asked him then. "Because I need help."

We had a new baby, and he looked at her adoringly. Maybe this would be a chance to get some more Kody time for my family?

"No," I remember him telling me, "I don't have time." He reminded me that I could ask my sister wives for help. We did help each other. When Janelle had each of her babies, we would go to the hospital, and then I would help her when she got home. Kody would spend a couple of days with Janelle after each birth.

After Robyn had Solomon in October 2011—about ten months after we moved to Vegas—Kody stayed with her for two weeks before the baby was born. He also stayed with her for two weeks after. *What?* I remember thinking. *That's not polygamy. That's not relying on your sister wives.* I wondered if Robyn was that much more helpless than the rest of us. Or maybe Kody finally listened to the midwife who had always told him he should spend more time bonding and helping?

Or did Robyn matter that much more?

Meri, Janelle, and I had always had kids to take care of, a family to run. Somebody's birthday was coming up or someone was getting married, and we needed to put aside our feelings. For the first ten years of the original marriages, Kody traveled for work, so the day-to-day operations were up to the wives. Even as Janelle and Meri avoided each other, they both knew they could depend on each other without question for family and emergencies.

I don't think Robyn ever experienced plural marriage. Rather than rely on her sister wives, Robyn had my Mykelti help with her kids. (Robyn and Mykelti had a wonderful relationship, and I was grateful for that.) Then Robyn's sister moved in to help, and then she had a nanny—we'll get to that (and to the T-shirt I wear when I work out). It always blew my mind that she relied on people other than her sister wives. She rarely asked for our help with anything. She didn't need to.

She was new, and maybe she didn't understand how it worked, I reasoned.

And, if I wanted to spend time with Kody, I needed to have a good relationship with Robyn. So, I invited her for lunch when Solomon and Truely were little. I remember she held baby Solomon in her arms as we filmed the scene at a restaurant we liked.

We talked about our relationship, and I told her that it had been tough when she showed up to the family—and that I had been jealous. I don't remember taking it out on her, but I'd heard that was how she took it.

In particular, she had been angry about Christmas.

We had been thoroughly stressed just before we moved to Las Vegas: As we welcomed Robyn into the family, we wondered if we could get out of Utah before the police arrested Kody. We decided to spend Christmas in the mountains to find some peace. I had always

loved planning holidays and parties, and I worked to include everyone's traditions. When Robyn came into the family, I told her that
we celebrated Joseph Smith's birthday on December 23, as I had
been raised to do. I carried that over into my marriage to Kody—it
was the piece I added to our holiday celebrations. Every December
24, Meri had Christmas Eve at her place. On Christmas morning,
Janelle made breakfast. I told Robyn about the traditions we had
settled into, but also asked her if she wanted to add a tradition to
bring a bit of home. To me, they were fun, inviting conversations.

Then I got a visit from Kody. Robyn told him she felt I had been
controlling, and he wanted to let me know I had been rude. Somehow, me trying to welcome her into the family got twisted into me
trying to put her in her place or telling her she had parameters she
needed to fit into.

I had been clueless. That first Christmas, Meri made her traditional Christmas pajamas for everyone, and Robyn created sweet
ornaments for each member of the family based on their personalities or hobbies. After the talk with Kody, I figured she and I just got
our wires crossed.

In any case, I apologized for any bad behavior that came from
my jealousy.

"I want you to know, during all of it, it was him I had a hard
time with," I said. "It wasn't you. It was Kody. I just felt left."

I told her I was sorry.

I meant it sincerely, no excuses. I came to that meeting hoping
to build a friendship. She started to cry.

"I thought you didn't like me," I remember her saying, or something similar.

No, I was angry about Kody.

"But I was worried you were angry with me."

Nope, Kody.

Pretty quickly, I understood that what I said to Robyn would go back to Kody, and there might be a twist to it.

Then, though the wives agreed that we wouldn't talk about what happened in the bedroom, Robyn somehow found out that I no longer gave Kody massages.

I didn't tell her.

"Why aren't you doing massages for Kody anymore?" she asked.

"He doesn't give back," I said. "So why would I do that?"

"Oh really? He's such a great husband."

Is he? I thought it was a betrayal that he would talk to her about our sex life. And that she would allow him to.

Deep breath.

That doesn't mean Robyn and I couldn't get along. I put on my big-girl (special Mormon under) pants, and we did things together. We bought special dishes for family functions, and that was fun. We threw parties and planned activities, and I enjoyed it. She added to Passover and made it lovely—I never liked doing Passover because I missed our Easter tradition that had disappeared when Kody decided it was pagan.

"What can we do to change this up a little bit?" Robyn asked, and then went for it. She added a scripture treasure hunt and morphed it into something our kids enjoyed. I was grateful and have some beautiful memories of that time, but I didn't let down my guard.

Chapter Nineteen

BRINGING THE BOY TO THE YARD

*H*aving our own homes allowed each of us to grow—and undoubtedly gave each of the wives the distance we needed to better understand ourselves as individuals, rather than as cogs in the family machine. I no longer coordinated parties, handled lesson plans, or mediated relationships. My role within the large family seemed to evaporate.

I felt like I could breathe for the first time in years—without walking on eggshells in my own living room. I loved it. If the kids hadn't been there, I would have danced, Tom Cruise–style, through the house in an oxford shirt and long Mormon underwear.

Janelle's kids came over all the time, and we all saw each other on the weekends or at family parties, and I knew my sister wives were there for emergencies. But we didn't have real conversations. Small talk? Sure. But we spent the whole workday in each other's space, and then we'd sit down on the couch, usually together, and listen to each other interpret our family. Think about that: When was the last time you dissected the deep meaning of a four-year-old's birthday party?

It was all so carefully orchestrated. What can I say that won't make this person angry, make this person cry, or make the audience think this person is mean? If I were just talking with Janelle, I could lay things out, for the most part. But on set? Forget it. It was exhausting and unrealistic. And by the time we saw each other outside the show, we were just done.

Our homes were sanctuaries.

When we lived together, I often felt as if my opinion, and my needs, didn't matter. In Vegas, I was essentially a single mom making her own decisions. Better still, I had some cash. Before the show, we lived in absolute poverty. If I needed money for the kids' shoes—or food to feed our children—I had to ask the family. Even though I worked, the money went in the family pot and often went to other things, so I never had enough, even for groceries.

But when the show started, TLC paid the family, and then each of us would be paid out of the family account. There was no set amount: We each told Kody how much we needed, and he wrote us a check. I had no idea how much anyone else got, and it never occurred to me to ask. Why would anyone need more than I did? I assumed anything left over would remain in the main account.

The sister wives and Kody met to talk about the family money, such as when one of the kids had a health expense, or when Meri wanted to buy her family's bed-and-breakfast. In that case, it was money we simply didn't have. The decisions could be painful—and difficult to understand because we didn't know the whole of our financial situation. Kody's name was on everything, including all our leases and the homes we owned, which complicated everything from trying to get financing to trying to file our taxes.

At one point, the family talked about taking a vacation using money from the show. But we didn't know how long the windfall would last. I thought a vacation wasn't the best use of the money—it didn't fit in with our family goals.

"Wait," I said, "none of us have yards." We had talked in the past about how we could create memories with our kids if we had a place for them to play outside.

"Can we talk about that as an option?"

I feel like it's one of the only times my voice was heard during a family committee: we each got a yard.

We also constantly tried to come up with other business ideas so we'd have something sustainable when the show ended. We talked about becoming Realtors, Meri and I started our own online shops selling clothing through a franchise, and Kody always had a scheme. Robyn created some neat jewelry and then developed the My Sister-wife's Closet concept. The pieces featured the elements—fire, water, air, and earth—or hearts and dragons, or claddaghs, and she built an online shop to sell them. We all did our best to promote them online, and we displayed them at a few trade shows, but the business never took off.

When I managed my own finances, I found I could budget well. It felt good to know I could take care of myself just fine, thank you, without asking the family's permission for potatoes and ground beef, or a trampoline for my backyard. I could put aside money for college funds and retirement—and not think about which item I would have to leave with the cashier when the total was more than I had in my wallet.

The kids had new backpacks and clothes for school. They could do extracurricular activities. We could go on trips. We got a nice TV. Our furniture didn't all come from a secondhand store. We started to play more.

I worked to take good care of my finances so we would be okay when the show ended. I felt solid and dependable for my people.

But even though we lived in separate homes with separate

finances, we always remembered we were Kody Brown's wives—we were each part of a couple.

I remember filming a trip to a furniture store in Vegas soon after Meri got her house. We got baby furniture for Robyn, and Meri made sure she had what she needed when the little ones were at her place. It was always about the whole family, even when Meri knew she likely wouldn't have more kids. But she also picked a living room set that she said she would never have picked on her own: Kody liked it. Technically, she could have picked something she preferred. But if she wanted Kody to spend time with her, she had to make sure he would enjoy being at her place. Yes, any couple will compromise on their decorating choices—but "compromise" and "bringing the boy to the yard" are different things.

I knew Kody wouldn't come to my home if the kids weren't well behaved, the food wasn't what he liked, and the house wasn't clean and decorated to his taste.

Dinner was ready, usually, when he arrived, but he was picky about what he ate—he liked only basic foods. It was all steak, sweet potatoes, brussels sprouts, and spinach. I usually had to make a different meal for the kids—and then Gwendlyn was a vegetarian, so it would be three meals. It could get complicated, especially if he didn't tell me he was coming in advance, which happened often and was one of our biggest fights. I needed to plan, and he felt I was trying to control him.

I wanted him to feel comfortable and relaxed while he was in my home, but it's funny to think about now: We all had the same job; the four wives handled childcare, shopping, cooking, and housework; and we each made sure the house was comfortable for Kody when he came over. Somehow, Kody was the busiest of all of us.

Then something happened that made everything that had come before—the eternal commitment, the moment he told me he loved me after our trip to Nauvoo, my identity as a wife—feel like a farce.

The sister wives wrote a book together published in 2012. For the book, Meri, Janelle, Kody, Robyn, and I each talked separately to a writer, who then weaved the story of our early years together, as well as Robyn's integration into the family. Talking with the writer took me straight back to my twenties, when I was young and crushing on Kody, and admiring Kody and Meri as a couple—so pre-Janelle, too.

Kody had a different memory.

Before we got married, Meri, Kody, and I had got caught in a snowstorm while driving from Salt Lake to Wyoming with a group of people for a retreat at Kody's parents' house. I loved seeing his family, and I felt like our bond as friends had grown stronger. We'd been in the car for hours after having to pull over and spend the night on the road. I was starving, and we ended up at a gas station. I ate a lot of junk food back then, and chili cheese nachos were my favorite thing.

"The sight of this chubby girl in my car devouring chili cheese nachos for breakfast put the brakes on our relationship," Kody wrote in the book.

Are you serious? I thought after reading the draft. *You were disgusted with me when I ate nachos? And you weren't attracted to me? Why did you marry me?*

This is what you tell the world about your wife? In your forties, when you absolutely know how hurtful it would be—or you should.

In *Becoming Sister Wives*, we found out stuff about each other that we didn't know, and it was brutal. I knew Meri and Janelle had struggled, but I didn't know the details. I felt heartbroken reading that book.

Mykelti read it, and she called me right after.

"I had no idea Dad felt that way about you," she said. She was so upset.

I was, too. We had been married for about eighteen years when I read the book, and I didn't know Kody had never been attracted to me. I felt so humiliated. The whole world knew almost before I did. And now my kids knew, too.

On camera, in front of the sister wives, Kody said, "I was not attracted to Christine in any kind of physical sense."

You can see the hurt on my face, even as I initially tried to make a joke of it.

"You were not attracted to Christine," the host repeated back.

"That's an understatement," Kody replied.

Janelle's face. Robyn's face. Horrified. I tried to smile through it, but it came out as more of a grimace. Oh, Kody. Gee. We just never know what he's going to say.

Why did you say you love me?

Why did you propose to me?

If you love me now, why would you hurt me so publicly?

A knife to the kidneys.

He played it like it was a tragedy—that he had to marry me. That wasn't the tragedy. The tragedy was that he kept me from someone who would love me. The tragedy was the narcissism of it, the belief that I wouldn't have moved on if he had laughed and said he wanted to keep me as a friend.

You're really putting this in a book?

Kody later said he felt like he had to marry me because I was "polygamy royalty" because of my grandfathers. Had to marry me why? Had to marry me because you thought it would make you look good while knowing I would be eternally married to someone who didn't love me?

I was heartbroken.

That new bit of knowledge didn't help our relationship. That he humiliated me also did not help. What else wasn't true? I felt as if I had been robbed of the ability to make a good life decision because he hadn't told me how he felt when he asked me to marry him. I also believed it was unfixable. Chemistry is there—or it isn't.

But because I had never had chemistry, I didn't understand how it was supposed to feel. I didn't know how it felt to be adored. He did his duty and stayed with me every fourth night, but staying the night didn't necessarily mean physical intimacy. If Kody showed up just before bed and left as soon as he got up, it could feel like punishment. It definitely didn't feel like companionship.

Chapter Twenty

KODY BROWN:
LORD OF THE RINGS

I was in deep. I loved our kids. I was building our future financially. I didn't want to tear my family away from stability again. I still dreamed that our eternal marriage would reach the stage where we all settled into a happy routine, enjoyed each other's company, and watched together as our children raised their children.

I have good memories of our moms in Vegas. I liked watching them together. One year, Kody took them all out for Mother's Day: Robyn's mom, Meri's mom, Janelle's mom, and my mom. They loved each other, and they loved Kody. We all became so close—one of the things I had hoped for when I became a sister wife.

Like every family, we had wonderful days and bad ones that melded together into years. There were times when Kody and I got along, and we were fine. We didn't have a true intimacy piece to the relationship, even if he still visited my bedroom, and that's undoubtedly why I never felt secure in our relationship. I loved him, but I didn't know what deep love felt like.

It's hard for me to remember the good, sometimes, but there were reasons to stay. Aspyn, my oldest, has a video of Kody and me swing-dancing in the kitchen.

She posted it on social: "This is my parents today."

It was cute.

In Vegas, we were still trying, even if it felt like everything was slipping sideways.

Things would come up on set that were painful—one of us, usually Kody, would say something that hurt. Or I remember Kody's rotating schedule came up because, while the schedule was generally every four nights, he might show up unexpectedly at one of the other wives' houses if he was withholding attention or a wife couldn't host him that night, and we wouldn't be ready for him. That could bring feelings of irritation or rejection because getting ready for Kody was a production, and he was never part of that production. He didn't help with the meals or the housework. So, our producer suggested we start to see a family therapist.

It did help. We sorted through some things before we had to do it on set, or we sorted through things after we were on set. It still didn't always feel safe, and some of those therapy sessions brought up things I didn't need to know.

For example, we'd had some drama over the years over rings. (I've been told the rings are a thing on the blogs. It's funny, to me, what people wonder about.)

Meri got Kody a wedding ring when they got married. One day, when he was shopping with Janelle about ten years after the wedding, Kody melted it down to add the gold to some of our girls' claddagh rings—he gave each of them one when they turned a certain age. But he hadn't talked to Meri about it, and they were rocky.

I was furious. Why would you do something like that? He felt frustrated that Meri had so much ownership of him—first wife, legal marriage. But good lord. Talk to her.

Then, a few months after he met Robyn, he started wearing another ring—some sort of signet ring.

"What's that ring?" I asked.

"Oh, Robyn gave it to me," he said.

"You're not even married yet," I said, "and you're wearing a ring from Robyn."

"Oh, yeah," he said. "She bought it a while back—she's had it for years, but she never had anyone to give it to. Now she feels like I earned it."

Right. Here's the thing: You can't melt down your ring with Meri and then wear a ring that your girlfriend gave you when you have three wives at home.

Maybe you can give her your letterman's jacket to wear, too?

At about the time Robyn joined the family, I saw a cool ring modeled after one Joseph Smith wore. It was a simple band with an oval engraved in it. I checked in with the sister wives to see if I should get it—I saw it as a cool ring that connected Kody to our founder, and not as something that connected Kody to me.

"Should we give him this ring?" I asked.

They all said they were fine with it. It was a gift from us, something I happened to see that had a cool story.

"Robyn gave me a ring, and you were mad," Kody said.

Check. Yes, I was.

"And then you gave me a ring, and for some reason, that was okay," he continued.

"Well, first, I was your wife when Robyn gave you the ring, and she was not," I said. "And the Joseph Smith ring wasn't meant to be anything other than something I happened to see that I thought you would like, and, after checking in with my sister wives, decided to get for you."

Nope. That was a bad decision, he (or someone) was mad, and he did not wear that ring for long.

I didn't know whether to feel bad or to be angry because all my sister wives had told me they were fine with me buying the ring. I acted on the information I had. But that's how it seemed sometimes—like everyone held on to little bits of information to either protect themselves or find control in a family dynamic that could change instantly. Each wife, including me, talked to Kody about the other wives, in part to try to resolve problems, but also to let off steam. Kody was like the grandmaster of information, and he used it for control, too.

But sometimes Kody was on the receiving end in our therapy sessions.

Kody found out I had chucked his diamond-less claddagh ring into a field during a particularly bad therapy session.

"You did what?" the therapist said.

"I threw it," I said.

"Maybe you could have talked about it a little bit more," she said.

"Yeah," I said, "I probably could have melted it down."

"No," I remember her saying, "that's not the right answer either."

I was legit angry that he had put a little diamond chip in Robyn's ring and not in mine after I had asked so many times, and I should have been, but she was right. There were better ways to handle it— for both of us.

In Vegas, the four sister wives went in on a claddagh ring for Kody. It could represent all four of us.

And, at some point, Meri and Robyn got a claddagh ring together, too.

Then, when Robyn started My Sisterwife's Closet, her jewelry company, Kody designed a ring to sell. It was crazy expensive.

Dude, I remember thinking. *No one can afford a ring like that.*

He designed it with a sapphire on the inside of the band—so you couldn't see it. To me, that meant he saw himself as having a secret life that was so special to him, only he should know about it. He began wearing the ring he designed with Robyn.

Kody Brown: Lord of the Rings.

Frodo was probably right.

Chapter Twenty-One

JUST WAIT FOR THE CREDITS

I'm a damn good mom. There's a learning curve, and I'm still rounding the bend, but being a good mom is what I've always loved most about myself. In Vegas, I realized being Mom was more important than trying to be attractive to Kody or working to be a good sister wife. My kids? And by extension our kids? I had time all day every day.

I knew that's where I could make the biggest difference, and I understood my role.

But I also understood their role: They kept me grounded. They reminded me what was important. They made me feel deeply loved.

As I realized from watching the show that I could be a better listener for my kids, my dad told me a story.

He came home from work one day when I was three or four, and I said, "Dad, I need to show you something!" Usually, he was too busy, but this time he let me take his hand and lead him outside, he told me. I showed him that I could pump myself on the swing set, yellow towel flowing behind me, giggling and grinning and so excited by his attention.

He told me later that he felt grateful for that moment, for the time he took for his little girl.

I made myself a promise: If the kids ever said to me, "Can I talk to you for a moment?" I would stop everything. "Yeah. Let's go. Let's talk. Let's do it right now." I'd turn off the burner, push off the errand, or have the child stand nearby until I finished whatever I was doing.

Stop. Adjust. Eye level with a toddler or a teen.

"Okay. What's on your mind?"

Like my dad, I'm grateful for those moments.

Each mom had moments when different kids would seek them out, but my six kids, Janelle's six kids, and Leon always knew they could come talk to me. I had a couch in my room specifically for that purpose in the Vegas cul-de-sac. On my couch, the kids talked about school, or life, or love, or something that happened with their friends.

In Vegas, I figured out the love languages of all our kids. Quick primer: Some people like words: you have the most beautiful heart, and I love you. Some like gifts: I was at the stationery store and found this fun pen with bears on it. Some like acts of service (that's me): I made you pancakes and sewed a star patch on the hole in your jeans. Some like quality time: Let's go, just you and me, to that action movie you've been wanting to see. And some like touch: Come sit with me and I'll brush your hair.

In my home, rather than sharing a house with my sister wives, I could parent how I wanted.

I didn't want the kids to come to my house and feel like they needed to do chores. I wanted them to hang out, play games, bond with each other. The house will get clean eventually. They didn't have to finish all the food on their plates. Dinner didn't need to be a big production with a house full of teenagers. They weren't allowed to eat food that looked like I was going to use it for a recipe. They could have cold cereal only as a snack because I didn't want them to sugar-crash at school. They weren't allowed to make a mess with honey.

A woman's gotta have some rules.

They know I'm an ogre after nine p.m.—you don't want to mess with me after nine. In fact, everyone knows that.

One night, after we had all moved to the cul-de-sac in Vegas, the girls were sleeping across the street at Robyn's. At about midnight, all of them—Gwendlyn, Ysabel, Aurora, and Breanna—decided they wanted to sleep at my house.

They banged stuff around and ran up and down the stairs, and the whole house was just filled with noise.

"What are you doing here?" I asked them.

"We wanted to come back home and sleep here," my girls told me.

"No," I said. "Get out of my house."

"What?"

"You can't sleep here," I said. "You said you were gonna sleep at Robyn's, so you go back over there right now."

I watched as they all traipsed back across the street. I'm sure they were all thinking that I was a bit out of control.

The next morning Robyn called me.

"I told them not to go over there," she said. She was laughing so hard she could barely get the words out. "'Your mom's not gonna like that.' They did not listen to me."

She told me she watched them cross the street, and then she watched them cross it again a few minutes later.

By then, we were both laughing.

During reasonable hours I belonged to the kids. Once a month, I took one of my kids out on a date. With six kids, that may not seem like much, but they remember those nights when they had me all to themselves. I remember telling Paedon it was his night, but he didn't want to go anywhere. He wanted to stay home and watch a movie. We popped popcorn and snuggled up on my bed. One of the other kids knocked on the door and asked if they could come in.

"No, sweetie, it's my date with Paedon," I called out.

He glowed.

Check! I thought. *He'll remember this.*

Paedon and I didn't get along well from when he was fourteen to when he was sixteen, in part because Kody had gone from being an incredible dad to a disappearing act. When that happens, you look for solutions: Paedon and I needed a way to connect—something safe to talk about—so we started playing *Halo*.

After he jumped behind me and ripped off my head, I refused to play with him unless we played on a team together.

"I don't know what subconscious thing is happening right now, but you literally just ripped out my spine," I said.

Then we started playing *Lego Star Wars*: I made him call me "Mom Solo."

"I'm not calling you that," he said.

"Then I'm not gonna play!" I said, and I ran out of the room.

"Mom! You child!"

That one-on-one time was the most important thing I could give them.

But the time with all six felt like magic. I loved to see how their minds worked with their wisecracks and stories. It melted my heart to see them include tiny True in teen games. They soothed, teased, played, and loved. I could feel grateful and whole in those moments.

Some moments were more predictable than others.

Every time we watch a movie, to this day, just as it's about to end and the credits are ready to roll and it's finally time for the kiss at the end of the love story and you know it's going to be really, really good, my kids start roughhousing. Without fail. They start losing their brains, jumping all over.

"Oh my gosh! Stop it!"

If you're a mom (or a human), you know that never works.

"Just wait for the credits," I'll say. "We will dance at the end credits."

We would watch the rest of the movie. It's possible that the importance of a good love story in my life is obvious. The kids would sit silently, holding their collective breath.

As soon as the credits began to roll, we danced. That's the true ending of each and every movie I watch with my kids: happily ever after and a dance party.

Chapter Twenty-Two

I STOPPED EATING
MY EMOTIONS

When we moved to a cul-de-sac in Las Vegas where our four houses were within steps of each other, I thought for sure me and my kids would see Kody more. It would be hard for him to hide where he spent his time if we could all see each other's houses from the front window.

But Janelle's kids would come to my house looking for Kody, and he wouldn't be there. We knew he wasn't with Meri because they'd had a falling out.

Oh, I realized, *everyone's getting scraps, not just me.*

Kody spent so little time with us that Paedon began referring to himself as the "man of the house." He was my protector, still is, but we had to talk about why Mom still made the decisions.

We talked about Kody's absence in therapy. "My kids always talk about how much they miss Kody," I remember Robyn saying.

Girl, please. Your kids are secure. They know they're loved. Your kids all know who their dad is—my kids don't.

"How can you say that when we can see where he is?" I asked.

I don't believe plural marriages can work when there's a favorite. And I wasn't going to be close to Robyn because I couldn't trust her.

"I don't know where Kody is either," she'd say.

The move had been a big deal. Two years after we got to Vegas, in December 2012, we each moved into four custom-built homes with the same base floor plan, but that looked different from the outside—mine had a turret and a moat. As a family, we believed it would move us closer to what we had in Wyoming or the Lehi house, without having to live in the same building. While we were physically closer, our relationships did not improve.

By the end of each day in Vegas, I'd had enough of the emotional togetherness, the talking on set. I felt constantly on edge, constantly uncertain, constantly worried about the next thing that might pop out of someone's mouth. The questions were hard and often about things the producers noticed that they then wanted to dive into, and it might be about the way I side-eyed Kody when he said something that wasn't true, and then I'd have to come up with a diplomatic way to be kind about it. It was like gaslighting myself.

I don't think any of us wanted to spend time with each other in the evenings, but at first, I didn't know anybody else. Because I grew up in a closed community, I didn't know how to make friends. I remember asking my neighbor Deirdre, "How is Truely supposed to make friends?" Deirdre explained "playdates" to me: You invite people to come over. Or you take Truely to other people's homes.

Then, they hang out.

What? Rubbish!

Is that really how it works?

When I was little, we made friends through church—or through our dozens of brothers and sisters and cousins. There were kids everywhere, and it wasn't a matter of making friends so much as just showing up.

Our kids figured it out quickly. They went to school and they made friends. Ta-da! But then I'd hit it off with their parents. We'd hang out while our kids played. Crazy, right?

I worried, for the first time in my life, whether people would like me. I had to say things like, "You want to come over this weekend? We have a pool in the backyard," but also, "It's always a little bit extra in the Brown household."

Most of the time it was fine. But one time we were invited to a birthday party. When we got to the house, there was no party, but there was a huge hole in the roof of the house. Meth lab fire. No more playdates with that family. That's a problem everywhere, but Vegas has maybe a wider variety of people.

Because we were on a reality show, we also had to watch out for people pretending to be friends because they thought they could become famous through us. I learned how to filter.

In part because of the new friendships and socializing, I also started to drink a bit more in Vegas. I'm pretty sure you guys noticed. After a hard conversation, Janelle popped out on one episode with, "I feel like we should have alcoholic beverages," and the whole state of Utah gasped. And then when TLC started having to bleep us? Oh. My. Heck. In Utah, our crowd didn't cuss and didn't drink. Vegas is different that way, but if you're a sister wife, what you say or drink in Vegas definitely doesn't stay there.

I started having friends over to my house and going to their parties, and it felt good to relax and talk to people I wouldn't be living with in 250 years because we were eternally linked.

But I started to come home from the set feeling like I needed a beer. *Need* is the right word—I needed something to take the edge off the day so I could be a good mom. I found that if I drank just a little, just one bottle of beer or cider, I could make dinner, have great conversations, and help the kids with their homework. It wasn't a lot, but it was a crutch, and it was something I would have to deal with.

As the constant rejection continued outside my window, and as I worked to get through the humiliation of being the chubby nacho girl, I went through some tough body image and self-esteem issues. I've always been a bigger girl, always been overweight. It's part of who I was. But when I got pregnant with Truely, I gained a lot of weight. I went on a diet after and didn't gain it back, which was great. But then, in the book we wrote together, Kody called me "dumpy."

To heck with that, I thought, and I started to eat junk food because why not? But that also seemed ridiculous.

The show didn't help. I remember my friends saying, after guest appearances on the show, "Oooh. I don't like the way I look on camera." No one does. It's hard. You realize you have certain facial expressions no one else notices, or that your left eyebrow isn't perfectly symmetrical with your right, or some other ridiculous little thing. But I hadn't clocked my weight until we went public.

Oh my gosh, I thought. *I can't believe this. You're on TV. Things need to change.*

When I lived in Lehi, I had a miscarriage. It was terrible. Terrible. Dr. Bean performed the D and C procedure afterward, but he was also the one who delivered Truely, then treated my postpartum depression.

When I started to go downhill in the cul-de-sac, I called Dr. Bean: "I'm spinning out of control, and Kody has a new wife, and Kody was never attracted to me . . ."

"What are you doing?" he asked.

"I'm eating everything," I said.

"Okay," he said, "maybe there's something else we can try."

That's when I started my fitness journey, but true inspiration came from Janelle. When we lived in the cul-de-sac, Janelle worked out every day, and she didn't seem worried so much about how she looked as she did about being strong. She loves camping and hiking, and those things are so much more fun when you don't lose your breath or feel your heart rate going up.

Why am I not respecting and honoring my body? I started to wonder, after seeing Janelle's progress. *Why do I not love it like I should? It's gotten me this far.*

When Janelle started working out, she became empowered. Her self-esteem increased, and she was strong.

That was when I started to work on loving myself for me, and not for Kody or anyone else. I wanted to feel good. He's not attracted to me? Okay. Fine. I'm still going to look good for me. I started to watch what I ate. I started to work out. I hired a trainer after working out with Janelle a couple of times. We started with a weigh-in and then talked about form and musculature. The workouts—kettle bells, weights, medicine balls, battle ropes—left me exhausted.

I loved how I felt.

Oddly enough, I worked out with Kody sometimes. We'd go to the gym together and do our own workouts.

My trainer was lovely, and she would hike with me or plan a workout in my backyard. She helped me understand that when you make a decision to take care of yourself, it empowers you. You have the ability to make your own life better, but to do that, you have to like yourself enough to believe it's important.

I realized I do like myself. I've done the work, over the years, to be kind, to think instead of spout, to be curious and grow, and to be an excellent mom.

We started changing how we ate when Kody got into eating based on his blood type, which is the same as mine. No matter whether there's scientific evidence for it, it got us eating healthier food—protein-heavy, lots of veggies, and avoiding dairy.

Eat broccoli to lose weight.

That's hard to argue with.

When you have so many kids running through, searching for snacks, we each had to have extra food in the house at all times. Even if the snacks are healthy—popcorn, cheese, fruit—they're still caloric, and they aren't necessarily things I would keep if I lived on my own. Proximity means temptation.

We also had a swarm of people to feed, and healthy means more expensive. It's harder to buy fresh when you buy in bulk, so I had to think harder about options. Before dinner, we always made an appetizer—veggies and dip or something—because otherwise, they're going to come in like a horde of locusts and eat everything in their path. We did a lot of bar meals, like a pasta or pizza bar, or a sushi bar. We always had a salad bar. But we also did what was cheap, so we ate a lot of pasta and bread.

Not anymore—that stopped. Beans and brown rice are just as cheap as pasta (and can be fun with veggie sides and hot sauce), oatmeal could replace sugary cereal. A salad bar could include a protein-y grain, like quinoa or lentils. If it's a whole food—which means you're starting from scratch rather than something some-body else has already made into a chip, a mix, a bread, or a frozen dinner—it's healthier. Did you know that, according to the World Health Organization, we're never supposed to eat processed meats like salami or bacon because they can cause structural damage to our cells, leading to colon cancer? It's nuts.

I started to listen to my body. I ate mostly white meats, such as chicken and fish. Red meat makes me achy and sore, so I don't do that often. I stay away from milk because I don't digest it easily. Ice cream! Proof that there is a god! What happens to my belly after I eat ice cream? Proof that there is a devil.

I stopped eating my emotions.

I also learned that when I want to lose weight, I have to count calories—I don't care what supplements you take. There are tricks: Go for a twenty-minute walk and earn yourself a hundred calories. Smartphone apps will keep you accountable and do the math for you. Look for fun but low-calorie foods, like pickles or a lovely tomato salad. And allow yourself treats, like a square of dark chocolate or one of those hundred-calorie ice cream bars. But track your calories. I feel pretty good at 170 pounds, but it's different for everyone. That's where my clothes fit right.

I still love desserts, and I don't see the point if it's not chocolate. And I occasionally enjoy a massive plate of nachos. For some reason, I enjoy them more than I used to.

I thought, because I felt so great, that Kody and I would get better. I looked better, and my confidence was high. I felt happier, which meant I put less pressure on Kody. Every aspect of my life got better, so I thought my relationship would, too.

Chapter Twenty-Three

YOU'RE REALLY GONNA DO THAT?

*I*t didn't.

We rented a couple of RVs to drive to Montana for a family vacation, but our plans fell through, so Kody said, "Well, we can just go hang out with Ken." This Ken could beach! If we hung out with Ken, we could go to the lake in Ken's boat.

Ken was one of Kody's high school classmates. When Kody joined the polygamist church after performing his mission for the LDS church, Ken and another pal shunned Kody, complaining about his morality and calling him a sinner. Ken said he didn't want to be around Kody anymore.

They had been best friends.

Then they repaired their friendship a little bit. And Ken, being a generous man, told Kody, "We would welcome you back to the church with open arms, but you can only bring one wife."

Kody presented it to us as a joke, and then he started talking about how we could go boating with Ken, and blah, blah, blah.

I was livid.

"You're really calling Ken?" I said. "You're really gonna do that?"

Ken! Ken! Ken! and I threw a fit on the show. "He owes me an apology," I said. His behavior, to me, was unacceptable. "I'm beyond pissed that we're gonna go see him."

We'd seen him at a high school reunion, and Ken told Kody that finding out Kody was going to be a polygamist "brang in a lot of friction. I just thought he was stupid." I side-eyed him. Meri side-eyed him. He kept going. "It made no sense to me how he could do such a thing."

Neat. Sign me up to hang out. I can beach.

On our RV trip, I let Kody have it: "I don't know why he's allowed on our family vacation when he's against most of our family."

Kody's response?

"Well listen, he's always invited me to go boating. That's—"

Rubbish.

How did that end?

"Okay," I said. "It's fine."

The cameras caught all of it, of course.

We went to see Old Faithful and drove through Yellowstone. Beyond beautiful.

And then Kody said, "I tried to get a hold of Ken in spite of your complaints, Christine." Eye-roll on my part. "He is not available." We would not be going to visit.

"That's too bad," I said. Pursed lips.

And then Kody lectured us about how everyone has religious prejudices and told us that Mormons believe Mormonism is for everybody, while he, Kody, did not believe polygamy is for everyone. I asked, again, for an apology from Ken, and Kody said he would not ask for one—something about it making his testicles shrink.

I told him to sleep somewhere else that night. In front of my sister wives. They all went silent and looked away because that's how we kept our relationships separate.

On the show, Kody talked about the extraordinary size of my ego and said it was driven by my pride.

Telling this story now, none of it seems unreasonable to me. There are many ways to make your perspective clear without calling people "stupid" while using bad grammar, or without letting a portion of your best pal's family know they're not welcome. And Kody? Yeah, fight for our honor. What happened to my maverick? What happened to the guy in high school who went against traditional thinking?

I was thinking, at that time, *If you went back to the mainstream Mormon church, you'd take Robyn and leave the rest of us behind.*

I didn't want to be left behind, nor did I want to go somewhere I felt we weren't accepted. Ken apologized later—he called and said he understood he needed to clear the air, but he did that by saying it was just a joke.

And then we went to the lake to hang out with Ken, who had cleared his schedule so we could film with him. I felt frustrated and angry, and I didn't think we should be there or that we should film it.

But there was more to the story.

Kody convened a meeting at a picnic table as we headed to visit friends in Montana. I said I was worried everyone was mad at me for getting upset about Ken. Kody decided we should pray about it, and then said, on camera, that he would talk with me privately about it so he didn't embarrass me, which embarrassed me.

When he got me by myself (with the camera), he said my behavior was erratic, and then said, "Some people refer to it as 'PMS,' but I don't know what's going on."

I guess, as a woman, if I didn't agree with his take on the situation, it must have been temporary female insanity.

Hysteria and so on.

I did, however, feel out of control. I did not feel as if I was being rational, and maybe that was because, normally, when I'm angry, I think about it for a bit before I say my piece. In this case, while I still feel like Ken's behavior was inappropriate and like I didn't want to be around someone who didn't approve of my family, I didn't like that I had just let loose. It didn't feel like me. It felt as if my insides were bouncing around, like my guts had imbibed too much caffeine. I couldn't sleep anymore.

While we were in Montana, we started chatting with a woman, a nurse, who talked about her menopause symptoms. Afterward, I opened up to her a bit about what was going on with me.

"Oh," she said, "you just need this progesterone cream and you'll be fine. You can find it in any health food store."

Whoa. Nobody talks about this stuff. And I was only forty. I hadn't even been thinking about the possibility of menopause. I was so grateful to her—I think she added years to my marriage. But here's what no one talks about: Before you even hit menopause, which is defined as one year without your period, you hit perimenopause, which usually lasts about four years but can last as long as eight. Perimenopause is sneaky. I think we all hear about hot flashes and lower sex drives, but I thought it happened in one go, like one day you wake up and you're just done.

We don't talk about menopause or perimenopause because we don't see it as normal—or sexy. But what if my ability that trip to say what I was thinking was simply my wisdom not being held back by my estrogen, because my estrogen's only concern was how I could get what I needed to have more babies?

So, that's one theory. The other is that my hormones were in disarray. It was like *Are You There God? It's Me, Margaret.* all over again, and it wasn't any more fun as an adult. The sneaky symptoms? Forgetfulness. Dryness. Waking up at night. Needing to open a window at night. Not wanting your partner to cuddle because it feels as if your skin will crawl off your body. Periods that last a day. Periods that last a month. No period. Feeling hungry. Feeling full. Feeling like you're about to get the flu. Feeling as if you're boiling on the inside. Reaching for a sweater two minutes later.

My menopause got worse. By the time I hit forty-five, my hot flashes were awful. Not everyone gets them. (Some people barely notice menopause.) The over-the-counter cream stopped being enough, and I started having a hard time with conversations and existing as a human.

I called Dr. Bean.

"I'm not okay," I said. "I don't know what to do."

He told me I probably needed stronger progesterone, and he gave me a prescription. And I went to see a natural care doctor who hooked me up with vitamins and supplements after I told her I felt like I needed a drink to be around my kids. When the hot flashes got out of control, I went to see Dr. Bean in person, and he started me on estrogen. Gosh, it was fun to see him again, and the estrogen was enough. Dr. Bean also taught me that you need to listen to your body. When I was pregnant with Truely, I told him, "I feel like she's smaller than the rest of my kids. What do you think?" He said, "I don't know—it's your body." From then on I was like, "Oh. I got this. I'm listening."

Now, when people request cameos for fortieth birthdays, I say, "Look, I know this is your birthday, and I'm going to sing to you, but I'm going to have a real conversation with you: Menopause sucks, and it's going to kick your butt, but when things stop making sense, you can get help for it. Go talk to your OB-GYN." It's my personal public service announcement. We need to talk about it.

Listen. If things start feeling off, you can go get your FSH levels checked, your doctor can tell you if you're in it, and then they can recommend hormone replacement treatment—yes, there was a scare about breast cancer and stroke risk with HRT, but newer research has shown the benefits often outweigh the risks. HRT can take care of all those sneaky symptoms, as well as helping your skin and sex life. There are a ton of natural options, too. Just know that it may hit earlier than you think, that lots of fancy-pants celebrities like Gwyneth, Drew, and Cindy are working to make talking about it normal, and that wisdom is incredibly, indisputably sexy.

That was a lesson I still needed to learn.

Chapter Twenty-Four

YOU JUST LOVE PEOPLE

*R*ight, so we started with Beach Ken and how Kody and the Sinful Barbies were going to hell, and now we're moving on to burning garments.

One day, as we traveled home from a group trip, Robyn made a request.

"I want to talk about garments," she said.

As a reminder, garments, otherwise known as temple garments or special Mormon underwear, are underclothes that have been blessed.

But you guys, they're hot—especially our church's long-underwear version. In Las Vegas. They may have been protecting us from evil, but they weren't doing much for heat exhaustion.

"I'm never going to wear them again," I said.

I think they're a form of control specifically aimed at women. I believe that if you don't like how you look, then you're being controlled. The cut of the garments forced us to wear long, frumpy clothes that were never in fashion, and when I look at my photos over the years, I was a frumpy girl. I don't want to be a frumpy girl.

I don't want to be uncomfortable. I don't want to be controlled. In fact, I refuse to be controlled.

Everyone else said they hadn't been wearing them because it was hot, but that they loved the church, and they loved their garments. We all took them off for filming, because the lights were hot, and wearing garments on set felt like sitting in a plastic baggie. On media tours, we took them off to film because our clothes fit better, and then we put them on afterward. I had always loved putting them back on—they were like extra protection.

Before we left Utah, Kody co-taught Sunday school lessons.

The lessons were more about being Christ-like and less about the fundamentals of our church.

In Vegas, we didn't have a local church. We had Truely baptized, we went to one more church service in Utah, and then things petered out.

Over the years, I had questioned my faith. I felt sure my garments didn't make me a better Christian. I understood that membership in our tiny church didn't give us a monopoly on doing good deeds. And I didn't believe God would create one true religion, then leave a billion humans to fight for their spot in a game of divinity musical chairs.

Also. According to our church, God said, "Men are in charge." Seriously? What kind of god would come up with that plan? I started to question members of our leadership—I didn't find them honorable, and on a personal level, I didn't care for them. The actor Virginia Hill accused them of stealing more than one million dollars from her, and a civil court ruled in her favor, as well as holding that church leaders embezzled tithing money. The church chose replacement leaders who were so strict that our children hated them.

They wanted Kody to cut his hair. They said he couldn't pass the sacrament—bless and pass ceremonial bread—if he didn't.

Cuz Jesus had a crew cut.

Then we found out we weren't supposed to wear earrings. Church teachings became more about previous prophets—previous church leaders—than about scriptural doctrine.

I told Kody I didn't think I could teach Sunday school anymore to our kids. I told him I didn't believe our Articles of Faith were the word of God.

"Those are conditions of our religion," he said.

"I know," I said. "I just don't think they're true."

It was hard, and it took a long time to understand it myself, because I loved being in the church, and I loved my friends there. But I had lost my faith—I couldn't erase that. I couldn't be a hypocrite when that was one of my own complaints.

The LDS church has what they call a "Temple Recommend," where the bishop interviews you to make sure you're paying your tithing and not drinking alcohol or having premarital sex, and that you still believe the tenets of the church. If you're doing everything you're supposed to, you can go to the temple. That's why gentiles can't go to Mormon weddings—you have to be a Mormon in good standing to enter the building.

Our church had an "Activities Recommend," which is similar, but prohibits a person from attending church activities if they don't tithe or believe in the tenets of the faith.

As I struggled through my religious crisis soon after our garment conversation, I planned to go to girls' camp with Ysabel. I asked my sister if she would be a camp counselor with me. Sure, of course. But then two months before we were supposed to go, I had to update my Activities Recommend—they expire—and I knew I would have to lie. I couldn't lie to the bishop just so my daughter could go to camp.

I called my sister.

"I'm sorry," I said. "I can't go with you."

She understood. She's still part of the church and loves it, but I couldn't keep pretending. I stopped teaching Sunday school. I put in my earrings. I ditched my garments. I told Kody, and he asked how God felt about it. I told him my relationship with God was fine. Kody said okay. It took me about six months to process everything. At some point, I had to tell my kids I was struggling after spending their whole lives convincing them it was all true. Just as my mom had done for me.

Man.

I told Ysabel I wasn't going to girls' camp anymore.

"That means I'm not going to girls' camp," she said. I told her she could do what she wanted.

But my girls are different from the other girls at church. Once, on the way home from camp, Gwendlyn knocked the wind out of me.

"All these girls want to do is have babies," she told me. "They don't want to go to college."

"Oh," I said, my words gone. These kids didn't even need the threat of apocalypse to avoid higher education.

"I don't have anything in common with them," she said.

It was a wake-up call for me that—as much as I wanted my kids to hang around kids with a similarly modest upbringing, and as much as I wanted them to be a part of supervised activities, and as much as I wanted them to have all the fun I had in the church growing up—we'd raised children who were different. We told them they could choose polygamy or not. We exposed them to other religions. We raised them to want an education and to have friends outside the church, which the camp kids also didn't do. The church kids didn't, for the most part, watch movies. They didn't listen to music.

It started to dawn on me.

Our leader was the only one who knew the rule of God. I was required to follow, without question, a strict list of rules. I grew up afraid of the outside world in a sheltered community. We judged and even ostracized those who left the church.

Check, check, check, and check.

I believe I grew up in a cult.

I believe I raised my children in a cult.

I grew up with friends and family who did and said and believed the same things I did. It was my normal. I knew what cults were— had even talked about how crazy and weird they were. But I don't have horrible memories of abuse, ostracism, and being unable to leave. We stayed because we liked the people, and we liked the ideas.

I had freedom. I felt safe. I had so much fun. I loved having a big family and my church community. When I chose to live plural marriage, it was an educated decision. I hadn't been brainwashed. But just like everyone else, I had a tunnel of thoughts with a particular set of boundaries. Even before I believed we were in a cult, some of my kids figured it out as young adults. I had taught them not to live in fear.

I looked at other religions, hoping for something that made sense for me, but I haven't been able to find one that doesn't teach that there's something to be afraid of—that there's a devil or punishment from God. I'd rather live my life with hope.

Losing my religion was a process, and I was doing it under the glow of a spotlight. I kept quiet as I tried to figure out how I felt and what I thought. I read Gabrielle Bernstein's *The Universe Has Your Back: Transform Fear to Faith*, which is about finding direction to live a divinely guided life while also trusting enough to let go, relax, and live joyfully. Napoleon Hill has an amazing book called *Outwitting the Devil*, which talks about how fear and jealousy hold you back from doing the good things you want to do. I read *The*

Screwtape Letters by C. S. Lewis, which is a funny way of looking at the things that tempt us. It was important to me to have a personal relationship with God, even as I began to understand I wasn't part of a religion. I still believed in God, and God's opinion of me mattered. Would God want me? Would God accept me? What kind of child of God am I?

I like having someone battle on my side, and I like having a god I can talk to.

"Are you okay with this?" I asked. "Is it okay that I'm leaving this church?"

The god I talk to is relatable. He's open-minded and understanding.

As I became stronger in my own identity, I thought, *God is fine with me, and I am fine with him.* I didn't need to be part of a church, and I didn't need to buy into ideas about men's place over women or pierced ears.

I'm sure losing one's faith is scary for some people, but for me, it was lovely. *Oh my gosh, I've been so backward*, I remember thinking. *The world is full of people not to be afraid of.* I believe most people are good, that they believe family is important, and that they're doing what they can to make life better. We all want love. We all want family. We all want a safe community in which to raise our kids. The world became more beautiful for me.

I decided to stay with the family, because having a family is separate from religion, but I was done with the church.

The good parts of me didn't go away with my Jesus jammies. I believe in treating people well and fairly. I believe all the things my mom taught me. I think there are many different gods and religions, and there's beauty in that. I like the idea that there's a presence, but what matters in my daily life is how I treat people—that I'm kind, open-minded, generous, and willing to give back.

When we had pitched the show to TLC, we argued that ours was a civil rights issue—that as consenting adults, we should be free to love anyone we wanted. As I shook off a close-minded religion, my kids helped me better understand the other communities that hoped for the same right.

When Leon told us they were gay, I remember thinking, *What a relief for them.* Leon must have felt so much anxiety but still felt safe enough to tell us. I realized that it didn't bother me at all—I just wanted what was best for them. I was relieved for myself, too, because I had always known, with eighteen kids, that someone would come out, and I didn't know how I would respond.

With love, I thought. *Nothing has changed.*

It remained the same when they came out as transgender. We had an incredible relationship in Vegas, and Leon was always at the house. I knew I loved them, and it didn't matter—and I hoped they would find someone who loved them as much as I do.

When Gwendlyn told us she was bisexual I felt grateful she'd told us and hoped she, too, would find happiness. I'm so proud of who she has become. Leon and Gwendlyn both now have wonderful partners.

I had believed sexuality was a choice, and our kids have opened my mind. I love the conversations that start with me saying, "Teach me how to say this in a way that isn't offensive because this is all new to me," or "What's a better way to phrase this so I sound as accepting as I feel?" Each time I've progressed, I've realized I wasn't as open-minded as I thought I was, and I keep working to be better.

My mom always had it right.

You just love people.

Chapter Twenty-Five

DON'T MAKE JOKES WITH OPRAH

*W*e sued the state of Utah to challenge its polygamy law in 2011. Our case stated that the law violated our First and Fourteenth Amendment rights—for freedom of religion and civil rights.

In October 2010, a few months before we filed the lawsuit in July, we found ourselves and our lawyer, Jonathan Turley, headed to the *Oprah* show to talk about why we had fled to Las Vegas.

"This is the worst time to do *Oprah*," I remember him telling us. "I'm just going to tell you straight up, Oprah can make it or break it. If you don't impress Oprah, your lawsuit is going to fail. Oprah needs to like you."

No stress.

"Don't make jokes," Jonathan told us. "Everyone thinks they can make jokes with Oprah: She's not going to understand. Don't make jokes with her—it makes it awkward for her. Just answer her questions and be yourself.

"Also, don't make jokes."

Got it. No jokes.

Oprah was lovely. She came out to the stage in these comfy-

looking shoes, and then she switched them out for pretty, uncomfortable ones when she sat down. We laughed about that, and she
said, "I can't walk in those, so I'm just not going to."

Suddenly, she seemed like a real person.

The show started, and we all chatted, and things seemed to be
going well. She asked me about being upset when I found out Robyn
and Kody had kissed before the wedding. She wanted to know why
I was okay with the idea that Janelle and Meri were having sex with
my husband, but a kiss from Robyn was upsetting. Oprah asked
hard questions, but we talked about it for a bit. Robyn was kissing
a married man. Meri and Janelle were married to the man they were
sleeping with. See? Simple.

Janelle said some of our best friends are monogamists, and
Oprah laughed. That loosened everybody up a bit.

And then Kody made a joke, and I can't remember what it was,
but I remember it wasn't funny at all.

"That's not funny, Kody," Oprah said.

Ooooh. Ouchiest of ouches.

"I don't know you," she continued, "and I don't know your sense
of humor."

The interview continued, all of us with our hearts in our throats.
Did Kody ruin it for polygamists everywhere by trying to make
Oprah laugh?

He was nervous—all of us were—and the attempt at a joke came
out as a defense response. We felt so bad for him.

"What were you thinking?" Jonathan said as soon as we left the
set. "You made a joke with Oprah! I told you you can't make a joke
with Oprah!"

"I saw a piece of paper before we went on," Kody said. "All
the questions were about sex, and I panicked! I didn't know what
to do!"

All in all, it was a wonderful experience. Oprah was one of my favorite hosts.

Vegas had been stress-free, as far as the law was concerned. Some neighbors made comments at first about the appropriateness of polygamy—and about how we were all going to hell—but they chilled out. We weren't the worst neighbors to have there. And the kids had done well outing themselves as members of a polygamist family at their public school. The other kids had questions, but then our kids became part of their normal. Our timing had been good. There had been such a massive shift in people's ideas about alternative lifestyles, and we benefited from that—and yes, I see the irony in that.

But we felt the fight in Utah was important. We drove up to see our friend Joe Darger, who was also a polygamist. That meant going back to Utah. As soon as we hit the mountains, all I could think was, *Oh! It's like we're home again!* Everyone talked about how much they missed the mountains, snow, and our families. It felt important to win that lawsuit so we could go back.

Joe has three wives, including two who are twins, and they all live in the same house. In our community, it's not unusual for sisters or friends to marry the same guy. They're all good friends and have served as role models for us: They're super organized and usually on time. They seem to get along even while living in one house and using one kitchen. And they deserve the credit for pushing for the decriminalization of polygamy in Utah, arguing the case, and protesting at the state capitol. They found a senator who was willing to push a law, so they had been more politically active than we had. They had even gone public before we did, writing a book about their family called *Love Times Three: Our True Story.* They're independent polygamists, so they're not affiliated with a church or particular religion.

I have no idea how old I am, but this is me as a little girl wearing a dress sewn by my mom. Love that ponytail!
Courtesy of Christine Brown Woolley

Dad's favorite photo of me. Mom put my hair in pigtails and couldn't take her eyes off me. Probably because I moved around all the time. *Courtesy of Christine Brown Woolley*

An Easter Day portrait taken before my baptism in one of my favorite dresses.
Courtesy of Christine Brown Woolley

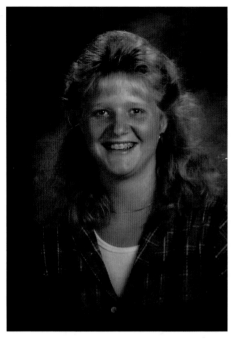

I got braces in eighth grade. I love that outfit. The shirt belonged to my other mother, who was always so cool.
Courtesy of Christine Brown Woolley

High school graduation day with Granny, who everyone says I look like. Left to right: Granny, Dad, me, and Mom. *Courtesy of Christine Brown Woolley*

Wedding day with Kody.
Photograph by Tana Allred

Pregnant with Mykelti.
Photograph by Lifetouch

Me with Kody, a couple
months after being married.
Photograph by Lifetouch

The family portrait with Aspyn
(left) and Mykelti that Robyn
used to create a drawing of
Kody and her young children.
Photograph by Lifetouch

Pouring sand at the commitment celebration. Why are we doing this? Left to right: Me, Janelle, Robyn, and Meri.
Photograph by Fernando G de Cossío

Our commitment celebration. Look at Mykelti's hat. She's so glamorous. Left to right: Ysabel, Mykelti, Kody, me, Truely, Aspyn, Paedon, and Gwendlyn.
Photograph by Fernando G de Cossío

In Las Vegas with the wives and Kody. Left to right: Meri, Robyn, Janelle, and me. *Photograph by Wendy Vaughn*

Photo shoot with the immediate family. We wore jeans and had a red, black, and white theme. Left to right: Mykelti, Kody, me, Aspyn, Gwendlyn, Truely, Paedon, and Ysabel. *Photograph by Wendy Vaughn*

This was probably my favorite photo with Kody.
Photograph by Wendy Vaughn

Aspyn and Mitch's wedding. It's the last family photo we had done. Check out those beautiful hats that Mitch's mom, Hannah, made! *Photograph by Kali Poulsen*

Chatting with Dad on the day
I married my husband, David.
Courtesy of TLC

Paedon walking me down
the aisle. *Courtesy of TLC*

Mob boss wedding photo with
David—ready to take over the
world. *Courtesy of TLC*

When we sued Utah, it angered our church. By that point, they didn't feel like we represented them, and not all of us thought we did, either. I had spoken out against some of their practices, and they didn't want that limelight.

We won our lawsuit in 2013, with the court saying a man can't legally marry more than one person at a time, but there's nothing, constitutionally, that prohibits him from living with someone else. People do that all the time: you separate, you move in with someone else while you work out the divorce. But our case was later overturned on appeal on a technicality: We had never been prosecuted for polygamy, so our rights had not been violated. That, of course, meant we still couldn't go home because the threat of a felony offense would hang over our heads.

In 2017, the state upped the ante: they expanded the anti-bigamy law to make it a more serious second-degree, rather than third-degree, felony if domestic or sexual abuse was involved, and they exempted minors from prosecution. I'm all for coming down hard on abuse, but if people were afraid to report it before, toughening the penalties wouldn't help.

The new law also reworded the definition of bigamy: The old law said it's bigamy if a married man spiritually marries someone else or lives with them. The new law says it's bigamy if he lives with a "purported" spouse while legally married to someone else. The state said it would prosecute polygamy cases only if abuse were involved.

But it wasn't a guarantee.

The Dargers kept after it, explaining that abused family members feared coming forward because the laws were too restrictive. No wife will say she's being abused if she risks going to jail or sending her family to jail on a felony offense if she says she's a polygamist. Joe realized the rights argument wasn't going to convince Republicans in Utah, so they kept working the abuse angle.

In 2020, the Utah legislature passed a law that made polygamy among consenting adults an infraction, like a parking ticket. It's still a felony if you marry someone without telling your spouse or the person you plan to marry that you're married to someone else. It's still a second-degree felony if a person is found guilty of polygamy, as well as abuse. The governor said it was time to bring polygamous families out from hiding so they would be safe.

No matter what else happened with our family, I'm proud that we helped people see polygamy in a different light.

Chapter Twenty-Six

CAN I JUST BE WITH HER, PLEASE?

All the wives drove to San Francisco to look for dresses as a bonding experience for the Brown family commitment ceremony. The ceremony had come up in family therapy as a way to celebrate how far we had come, to acknowledge what we had learned in counseling, and to recommit to each other at a point when things seemed pretty precarious.

The shopping trip was fine, if awkward as far as the dresses went. The crew showed Kody back home completely clueless about how to feed and care for his seventeen children. By that point, our kids took care of each other or themselves, but Ysabel stubbed her toe and Kody burned the steaks, and that was the end of it. In San Francisco, we discovered that a) we couldn't all shop at the same store because of the size range of our bodies, and b) we couldn't talk on the phone with Kody in front of the other wives.

In reality, we had a great time—it was a fun trip.

Before we left, three-year-old Truely had been just sick enough for me to take her to an urgent care doctor, who said she probably had the flu and sent her home. While we were in San Francisco, Aspyn called me.

"Truely is sick," she said, sounding panicked. "Like really sick, and I don't know what to do."

I called Kody.

"The girls are there," he said. "They can take care of it."

"Kody, I really need you to help with Truely," I said.

"I have a lot to take care of at Robyn's house," I remember him saying. "I'll see what I can do."

Awesome. Thanks.

The evening I returned home, Truely was still sick. She wanted to sleep with Mykelti, and I went in to check on her, and her eyes were crossing. I ran her back to the urgent care.

"She needs glasses," he said.

No, really. That's what he said.

"You don't understand what's happening here," I said.

I immediately called my doctor, and he cleared his schedule: "Bring her in now."

He examined her. She was swollen and couldn't breathe right, and she could barely keep her eyes open—and she didn't seem to understand what was going on. I was terrified.

"Take her to the ER immediately," the doctor said. "She's in kidney failure."

Oh my god. We rushed her to the emergency room. I called Kody along the way, and he met us there. It was so scary. They ran some tests and said she was like an eighty-year-old woman on dialysis—at first, they thought the machine was broken.

They admitted her to the hospital, and I stayed there, with Kody leaving at night and coming back for a couple of hours during the day. But Truely wasn't getting any better, and they said she had to be on dialysis.

She was so skinny but also puffy, and she couldn't pee. Her bladder wasn't working, her kidneys weren't working. They kept drawing blood to do more tests. And at the time, we had no insurance because we were right in the middle of getting new insurance, so they kept coming to the door of Truely's room to say, "We need more money."

"Look," I remember saying. "My daughter's here. I don't have money for you. I can't help you. Can I just be with her, please?"

Then they would back off, and then come back, and I'd offer up more money. By the end of it, I would owe more than $200,000.

They wanted to do dialysis, and we had to decide whether we wanted to bring her to the hospital every day to hook her up to the machine or keep her in the hospital. She was so little, so of course we wanted to bring her home. That raised the risk of infection, but we decided to rent the dialysis machine and keep her in a familiar setting surrounded by those who love her.

They had to perform surgery on her abdomen—it's different for toddlers—to insert a catheter for the dialysis machine, and I remember waiting for them to take her back. The surgeon came in and looked at Truely's chart.

"How old is she?" she asked.

"She's three," I said.

"Why are you doing this surgery?"

I'm sure she could read the expression of *what?* on my face.

"We went through hours discussing this with the doctors, and they said this was the best option."

"There's a huge risk of infection," she said.

It wasn't the we'll-take-good-care-of-her pep talk I expected and needed.

"I don't have any answers for you," I said. "I don't know what to do."

She looked at the chart again, and then she looked at Truely's numbers.

"Oh," she said, "well, I guess this is the best surgery."

Cold.

Oh my god, this is the surgeon who will be taking care of my daughter.

The nurses and anesthetist got Truely ready, and then they started to wheel her off. Truely was screaming. Then the swinging doors closed behind them, and I realized it was out of my hands and in theirs. It was the worst feeling. There was nothing I could do for her.

She was in there for a couple of hours, and when she came out, she was puffy everywhere and looked terrible. I was so angry at the surgeon. I talked with a nurse who asked who it was.

"If my kids were going through anything, I would request her," she told me. "She's honestly the best there is."

The surgery went well, and I spent the night at the hospital. The next day, a doctor came to see Truely and asked how she was doing.

"I understand I really hurt your feelings yesterday," she said.

"Oh!" I said. "You're the surgeon."

There had been so many people and so much stress that I hadn't recognized her.

"Yeah, I'm really sorry," she said. "I get into surgeon mode, and it was just hard on me that she was so little. I could do it, but it was scary to me, too."

She was great. Truely was on dialysis for several more days in the hospital—they wouldn't let her go home until she urinated because they wanted to make sure everything was working properly.

Kody told me to draw a picture of Truely at Disneyland, all healthy and better, and then draw a picture of her in the hospital with all the tubes tied to her. I showed her the hospital picture, and we talked about it. She was still lucid and chatting, even though she was kind of out of it. I showed her the second picture and told her that as soon as she was well enough, we were going to Disneyland.

That night, she peed for the first time.

On the tenth day in the hospital, the nephrologist said we could go home—he said that while Truely's numbers weren't quite where they wanted them, she was healing fast, and that at her age, she would get better faster at home.

"What about dialysis?" I asked.

"She'll probably be fine," he said.

He told us we needed to be careful the first year and watch her like crazy. We expected to go to a million follow-up visits, but after four visits in the first month after she came home, her doctor said, "I don't think I need to see you again. If she gets sick again, let me know, but I think you're done."

They filmed us coming home from the hospital and her greeting everyone, and she looked like a stick figure.

She got sick twice more that year. On Christmas Day, she threw up. I looked at Kody.

"She's fine," he mouthed.

No, I thought. *I'm not doing this.* I took her to my bed, and that's where we spent Christmas Day, all snuggled up. I watched her like a hawk, but every time she got sick, she was fine. She never had a relapse. No one knows what caused it, beyond that she got the flu, she lived in Las Vegas, and she got dehydrated.

As always, we talked about the experience on the set.

"I needed your help," I told Kody, referring to the moment when Aspyn had called me in a panic.

He said he had been doing laundry at Robyn's house.

"You were gonna let our daughter die because you were doing laundry for Robyn," I said. I felt like we were last on his list.

Kody got so mad that he asked the crew to turn off the cameras because he knew just how bad it sounded. He hadn't been there when Truely and I needed him desperately.

"We're not filming this," he said.

I confided in Robyn about it later.

"If Truely had died, I would have left Kody," I said. "Because she didn't matter to him. Because he was more focused on doing laundry at your house than helping our daughter."

Robyn was beside herself. She was horrified at the idea of me leaving over the surgery. Breaking up over the death of a child doesn't make logical sense, but I think she understood that in that situation, it did because Kody wasn't there for Truely, he wasn't there for me, and he wasn't there for his oldest daughters who he left to deal with a scary situation.

Robyn told Kody, who got mad at me for talking to Robyn about it—rather than apologizing for not being there when we needed him. That was the last time I opened up to Robyn: I felt she betrayed my trust by telling Kody something I had said in confidence.

Truely, on the other hand, was fine. We took her to Disneyland after she got better, and she spent a long time talking with Rapunzel and Flynn Rider.

"Did it hurt when Mother Gothel stabbed you?" she asked Flynn Ryder. Truely had seen that happen in the movie *Tangled*.

"I have a scar," he said.

Still-skinny baby Truely, who had almost no hair because she had just cut it all off by herself, took a look at his scar, and then she lifted her shirt.

"So do I," she said.

Oh my gosh, their faces. They knew they were talking to a miracle baby.

"We have to talk to more kids, but afterward, do you want to walk with us through the castle?" they asked Truely.

"Sure," she said, obviously the coolest character in the bunch. And the cutest.

Joy.

They made a big production of it. Her confidence has always been amazing, and she walked through like she owned the place, like she was exactly where she was supposed to be.

Chapter Twenty-Seven

JUST BE NICE TO EACH OTHER

I wasn't excited about the commitment ceremony. Kody hadn't shown up, on multiple occasions, when I needed him. The kids felt deserted. And I understood that Kody was in love with Robyn, and that he didn't have much to spare for the rest of us.

Polygamists in our faith don't renew wedding vows because we've already been joined for eternity. How committed did we need to be? So we called it a celebration of our vows.

Our therapist helped us, for months and months, come up with a family mission statement that would serve as a backdrop for the ceremony. If it had been up to me, we would have made a poster that said "Just be nice to each other." We scribbled on large pads of paper, making sure everyone felt heard, and the adults spent time with our therapist trying to talk it all out while making sure we didn't hurt anyone's feelings or start any fights.

We were all—kids too—going to sign the mission statement during the ceremony. The whole thing was, as usual, done by committee, and I still felt like I didn't matter. I remember thinking that I didn't like living that way.

The whole season—season six, if you're keeping track—was about the ceremony, so week after week, they filmed us discussing what was important to our family. None of it lined up with real life.

Kody said the ceremony would remind us that we were one family, and that our houses in the cul-de-sac were one home. But that wasn't true.

On the set, I said I had to decide every day whether I was going to be a bad sister wife or a good sister wife. Looking back, that seems like a funny thing to say. Should it be that hard?

We hadn't been able to make any decisions on dresses while we were in San Francisco, so we decided to have our dresses made, but our timing was off, and our seamstress was still working on fittings the day before. By the day of the ceremony, Robyn's and Meri's dresses still weren't finished. Meri went shopping at the last minute and Robyn wore a dress she had.

The dressmaker said she'd thought about running away screaming. Kody said that she now understood what it was like to be a member of the Kody Brown family.

I did not want to be there.

Just before the ceremony, Kody got me another claddagh ring, to replace the one I'd hucked into a field. It didn't have a diamond. Instead, Kody had them put rose gold over the heart because he knows that's my favorite metal. I had seen the ring and liked it, but he did the rose gold on his own. It was beautiful.

I tried to think about what we'd come up with as a mission statement together.

We enjoy being together as a family because we have developed a safe, peaceful, and pleasant atmosphere where we love and respect one another.

We weren't there yet. We hadn't been able to keep the promises we'd made in therapy. I could still see Kody's car at Robyn's house.

Meri and Kody were still on the fritz. But yeah, sure, maybe this could spark a fresh start.

In front of the camera? "Oh my gosh, we made it!" I said. I mean, we had managed not to divorce each other.

Kody spent days stringing lights between all of our cul-de-sac houses to signify our connection. He said that if any of us misbehaved, we would be kicked out of the family.

Awesome.

We expected two hundred guests. Meri's sister and mom made seven thousand hors d'oeuvres.

During a rehearsal, I set up the stand with the placard that had our mission statement. The wind immediately knocked it over.

Uh-oh.

"Is that an omen?" I wondered, for the camera.

The guests arrived, and we sorted our dresses. We took hours of photos. Truely started to cry, and Kody's face turned bright red as he clenched his jaw.

"Look down the lens!" Kody yelled. "You look at him!"

"Kody, you sound so mean!" I said.

"I have been taking pictures for two hours," he said. "Everyone else has been doing it for like fifteen minutes."

Eternity.

The ceremony began. Kody said we embraced a spirit of abundance and affection. Janelle talked about making "conscious and responsible" choices. Robyn cried as she talked about "embracing one another with a covenant of an eternal nature." We all signed the statement in front of our friends and family.

And the cameras.

I remember thinking, *If I'm going to stay, it needs to look different from this.*

We—the sister wives—decided to do a sand-pouring ceremony. We would all pour different-colored sand from individual containers into a joint container to signify our togetherness.

In the middle of it, I thought, *This is ridiculous* . . .

I set down my little container after adding my sand to the mix.

I'm not even going to be staying.

The thought came out of nowhere.

The kids told us what it meant to be our children, then gave us roses. We planted a family tree. Kody's lights sparkled over the cul-de-sac. We danced.

Two weeks later, my little container tipped over and broke.

Chapter Twenty-Eight

ENDURE THROUGH THE END

I've never been particularly good at self-care. With eighteen kids (Robyn had Ariella in January of 2016), there wasn't time for that—and it felt selfish. We're not, as women, taught a) that we should take time to replenish our souls so that we can take good care of everybody else—because you always adjust your own oxygen mask first, and b) that taking time for ourselves isn't immoral.

You have to be self-aware and listen to yourself, you have to know being selfish isn't bad. If you don't put yourself first, you lose yourself. Who are you as a person? If you don't know, you don't set goals for yourself, and you don't grow as a human. We believed plural marriage would help us grow—but it was because it was a sacrifice. It'll make you the best person ever because you'll go through so many hard times.

Endure through the end, they always told us.

It's terrible, this "morality" they sell. Why can't we enjoy through the end? Also, isn't that a bit dramatic? Endure through the end? You do you, but I'm gonna choose to be happy. For the most part, I did that. I'm a cheerful person, and no matter what was going on, I thought, *We can handle this. We'll be fine.*

That's great and all, but "choosing to be happy" may have simply been the best way for me to be resilient in an unhappy marriage—another version of enduring through the end.

Oof.

Looking back, maybe "enduring through the end" isn't the best way to think about marriage and life.

Trashy Scottish romance novels were my thing for years and years and years. If you didn't know there's a trashy Scottish romance novel genre—maybe you've been too caught up in that whole romantasy thing?—you're missing out. Don't hit me with any time-travel rubbish. That's the worst. Hit me with the cheapest, trashiest potboiler you can find. Listen, I was dealing with real-world problems. All I wanted to worry about was whether the two people who obviously hated each other passionately would end up falling in love, after a forceful stolen kiss that made her feel some kind of way underneath her rage-filled indignation. (And yes, if anyone tried that with one of my kids, I'd knock their block off. So inappropriate.)

My kids would say, "What do you want for your birthday?" As if they had any doubt.

"I want a bath," I answered one year while we lived in Vegas. "I want to be left alone in the bathtub."

My tub was enormous and had jets. My kids cleaned my bathroom so it was spotless, ran the water to the perfect temperature, tossed in a bath bomb, and added some candles. Of course, they found me a brand-new trashy Scottish romance novel. The best part? Aspyn took the kids out for hours. I read the entire book.

Through the years, every Christmas, every birthday, and every Mother's Day, they would give me trashy Scottish romances. Or novels that were generally trashy in any way. If it was particularly horrifying, they would read from the back cover in front of the whole family, often using different accents. If we were filming, it was particularly funny because it was so embarrassing.

Even if I didn't know how to do self-care, my kids knew how to do it for me, and they didn't see any problem with me taking that time. I learned so much reading trashy novels.

We settled into a routine in Vegas that felt okay, mostly because the kids were all in a good place. As humans, we have a tendency to settle in and make the best of our normals.

In a literal sense, those normals, and my kids, saved my life, because things started getting harder in the Kody Brown family—and I hit a challenge harder than any other I had faced.

Kody divorced Meri legally but not spiritually in September 2014 so he could legally marry Robyn and then adopt her kids. Meri was kind about it, even though it took away her status as the "legal" wife. She thought her relationship with Kody would change, but it was only for the worse.

Not long after, Meri told us she had reached out to someone online who made her feel seen and loved. But that person, whom she'd been flirty and honest with, turned out to be a scam artist. A creep. She was mortified and heartbroken, and I hurt for her. No one should have to go through such a horrible betrayal, and I wish she'd had the chance to sort through that whole mess privately.

I don't think any of us wanted to talk about hard things like the catfishing scandal on camera, but I remember the director trying to encourage us by saying, "It seems like you're about to say something, and you get super, super close, and then you say nothing. We would like it if, maybe, you shared what was going on inside your mind."

It was just after "Brave" by Sara Bareilles came out: "Say what you wanna say and let the words fall out."

Oh no, I thought. *That's not going to happen.*

I have no doubt it would never have happened if Kody hadn't completely withdrawn his affection. I've been on the wrong side of Kody, and it's a lonely place. But from that point on, he blamed her for their relationship issues.

Janelle's daughter Maddie left Vegas to attend Utah State in 2015. Shortly after she left for school, she started dating Caleb, and it was fun to see them grow close, especially as the adult relationships in the family continued to implode. But after Caleb asked her to marry him, and as their June 2016 wedding grew closer, Maddie decided her own happiness depended on lifting me from an abyss.

I didn't talk about this for the cameras:

Just before Maddie and Caleb got married, I blew out my knee. I tore my ACL and my meniscus, and I had to have surgery. Kody brought me home from the hospital and then prepared to leave.

"What do I need to do?" I asked, wondering about meds and aftercare.

"I don't know," he said.

"They didn't give you any instructions?"

"No," he said. But he had gotten my prescription for pain pills filled, and he handed me the bag. My mom and daughters stayed to help.

I had never taken oxycodone before—if something hurt, I took ibuprofen or aspirin. Real pain indicates that something's wrong, and if I take something that masks the problem, I'm not going to fix the problem, so I generally avoid it. With the surgery, I had already fixed the problem, and it hurt, so I took my meds.

On the third day after the surgery, I felt like I had the flu. I was achy from head to toe. I took an oxycodone, and all the symptoms went away.

Oh, I thought. *I'm not taking this for my knee anymore. I'm taking it because I'm achy everywhere.*

And then.

It gave me the best high I ever felt. I was on top of the world, and I could accomplish everything!

I lived about two minutes away from the interview set, so I could take an oxycodone just before I left, drive to work before it hit, and then feel great on set. Oxy made the set fine. I could do anything on oxy.

About forty-five minutes later, I would feel the low coming, and I'd feel so sad. *You've got another couple hours before you can take another one*, I'd think. *You've just got to get through this.* All I could do was think about the next hit, and it was hours away.

It became this cycle of the best high ever, forty-five minutes of swimming along taking on the world, realizing the low was coming, hitting the low, then fixating on the next hit—when I would start the exact same cycle again.

About two weeks into this shambles where I couldn't even think clearly enough to get myself out, Maddie came over and sat on the couch with me in my room.

"Caleb's coming over," she said, "and you're a mess. I miss you—we all miss you. We all need you back, so whatever you're doing, figure it out."

I told her I'd get off it and that everything was going to be okay.

I talked to Kody.

"I have an addiction to oxycodone," I told him. "I'm going to need your help to get off this."

I broke the capsules in half. I gave half of them to Aspyn because I knew it would be mortifying to have to ask her for more. After I started taking the half dose, I never had the high again and I never had the low. After about a week of that, Kody took all of the young girls out of town, and I spent the weekend in bed sobbing, watching *Pretty Woman* over and over and sobbing. I couldn't handle my life,

I couldn't handle anything. My mom stayed with me and took care of me.

At the end, I gave the rest of the oxycodone to my mom. You can take them to your local pharmacy and they'll dispose of them. You don't want to flush them into the city sewage system because it can contaminate local waterways and the water supply. But I was still so unbalanced for maybe six months after that. I didn't feel like me, and all I wanted was oxycodone. I couldn't get it, and that made me angry. I knew I would never feel that high again.

It was that fast to become addicted, and then that long to find myself again.

I decided to tell my kids about it, to be open about what had happened. If it could happen to me, it could happen to them, and what kind of mom would I be if I didn't warn them? That being said, medical professionals will also tell you that you will heal better after a surgery if you're not in pain. But as soon as ibuprofen will suffice, stop with the oxy.

The memory of that high still tempts me. I had a root canal not long ago, and I told them I couldn't have oxycodone. I took Tylenol instead, and I was just fine.

When I think back to that time, I don't know what might have happened if Maddie hadn't felt comfortable coming to me—if we hadn't had all those years of sitting on the couch and talking about everything from lost teeth to first kisses. And I don't know if I would have been strong enough to get out of it if I hadn't already discovered that I loved myself enough to want me back.

But my kids weren't done with me.

Mykelti moved to St. George, Utah. There, a friend introduced her to Tony Padron. Soon after, she got her associate's at UNLV, and they came home and announced that they wanted to get married. We had met him only a few times, and I handled it poorly.

I was in shock. I thought she would come back to Vegas to go to fashion school. She was nineteen. I didn't know they were a serious couple.

But it also sent me straight back in time. I realized I wished I'd had more time to date Kody, and I worried for her. I thought Kody and I should have taken the time to get to know each other in a more intimate, romantic way. Maybe he would have figured out he wasn't that into me—or maybe I would have.

I wanted Mykelti to fall in love. I wanted her to have passion. I worried that she had done what I always had told her to do: find a friend, build a partnership, love is a gradual thing and will come. I knew that if she didn't have that passion when she got married, she would miss something important. I didn't think they had it. I didn't see any romance.

Then we played this silly couples game, and Mykelti and Tony knew each other better than any of the rest of us knew each other after being together for decades.

They'll be fine, I thought.

They talked to each other constantly about everything, and they felt comfortable doing it. It took them a month to figure out all these things they knew about each other that I still didn't know about Kody.

It hit me hard, how Kody was with Robyn, and Maddie was with Caleb, and then how Mykelti was with Tony—especially with Mykelti because she'd found love so quickly.

Oh, I thought. *These are soulmates, and Kody and I just don't have it.*

Chapter Twenty-Nine

I COULD MOVE HERE

*M*addie and Mykelti got married while we were in Vegas. And then Aspyn got married, and I loved being near her and seeing her as a new wife. My kids were all doing well in the schools there and planning to go to college at the University of Nevada, Las Vegas, so they'd be close to home with in-state tuition.

As long as the kids were close, I was fine. Being upset about things, being jealous about things, being angry about things—what good does that do anyone? I wanted the kids to have a good relationship with their dad. For that to happen, I had to push my own feelings down.

And then, in 2017, we found out the Oakland Raiders were moving to Vegas. Everything was going to go to hell, Kody grumbled, and the kids wouldn't be safe, and traffic would be bad and . . .

Seriously? We lived in Las Vegas. It's not known as the city of morality—a football team seemed like the least of our worries. But then the family started talking about the schools not being safe. My kids were fine. My kids were excellent. Janelle's kids? Great. No fears. Lots of friends. Great teachers.

One day, out of nowhere, Kody sat us all down and explained that we needed to leave Vegas, saying it would be safer and better for us financially. He presented a plan, but said we could pick where we ended up.

As it turned out, even the picking of the place had been preordained.

As a family, which meant everyone but Meri, Janelle, and me, we decided to move to Flagstaff. *All right,* I remember thinking, *I guess that's what we're doing.*

I was furious. I did not want to take the kids away from their friends and schools. But we were a family, and I wanted to be a team player, so I decided to be open-minded about it—even though I thought it was ridiculous. Why on earth would we uproot our family again?

Janelle was equally uninterested in going. I hadn't realized how independent Janelle was until we moved to Vegas. She traveled by herself, and she made plans with her kids without worrying about Kody: "I let him know. If he wants to come, he can."

When Kody started talking about moving, she had other plans.

"Why don't we stay here?" she asked me. Janelle had stayed behind in the past, waiting until we all got settled. We could keep our kids in school. I could be near Aspyn and Maddie. I could be there when the kids went to college.

For a moment, I thought, *Why don't we stay here?*

But I couldn't split up the family. I believed this was my kids' best chance to have a good relationship with their dad. At that point Kody was saying, "I don't care where we go, we just have to get away from the Raiders." My kids should all be Raiders for Halloween one year. It seems it would be terrifying. Anyway, Kody kept throwing out Flagstaff as a possibility.

I had never been, so we went to Flagstaff for my birthday, and he showed me different places. Then he showed me the property at Coyote Pass, where he thought the family should move. It was a fourteen-acre undeveloped lot that looked out over the mountains. I fell in love with the view and immediately understood how wonderful it would be to have us all settled there on our own lots. I imagined us each in our corners of the lot in our own homes, hanging out somewhere in the middle. We would transplant the cul-de-sac. It seemed magical and amazing, and a way to get a reset.

"I could move here," I said.

I'm sure you all know the saying "insanity is doing the same thing over and over and expecting a different result." So you're probably also thinking, *What in the actual hell was Christine thinking?*

I thought Kody would realize what he was missing. He and Robyn had been together for a few years, so maybe the shine had worn off enough for him to remember his other families. The big family picture had always been important to him, and I would think, *You're gonna realize how incredible your kids are and you're gonna want to be in their lives again, because what we had in Wyoming was so good and so cool.*

We'd gone on television because we knew our family was special, so I wanted us to be special again.

I honestly thought we would balance out. I saw Coyote Pass as the solution.

Kody talked to Meri about the possibility of a new start in their relationship. And then she was in. Janelle may have fallen harder for the property than any of us, but the three of us believed in Kody and his promise of a reset.

Still, I was so sad leaving Aspyn and Maddie behind. Aspyn had just gotten married in December 2018, and she struggled with the idea of us leaving—she didn't understand why we needed to go, and I couldn't explain it.

"So we're just gonna be alone?" I remember her saying.

Talking to her about it broke my heart, and it broke hers, too. Dad just felt like we needed to go.

Maybe we should have stayed in Vegas, Janelle and me. Maybe we should have let our kids finish school there. Maybe I should have stayed with Janelle and cultivated that friendship. But maybe neither of us would have gotten the finality we needed. Still, the more I think about it now, the more frustrated I get that I didn't stay with Janelle and our girls.

About a month after we moved in 2018, we learned that Dayton, Robyn and Kody's son, had been accepted to the university in Flagstaff.

I was furious. Was that why we moved? So Robyn could be closer to her son while I was pulled farther from my children?

This may surprise you, but things didn't improve for the Kody Brown family from there.

We settled into our new places, most of us focused on finding something affordable because we had to pay off Coyote Pass before we could begin to build there—but maybe even more so now that we believed we had moved under false pretenses: It seemed like we weren't worried about the Raiders. It seemed like we were worried about Dayton going to college in Flagstaff.

Kody still controlled the family money, as well as the payment for the property. I continued to tell Kody what I needed, and to then receive a check. I believed everything extra would be put toward Coyote Pass, as did Meri. Janelle handled our books, so she could see where most of the money went.

Janelle rented a small apartment, and Robyn rented a large house. Meri found a place to rent, but then had to move again because her landlord said the neighbors were uncomfortable having someone who lives polygamy around. And because I couldn't find a rental that worked for my kids, I bought a house. We could sell it when it was time to move and invest it in Coyote Pass.

I remember constantly asking Kody why we hadn't paid off the property and why we hadn't started building anything. About six months after we moved to Flagstaff, he gathered us all for a major presentation. He was excited, hair flopping, ready to hit us with yet another big idea. He unveiled the one-house plan—this idea that, as we had in Lehi, we would all have separate apartments in one big house. Kody would have his own separate space with a gorgeous view and grand windows, and our apartments would be afterthoughts.

No way, I remember thinking. *No.*

I could never leave.

The idea horrified me. I had gained autonomy as a mom. I'd been able to give my kids this amazing life. I was not going to share a house again. It would be a trap.

In addition to Kody's private quarters in the middle of the house, he planned to have a cabin on another one of our plots so he could escape.

Okay, I thought, *so you obviously don't like the idea of all of us together in one house, either.*

"I'm not really interested in doing that," I said.

I didn't give in.

I didn't try to be a "team player" on the committee that ignored my needs.

I didn't say, "It's fine."

It wasn't.

Kody asked why I wasn't into it. I told him I felt like it was a step backward and it would mean I didn't have anything in my name.

TLC paid all of us in a lump sum, which went into a business we created. But, once again, there never seemed to be enough money to take care of our big expenses. It was weird and frustrating because I knew how much money we were getting, and we should have been fine. While the rest of us needed to get approval from the family to spend extra money beyond our monthly payroll, Kody, it seemed to me, could spend however much he wanted without our approval.

"Kody would just take out funds, and I don't know what for," Janelle told me recently on camera. "And the money was just being spent—lots of it."

It horrified her.

The family money didn't seem to be going into paying off the property. I didn't want to go back to the days of being told there was no money for groceries to feed my kids, but plenty for a sports car for Kody.

Or a diamond for Robyn's ring.

But with the one-house plan, I also understood that Kody having his own space meant he would never be at my place.

"No, I wouldn't," he said, "because I'd have my own house."

"You would always be at Robyn's house," I said.

"Well, she has young kids," he said.

"Truely is a year and a half older than Solomon," I said.

This would not be a fresh start. This would not be Wyoming. Why had I stayed?

Meri was interested in the one-house idea. Kody had led her to believe he wanted to reconcile, and maybe this was her chance. But I didn't want to live near Meri again.

Our relationship had not improved. We both worked for the same company—she had brought me in—so we went on a cruise together. Maddie and Audrey, Leon's partner, also went. I thought this was a chance to see if anything had changed and, maybe, have some fun. As my sponsor, she was supposed to introduce me around, teach me about the company culture, and get me excited about the opportunities, and I looked forward to giving our friendship another shot.

Early in the trip, Meri thought I had ignored her. I told her I hadn't—I hadn't seen her.

Too late.

For the rest of the trip I remember that she ignored me completely, snubbed me, insulted me, or hit me with little barbs in front of other people. It was bizarre—and also exactly why I had ended the friendship the first time around.

Afterward, she called me. Here's how I remember the conversation:

"I want to be friends," she said.

"Seriously?" I said. "No."

"I know," she said. "But it was a long time ago."

"You were mean to me two months ago on the cruise," I said.

No.

I know she went through some rough times, but being nice is important, and treating people with kindness is important. I also know she has friends now who love her and watch out for her, which makes me think she must be a good friend back to them. I'm glad for that. But the thought of living in the same house again with her in Flagstaff made me feel anxious.

I also knew I didn't trust Robyn—so I didn't want to set up house on the other side of a wall. Besides, if I could see what was going on across the cul-de-sac, it likely wouldn't be better across the hallway. Janelle would want to create a massive garden, and she would want my help. And I hate gardening. I also didn't want to have to take care of the family lawn-mowing and landscaping, as I had done in our other shared homes. I wanted my own little space where I could make decisions for me and my family.

Worse, I understood Kody was an absent dad. I worried about my family's future. If I moved into the big house, there would be no escape: all our money would be tied up in that property.

About six months after we moved to Flagstaff, I realized Kody would sometimes do things with Janelle and her kids, but she didn't seem to care either way. She'd say, "We're going to do such and such this weekend." I'd ask, "Is Kody going with you?" "I don't know," she'd say. "He can do whatever he wants to."

Oh.

In my mind, it wouldn't be fun without Kody, and it stopped us from doing things. In Vegas, we lived just a few hours away from the beach, but I would wait for him. I wanted my kids to have that well-rounded, having-a-dad-around vacation with Kody. We went on a few trips over the years: The Nauvoo, Illinois, road trip that Kody, the kids, and I had taken. And we'd go up to see my dad in Idaho Falls about once a year. But in general, when we did trips, it would be with the whole family—all the wives.

Then we moved to Flagstaff, and I finally realized he wasn't going to do anything with us. He hadn't done anything with us in Vegas. The situation with Robyn wasn't changing. He wasn't going to do anything with us in Flagstaff.

One snowy February day, I had an epiphany.

You know what? I thought. *I'm just gonna do it.* The mountains shimmered with a fresh coat of white, and I didn't want to miss it, so I took the kids sledding. We just went. Kody or no, we had a fantastic day. From then on, I didn't think twice. I invited him all the time, with Janelle as my example, but I didn't make a decision based on whether he might be able to go with us another day.

Then I realized it was much easier without him. Kody could be pretty dramatic, making it hard when he was around—we had to plan the right foods, and stuff had to be packed in the right order, and he needed the proper number of running shoes, and we had to be back in time for him to kiss Robyn's kids good night, and so on. We would spend the day wondering if it would be enough. I preferred it when we did things without him.

By the time we had been in Flagstaff a year, I constantly did things on my own with my girls (Paedon had graduated from high school and moved to St. George before we left Vegas), and we had more fun. We played all the time. If they asked about Kody, I said, "Look, I don't think so, so let's do it on our own. We're fine. We can do it without him."

Aspyn and her husband, Mitch, and Mykelti and Tony had moved to Utah, and we went to visit. My kids loved it. We took Janelle's kids hiking with us in Flagstaff, and Robyn even sent Dayton with us. We started hiking and going on daily adventures. And Janelle and I did more together with our kids than we ever had—we hiked almost every weekend and kayaked several times a week when we had good weather.

We traveled more. We spent weekends in Vegas. We lived more independently.

But I still felt frustrated that I had to do so much alone. I wondered if I wanted to be on my own for the rest of eternity in my sacred marriage to Kody, Meri, Janelle, and Robyn. I wasn't sure if they would have kayaks in the Celestial Kingdom, but what if I had to spend the rest of time in a boat by myself?

I had been watching my life pass me by waiting for Kody to say yes.

Before this realization, I made excuses. I remember standing in the hallway one day as I told the kids we were going kayaking.

"Is Dad gonna come?" Gwendlyn asked.

I started my spiel.

"Gosh, he wishes he could come," I said. "He loves spending time with you."

Gwendlyn and Ysabel looked at me. I could tell they thought I was full of it.

I stopped lying for him.

"He's not coming," I said.

"Okay," they said.

"Look, I don't think he's ever gonna come," I said. "If he does, we'll just see how the day goes."

They were better with that than with me trying to manage their beliefs about a father who never showed up.

That conversation also helped me stand up for myself more. If I wasn't painting a false front on his image for the girls, I sure as hell wasn't going to gaslight myself anymore.

I realized I had a voice, that I could speak my mind, and that it was okay to be selfish about my time with my girls. I needed to be straight with all of us.

He actually did go kayaking with us for Father's Day, but he didn't change out of his jeans, and he didn't get in the water. He watched from the beach for about an hour.

"Okay," he said. "I have to go."

That was somehow worse than him simply not showing up at all—the girls could see he didn't want to be there.

After that, they didn't ask. They felt like they didn't have a dad, and I didn't have a husband.

Truely would still ask him occasionally if he was coming. "Nope. Not today."

C'mon, Truely. Let's go play.

I didn't realize how much of my life I focused on Kody at the expense of me and my kids until I moved to Flagstaff. Even as we rearranged our time, eating habits, and even furniture to meet his needs, he didn't do anything to make us want to spend more time with him. That's not a partnership.

As I spent more time on my own and with my girls, I became more independent. I learned that I liked myself as a woman. I loved myself as a woman.

Kody didn't love me as a woman.

A funny thing happened soon after: I began to understand that leaving was a real possibility.

WOMAN

Chapter Thirty

I JUST NEED MY DADDY

We had divided the plots at Coyote Pass and agreed on which ones we wanted. But the ownership of the four plots had been assigned oddly: Kody, Robyn, and I had a plot; Kody, Janelle, and Meri had a plot; Kody and Janelle had a plot; and Kody and Robyn had a plot. Weird, huh? I don't know why he decided to do it that way—apparently, he didn't tell anybody, and we weren't there when it was done. We didn't understand why each wife didn't have a plot, or why any of the plots needed more than two names. Like, why was Robyn on my piece? I still don't understand that.

Kody had us out to meet with a surveyor he had hired, unknown to us, for the property. As we walked the perimeter of the land we'd bought as a family in Flagstaff to look at the plots we'd each chosen for our homes, Kody hit us with a bombshell: the plot I had chosen on the hill with the most incredible view was no longer mine. I was so upset. It felt as if he was removing me from the property, as if he didn't want me in the family anymore.

And once again, I felt like I had no say.

That Kody spent most of his time with Robyn was no longer a secret—the whole family could see that Kody had used COVID to effectively live with Robyn and haphazardly visit or ignore the rest of us, including his kids. Everything I complained about in Vegas turned out to be true.

Before COVID, Janelle had gathered us in a restaurant in Flagstaff.

"Do we want to be sister wives, really?" she asked.

Yes, we all agreed.

For the first year in Flagstaff, I still believed we would be fine if we could get our homes built on the property. "Fine," of course, is relative.

And then COVID hit and changed everything. It brought out the truth of our situation. As people cozied in with their loved ones, Kody picked Robyn and her kids. It brought out all the favoritism—and that Kody had found his soulmate.

Kody just wanted to be married to Robyn. Ultimately, that's okay. Dragging us along as pawns to keep the show going and money flowing into his pot?

Not okay.

By month eight, as we worried that the property would be repossessed if we didn't make our payments, Kody and Robyn had paid a large chunk of money on her house. She needed more, and Janelle and I worried we wouldn't pay off the property by a deadline we had all agreed to. If we missed it, we would lose Coyote Pass.

Janelle tried to force the issue by buying an RV and installing it there to live in, shuttling water and propane gas while Kody said he refused to limit his living situation based on her choices. He used it as an excuse to stay away.

Kody started to talk about morals and values that we all needed to live by to be "loyal" to him—and said that he couldn't live in a family that didn't support them—but none of us had agreed to them or even knew what they were. They came out of nowhere.

In August 2020, I sat down with our therapist. She told me to make a list of the things that were important to me in a marriage. Kody came over that night and asked what we had talked about. I asked him if he wanted to hear the list, and then I read it to him: A companion. Someone who was attracted to me. Someone who put my kids first. Someone who wanted to be around me. Someone who would be a partner in my home.

"I'm none of those things for you," he said.

I knew that. I did not expect affirmation. And I didn't expect affirmation to hurt so much.

But it extinguished any hope I had of our marriage or my kids having a good dad.

"No," I said. "You're none of those things."

The kids had quickly grown frustrated by his rules, believing that as the rest of the country was able to get jobs, go to school, and date, they should be able to as well—especially as the COVID vaccines became available. But any child who didn't follow the rules was ostracized and accused of being disloyal. In Janelle's case, Kody insisted she choose between him and her kids.

Easy-peasy.

About seven months into COVID, as our family struggled to stay connected, Ysabel desperately needed surgery. It would become a defining moment.

We had known for years her surgery was inevitable: her back curved at seventy-seven degrees, causing her spine to look like an S. That curve affected everything, from how her muscles developed to her posture—causing her to lose a couple of inches of height. And it hurt. Every day, that kid was in pain. I could see it in her face.

Something as simple as sitting to do her homework looked as if it tortured her.

We had hoped to wait until after the pandemic, and until after she had finished growing so she could have a different surgery from the typical steel-rod version that would limit her movement for the rest of her life. For months, she had performed her exercises and stretches, hoping to slow the progress of the curve—and she had done wonderfully well. But the stretches couldn't postpone the inevitable.

Kody kept talking about how I was "traveling," as if I'd been on vacation and not worried about putting the family at risk. And Ysabel's surgery was not elective. She hurt all the time.

"It's time," her doctor said.

The surgical center required us to be on the East Coast and quarantined for two weeks before Ysabel could go in. It was only an hour from my sister's house, so, in September 2020, we stayed with her for the two weeks—she agreed to quarantine with us.

I thought Kody would come with us because it was a major surgery and because he had talked before about being there for her. Ysabel and I met with him outside the house, as usual, to tell him.

"Well, I'm not going to go," he immediately said, as the cameras rolled.

"Oh," Ysabel said. I could see the gut punch on her face.

"I can't leave my family for three weeks," he said.

His family. Robyn.

Ysabel just looked at me in shock.

Oh, my heart. This was arguably the scariest thing she had ever faced, but he needed to put Robyn's kids to bed. The dad with the posse of kids in matching tool belts—the one I had loved in Wyoming—was gone.

"Why do you have to go?" Kody asked me. "Isn't it really close to your sister's house? She can watch her."

"She's seventeen," I said, trying to keep my voice steady. "This is a major surgery, and I'm going to be there."

"Well, I can't go," Kody said. "I think you're going because you know it's COVID and you know I can't go."

But Ysabel's surgery wasn't about Kody.

"I thought you were going because when we talked about it before, you said you would," I said. He'd come to several of her doctors' appointments, including in Michigan. He'd been there when she was tested after all her exercises.

"I need to go inside now," Ysabel said. It kills me that she looked so vulnerable, and that so many people saw her pain.

Kody left, I went inside, and Ysabel looked so sad.

"What does he mean he can't go to my surgery?" she asked.

"I don't know, but I'm going to be there," I said.

"I thought we were his family," she said.

I did, too.

I decided we would make the best of it, and I would choose to be positive. My kid needed me. She needed to believe that her dad wanted to be there. She needed to get through a major surgery with a long, painful recovery.

I took the kids out of school, and we rented a house on the ocean in New Jersey, and we walked to the beach every day. We had a lovely time hanging out together.

I realized, while we were at that beach house, how easy it was and how fine I was. I wish Kody had been there for her, but I didn't need him there, and it was easier without him.

The morning of the surgery, I French-braided Ysabel's lovely hair, and we talked about how excited and happy she was to fix her back. It was the coolest surgery ever: They went in through the side—so she has a wicked scar she's extraordinarily proud of—and they collapsed one of her lungs so they could get to her spine. Then they used screws to attach two nylon-fiber ropes all the way up on both sides of her spine to straighten it, like a zipper. I was excited for her, and a little terrified.

Once again, I watched as the medical team wheeled one of my girls through metal swinging doors, and I trusted that they would take good care of her.

"Where's my dad?" she said, as soon as she woke.

"He'll be here in a minute, sweetie," the nurse said. "Don't worry."

They didn't know he wasn't coming.

"I just need my daddy," Ysabel said.

I was there.

"Your dad can't be here," I told her.

She asked for him all through the night.

"Where's my dad?" she kept saying.

The next morning, before she asked about her surgery, she said, "My dad's not going to come."

"No," I said. "He can't."

She must have figured he would surprise her, that he wouldn't let her down.

She asked if she could call him, and I handed her the phone.

"Will you sing me a song?" she said when he answered.

"No," I remember him saying, "I don't feel like singing."

I almost lost my mind.

The nurses kept asking, "Who else is here with you?"

"It's just me," I'd answer. And I realized that was fine, too.

The surgery went great. Ysabel still has a bit of a rib hump from the twist in her spine, and she may always have it. But her curve went down to seventeen percent, so just a breath of a curve. The S is gone, and she has one hundred percent range of motion, which she would not have had with the rod. It felt like one of the best things I've done as a mom.

We stayed at the hospital for five days, and then we went to my sister's house. Ysabel was in pain for a while—months—after the surgery, but I could tell she felt hopeful that it would improve, rather than steadily get worse as had been the situation before.

And I realized I could handle it on my own just fine.

"Fine." But I meant it. Not "fine" like I didn't want to talk about it. Not "fine" like I would struggle through. "Fine" like I was enough. I didn't need Kody there, and it was much less complicated without him. I'd always wondered if I would be okay alone. I'd heard Meri through the years say "I'm okay alone," but it didn't seem like she was. She didn't like it, and it was imposed on her, I thought. I didn't want to fake being fine.

But I was fine alone.

Kody hadn't wanted to be away from Robyn and the kids for the three and a half weeks we were gone, but he could have come for part of it. He could have been a guest at the hospital afterward. He also could have come to see her at my sister's house.

When we got back to Flagstaff, Kody visited Ysabel a few times. We had a reclining folding chair she could sit in as she recovered, and we'd take her outside and bundle her up, and he would hang out with her.

Aspyn, Mitch, and Hunter did come out after the surgery to spend time at my sister's house. Kody didn't know that until he saw the episode. It made him look bad.

Really bad. It shouldn't have mattered: Ysabel already knew.

Chapter Thirty-One

YOU'RE NOT ALLOWED
IN MY ROOM

*D*uring COVID, I'd locked myself in, bought masks, fretted over every runny nose, and figured it would all be over quickly. In the meantime, I cozied into my home with my girls and my thoughts. It was the first time I'd had time to think in years.

In our church, we're taught that if we live plural marriage, we'll be rewarded. We'll create worlds together for eternity.

Not long after Ysabel's surgery, as I walked down the stairs from my bedroom loft to the main floor, I had an epiphany.

I'm going to create worlds with Kody, Robyn, Meri, and Janelle, I thought. *For eternity.*

I felt as if my heart flip-flopped like a spastic, angry little fish.

I don't want to create worlds with these people, I thought. *I don't want to be doing this for eternity.* For all eternity, my opinion and needs wouldn't matter. I couldn't make it fit.

I sat down hard on the stairs.

The loft had been a family room, so there was no door at the bottom of the stairs. Floor-to-ceiling windows framed a stunning view in the loft, so my kids weren't thrilled when they found out it wouldn't be a communal space. I loved it. But we didn't have any privacy without a door.

"Let's put in a door," Kody said soon after my epiphany.

Could this mean we might be moving toward a physical marriage? I was in a bit of shock because I had just had my epiphany, because he had already told me he couldn't give me what I needed, and because he had so thoroughly deserted us during Ysabel's surgery. Was he trying to make amends?

He had been coming over at five or six at night, based on whether we'd quarantined and showed no signs of illness, and we'd hang out with the kids, eat dinner, and play a game. The kids knew to be on their best behavior, and we'd discuss what they might tell Kody while he was there—a story from school, a book they read. But he'd be on his phone the whole time, even during dinner, disengaged from all of us.

"Can you not do that at dinner?" I'd ask.

He'd get upset and frustrated.

"I have to watch this," he'd say, and go back to his phone to watch some video.

It was awkward between us. Sometimes we tried. We watched a few television series together. On the weekend, he'd still come over at five or six—never during the day. He'd play a game with Truely, or we'd all watch a movie together.

Then he and I would go upstairs to my bedroom. He would sit in his chair with his phone, and I would go to bed. That was our routine.

But a door would mean the children couldn't hear us or inadvertently walk in. Did he want to be my husband with benefits? It had been a minute.

A door.

"This will be great because then Zelda can't get up here," Kody said, as we framed the entrance at the bottom of the stairs.

Zelda. The cat.

I suddenly understood: It wasn't about intimacy. It was about fur. I wanted clarification, maybe to force a decision.

"You know, you talked a lot about Zelda and keeping her downstairs," I said, after we finished the job. "I thought we were putting the door in so we could have the intimate part of our marriage back."

"I'm not really interested in that with you," he said.

"What?" I said. After everything, I still felt sick. Twenty-five years.

"I never have been."

I'd known he had hadn't found me physically attractive at the beginning of our marriage, especially after the comments in *Becoming Sister Wives* about how disgusted he was when I ate nachos in his car, but I thought that had changed over the years—especially after I had gotten my weight down.

"I don't like how you treat your sister wives," he said. Wait. He's never been interested in me because he doesn't like the way I treat my sister wives? This is the man who said I saved the family's bacon because I had helped mediate between Meri and Janelle.

"I don't like how you treat Robyn," he said.

Oh. There it is.

But blaming my relationship with Robyn also sounded like a whole lot of horseshit to me. What in the world did him never being attracted to me have to do with how I got along with my sister wives? Nothing. Nothing at all. He'd known from the beginning, and he'd decided to marry me anyway—to take away the possibility of me finding someone who did love me and did find me attractive. For eternity. It was beyond selfish.

"There are a lot of people we know who have separate marriages," he said.

Gosh. So Kody could go to one of his other wives, but I would be eternally fated to no sex?

Sounds great.

I didn't get married because I wanted eternal abstinence.

"You shouldn't have proposed to me," I told him. "You shouldn't have told me you loved me."

I went to bed, and when I woke up the next morning, I sent him on his way. The girls and I went out of town, and we were doing the two-week quarantine thing, so he didn't come over again for about six weeks.

Then he came over to spend time with the kids, and as we all hung around outside, six feet away from each other, I asked if we could talk alone.

"I don't want you sleeping in my bed anymore," I said. "You're not allowed in my room."

"Whoa, wait," he said.

"No. I only want people in my room who want to be there, and right now, that's me," I said.

He didn't say anything—or anything I remember. He left soon after.

When I went back to my room, I realized his stuff was every-where, and it made me feel nauseated.

I don't even want him in my room to pack up his stuff, I realized. *I don't want him in my space.*

When he came over, I wanted him to spend time with the girls, not packing. I knew it would take him forever. I remembered watching how things had shaken out with Meri, how every time we'd move Meri, he would find a box of his stuff, and he would keep it in his truck—slowly moving out without saying he was moving out.

I wasn't going to give him that control.

He doesn't get to decide, I thought.

I spent every morning, before the girls woke up, packing his stuff and taking it to the garage.

Weeks later, he came over and started heading up the stairs to my bedroom.

"You're not allowed to come up to my room," I said.

"All my stuff is up there," he said.

I told him it was in the garage.

"What am I supposed to do with it?" he asked.

Don't know, don't care.

"Where am I supposed to stay?"

"You're the one who wanted a separate marriage," I said. "You have other houses. Go to one of them."

"So what am I going to do, just come here and hang out with the kids and leave?"

"That's exactly what you're going to do."

I told him our marriage was over. I told him I would be moving back to Utah.

Funny thing about living life on a reality show: I found out later that he had already filmed himself in the garage discovering all his boxes. He even counted them.

After I told him he wasn't allowed in my room anymore, I went around the corner of the house and let out a primal scream.

AAAAAAAAAHHHH!

I didn't realize he hadn't left yet.

Oops.

It felt so good. It was my moment. MY moment, when I felt strong.

Then I went up to my room, and I was so excited to have my space be my space. He existed in such a dark cloud, and I didn't have to deal with it in my safe place anymore. I just got to be me.

In our church, you're supposed to get what's called a "spiritual release" if you want a divorce. We obviously weren't legally married, but to stay on good terms with the church, they want to be the final authority. But I had already left the church, so I just think of that day—my primal-scream day—as the day we got divorced. It's my mental divorce day. In my calendar, on November 2, 2020, it simply says "freedom."

There was no committee.

I got to say when we were done.

I am nacho wife anymore.

Chapter Thirty-Two

WHAT. DID. THE. NANNY. DO?

I know we frustrated the TLC team—and our viewers—sometimes. We went from this seemingly happy family to, oh wait, Meri and Kody haven't been together in years? Kody spends all his time with Robyn? Kody doesn't help out with the kids? The wives aren't best friends? The director eventually resorted to asking questions the audience can hear just so you know he's trying—that he had the same questions viewers did.

We wanted to be respectful. We still tried not to fight or be catty while on camera. This wasn't *Desperate Housewives of Polygamy*. But where there had been cracks before, chasms developed in Flagstaff.

We didn't see each other as often because of COVID, which meant we often learned things through family gossip, or, worse, through the end-of-season tell-alls.

I love Suki—Sukanya Krishnan—who does our one-on-one interviews for TLC, but we never knew what she was going to hit us with. Those interviews were the hardest thing we had to do because it felt like they were looking for "gotcha" moments. They got them. It got spicy and that's good for ratings, but not good for my head.

COVID pushed everything into weird. TLC sent out seventeen pages of rules for the cast and crew to abide by to keep everyone safe during filming. I bought a bunch of new clothes that better fit my body and my move away from frump, and then I would have to try on the clothes and send pictures to TLC to approve for different interview looks. The producers had pre-approved our outfits before, but it became even more important during the pandemic. Since we wouldn't be sitting together, or even seeing each other, they wanted to make sure we weren't all wearing Metallica T-shirts.

Or whatever.

We did come up with some outlandish stuff, and they finally started picking our outfits for us based on what we had.

They also taught us how to do our own makeup. I'm sure that was obvious. In Vegas, we had all glammed up a bit with eyelashes and so forth on set, but in Flagstaff, there would be no makeup person.

Can we just talk about Janelle for a minute?

She could have gotten by with no makeup at all. It was hard not to think, *You suck. People* magazine? She looked so freaking good on the cover.

They wanted us to do our hair the same way each time we were on camera, too. So reality TV, but a little different from reality because most of the time I'm bare-faced and in a ponytail.

These were strange things to think about as I worked on my escape, but by this time, I was pretty used to the focus on appearance.

After three months of living separately from everyone, Janelle and I had formed our own little COVID pod. We tested, masked, and followed the CDC rules. Especially during filming weeks, when we had to follow an extreme protocol, we felt comfortable spending time together.

In the meantime, Kody and Robyn had a nanny for her kids. This irked me because the three original sister wives had always helped with childcare, and Kody had always told us to ask each other for help, rather than pay someone to do it.

It also meant they had someone who lived outside the house coming in daily during the pandemic.

Janelle and I wondered, soon after Ysabel and I got back from her surgery, why we couldn't hang out with the rest of the family—especially since the nanny could. What were the rules for her? Did she wear a plastic suit at all times when not at Robyn's house? Did she go through a disinfection tunnel before entering Robyn's home? Did she have a mutant gene that left her permanently inoculated? We had a family meeting just before Thanksgiving in 2020 to talk about whether we would spend it together.

I told Janelle I would just ask.

What. Does. The. Nanny. Do?

(You know I saw the memes you guys came up with. LOL.)

It was a big question—big enough that I had it emblazoned on a T-shirt that I wear for my morning workouts.

What does the nanny do?

Why was the nanny allowed in the house but the family wasn't?

That's when Kody gave us his list of rules.

No jobs, no visits to girlfriends, bleach your mail.

Wrap yourself in Saran Wrap before you leave the house.

He didn't change his rules when the CDC did. In fact, when Janelle and I got our vaccinations in December of that year, he said he didn't want us around because we had infected ourselves with the virus. We got the shot so we could all hang out—but he didn't.

"No, no," he said. "I've read enough stuff on it. They say it's not backed by science."

Kody's phone was a huge source of contention at my house. He would send me the latest video, and I would say, "I'm never going to watch the videos you send me."

He sent the conspiracy stuff, but also videos about relationships. Perhaps we could talk face-to-face instead?

In any case, he was extremely paranoid about getting COVID. Robyn had to play by the rules because Kody spent all his time there, though I do think they came up with the rules together. That's how most households did it. We were not a part of that household, and, for the first nine months of the pandemic, Kody and Robyn were the only ones who knew the rules. Everybody else?

"Do whatever you need to do for your own household," Kody said.

Roger that.

(Two months later, the nanny got COVID. She was fine.)

In any case, I told Kody that my kids wouldn't be there for Thanksgiving. They couldn't follow the rules and keep their jobs and relationships. I would be with my kids.

That was the first year I wasn't with everyone for Thanksgiving.

Janelle did the same. We planned to hang out with her family, but then her sister got COVID. Instead, I went to Aspyn's. That was amazing. Thanksgiving had always been stressful because it had been so many people—even if I had enjoyed the bustle and sisterhood of it. Pies with Janelle? Anytime.

I asked Aspyn what time she wanted to have dinner.

"Oh, I don't know," she said. "Why don't you come over and we'll cook and when it's done, we'll eat."

Whoa.

I went over Thanksgiving morning.

"Let's just have a mimosa," Aspyn said.

We started to cook, and she had this connoisseur experience planned. Every meal at her house is perfection. Last night? Chicken parmesan with lemon caper sauce and roasted vegetables.

We chatted about past Thanksgivings where everyone ran amok, and where I never got a chance to sit down for the meal and it felt like it was all over before it began.

We tasted and played, and we even sat.

"Why don't we just have some wine?" Aspyn said, as she opened a bottle. We drank wine and we cooked, and the whole experience was magical. I wasn't worried about what time anything had to be on the table. There was no stress. There was wine.

Mitch? Her husband? That man can cook a turkey. All the food was delicious—and we savored it slowly.

Did I miss the madness? Yes. Did I enjoy sitting down through the meal and having real conversations and feeling relaxed?

Oh yeah.

All that goodness helped me prepare for the things that needed to come next.

Chapter Thirty-Three

YOU ALREADY KNOW
WHAT YOU NEED TO DO

*Y*ou know I love a good fairy tale. Ursula. Bare-chested Scottish lords. The yellow towel that made me feel like Rapunzel. The whole-hearted love of my father, who called me "princess."

Kody called me a princess "issuing an ultimatum" when I said I wanted to move to Utah.

It could have been another gut punch. *Is this really who I am? Someone who makes unfair demands and throws emotional temper tantrums?* But by then, I knew exactly how hard I had tried. Even better, I knew exactly who I was. My whole life I had been the fun one, the one who provided the levity to keep our pre-Robyn triumvirate together.

After I left our religion, I began to believe that we have one life, and in that one life, I want to be kind—to send out every bit of good energy I've got while I'm here—but I also want to live a life that's good for me. In wanting to move to Utah, I was thinking about my future castle.

To be fair, I may have been thinking more about the moat.

I had evicted Kody from my bedroom and stopped needing him as a partner for activities with our kids. I had left my religion, and

I had begun my fitness journey. I knew I didn't want to live in the same house as my family. I didn't even want to be in the same town with anyone but Janelle and any of the kids. I desperately wanted to move to Utah to be near my adult kids and my mom.

I needed a nudge, a reminder of the woman I had worked so hard to become.

I called my mom.

"I gotta leave Kody," I told her. I'm not sure what I expected, but I wanted to start with the truth. "I don't know how to do it. I don't know how to leave."

Her response was immediate, almost as if she'd been waiting for me to call her—or like she's my mom and loves me and will always know what I need.

"Okay," she said. "You're going to put both of your feet firmly on the ground, and you're going to take a deep breath. And then you're going to start moving forward.

"You already know what you need to do."

Oh.

It's impossible to describe how it felt to have her so immediately there for me. I could weep with her, but there was comfort in it now.

"What do you need to do?" she asked.

"Well, I need to move to Utah," I said. I needed to be close to my kids. I felt that in my bones. Mykelti lived six hours from Aspyn, so somewhere in between. My dad and siblings all lived in Utah.

"What is it going to take to move to Utah?" my mom asked, and she helped me with the basics.

Then she said, "You need to start making decisions based on joy, not fear. Start making decisions for you."

I remembered believing she was selfish when she put herself first to leave my dad. I was so worried about what my kids would think. But we had come so far since Mom and I had started those honest conversations after Kody and I got married. I felt like I could tell her anything, so I did.

"I feel like I'm being selfish," I said.

"It's your life," my mom said. "Yours. It's not selfish to want a good life—you have to look out for yourself. It's self. It's love. It's not selfish."

She was incredible. And it was crazy for me to hear it from her because she loves Kody. When she sees him, she gives him a big hug, and I doubt that will ever change. She hugs Robyn. She hugs all the kids. She's the most loving person. But she's clear that loving Kody doesn't mean he's the best one for her daughter.

In fact, I thought she had been happy when I married him. She hadn't. I knew things had felt awkward every time we came to town, but at first, that was because I was still working on my relationship with Mom. And then, maybe it was because I dragged a circus along with me. But that wasn't it. She struggled with him as my husband. She saw that I always put him first—not my kids and not me. And she saw that he liked it that way.

"You never had a good marriage," she told me.

She was ready for me to put myself first.

"They're manipulating you," she told me as I talked about my fears of leaving the family.

"Naw," I said. "Of course they're not. They're fine."

We talked about some of the things that had been going on with the property, the kids, and my finances, and she said, "That's manipulation."

"Oh wow."

She helped me see clearly why my gut desperately wanted me out of there.

And then I talked with Janelle. Janelle and I had grown close, especially when she moved into her RV on the Coyote Pass property.

With Janelle was born one of my favorite rituals—and one that had been banned by my faith.

Mormons, both mainstream and fundamentalists, don't drink coffee because it's banned in the Words of Wisdom, which advises against anything that can lead to addiction. You could lose your Activities Recommend for drinking coffee, so it was a big deal.

Janelle, our rebel, had the first coffeemaker of the sister wives. In Flagstaff, when she lived in the RV, she would come over and have a cup of coffee. That changed our relationship entirely.

So, over a cup of coffee, I told Janelle I wanted to leave Kody. It wasn't the first time we had talked about it, and in her mind, it may have been a hypothetical.

"You can't leave Kody until you create your own source of income," she said immediately.

She's pragmatic, but that was not the response I expected.

"You need to be able to support yourself financially because otherwise, what will you do?"

It wasn't that she was thinking along the same lines herself. She was full in on Coyote Pass and felt her relationship with Kody was fine, though she wasn't happy about the COVID situation with her kids. But she fully supported me—even when I had started trying to sort through it in Vegas.

She did have questions.

"I've only raised my kids with you," I remember her saying. "What does this mean for us?"

Janelle and I hadn't always been on the same page when we were younger, but we had developed something true. I trust her and trust her absolutely with my kids.

Janelle will always be my sister wife, and I believe our children will always think of both of us as "Mom." I hope so. Janelle helped me think through everything that would need to happen for me to leave Kody and move to Utah.

I still needed to have a conversation with the big guy.

Not the one with the ringlets.

I didn't believe in a "testimony" like I had with Robyn. But I was a religious person who loved Jesus even if I no longer believed Joseph Smith was a prophet or in the Book of Mormon. Deciding to leave Kody felt spiritual to me because I felt I needed to have a strong connection with God to do it. I didn't want God to be upset with me or to be sad, so I talked with him.

"Dear God, it's me, Christine. You good with this?"

"Yo, Christine. You're a parent, just like I am, and I want to see you happy, just like you want to see your kids happy."

It was that simple. If God is a loving, nurturing entity, then why would he bind me to Kody and friends for all eternity?

That was my second-strongest "testimony." My strongest was still that Robyn should be part of the family. But when you think about it, they're related. Maybe God was sending the same message both times: Robyn should be with Kody. You should not be with Kody. You should both be with your soulmates—or at least with people who love you as much as you love them.

I sat down with my journal, trying not to panic about all I would need to do to leave Kody. My goal was to move to Utah in September, so I backtracked on what needed to happen before then. That gave me about nine months.

I needed to get out of Flagstaff. All my bad memories live in Flagstaff. Oh my gosh, I have great friends in Flagstaff—they're lovely. But I needed to move to Utah, and I needed to create a plan to make that happen. I had to get my finances in order and create a strict budget so I could save enough money for us to move because it's so friggin' expensive. I needed to downsize so everything would fit into one moving truck. I needed to find a place to live and sell my house—or rent it. I had to figure out if Gwendlyn would come with me to Utah for school, how it would work for Ysabel who would be graduating, what to do with my plot of Coyote Pass, what kind of visitation Kody would want with Truely, and how to tell the family. And then I would need to plan Ysabel's graduation party.

I tackled my finances first.

With money, everything had been done as a family. We each had a separate bank account, but if someone came up short or had an emergency, we would pull resources. We had a committee that would essentially vote to make a decision. In the early days, Janelle was one of our breadwinners, and her car broke down. The rest of us handed over cash to take care of it. Sometimes the decisions were harder, like when Meri wanted to buy a bed and breakfast—a lovely idea because the house had belonged to her great-grandparents—but it was a lot of money that we didn't have. Because our finances were so tied up with Kody's, that further complicated matters. We always tossed around ideas for businesses that could make money, from gyms to jewelry to real estate.

I would need to disentangle myself, but we'd all become much more independent after we left Lehi.

I think many women fear leaving their spouses because of the money issue, but so many women have talked to me and said things got better in every way, including financially, after they left. I think that comes from knowing what you can depend on and planning your own budget, which I'd already tasted. I couldn't rely on Kody for groceries with our committee dynamic, but I could depend on myself.

Polygamous marriages are tough because there is no legal documentation. The house was in my name and Kody's. The plot on Coyote Pass was in my name—and Kody's and Robyn's. I couldn't ask for half of anything, but Robyn could because she legally married Kody. She could ask for a portion of my house if she left Kody. All the money I had already contributed to the family account or family property would stay there. That's why the sister wives started talking about our legacy for the kids.

As soon as we moved to Flagstaff, I started selling a women's clothing line. Meri did too. I started making enough money that I could survive just on that. But I still owed thousands on Truely's hospital bills. I worked my butt off to pay it off with the clothing business. Then Ysabel's back surgery needed to be paid—it was a $50,000 deductible—but I got some family money for that one. Once I paid off my big debts, I realized, *Okay. Now I can think logistically about leaving.*

I went on vacations with my kids—usually family reunions. I went to some Brown family reunions. I made sure my family was in a place to feel comfortable.

With each step, I found peace and security. I had always looked for security in my family, but it eluded me. But when it was just me and my space, it was wonderful. I continued to work on me, to become more confident and secure. I felt calm and ready, even while I didn't know my future or what obstacles might arise. I didn't know if the show would continue. I didn't know if my kids would be okay with the change.

But I laid out a goal to achieve every month.

Check.

Check.

Check.

My conversations with Janelle and my mom got me there. Once I had a plan I could act on, rather than this vague idea that I wanted to maybe leave someday, it became real. I made every decision with

joy. I was one step closer toward my kids and the possibility of happiness, whatever that might look like.

I didn't know it would be so great to live my life for myself and
for my kids. It felt simple, a whole new dynamic—different from
anything I'd had before.

I felt myself become more powerful with each step, and I realized it had started even before my conversation with my mom. I had
already come to terms with my faith and figured out that God and I
were good, and I had already reclaimed my space.

To prepare my house for sale, I took care of the repairs myself,
met with a Realtor by myself, and cleaned the house myself so a
photographer could come in.

I sold my bedroom set. I did not need to bring that bad juju to
my new space. I posted pictures and kept it as nondescript as possible to keep my identity private. If people figured out I was selling
my stuff, they might figure out I was leaving before I told the rest of
the family. I didn't need for them to find out on the internet.

Kody and I had picked the set together and filmed it for the
show. It was Old World, and I loved it. I had tapestries up, and a lot
of gold and matching bedding, and it was a beautiful room. When
I was pregnant with Mykelti, Kody got me a picture of a woman
on horseback with a knight standing near. I love the Pre-Raphaelite
fair maiden stuff, but I didn't know what to do with that one or the
others I had. They're from the past and they felt important, but they
didn't feel like me anymore. I realized all of it symbolized a relationship where we tried for a long time, but no one should have to try so
hard in a relationship. I donated all of it.

Ultimately, every decision I made needed to help me toward my
goal of fitting everything in the U-Haul.

By the time I was done, I had a few odds and ends, as well as
the snow blower, which I didn't want to get rid of until I knew

I didn't need to clear out the driveway for people looking at the house.

Kody had already laid some of his cards out on the table. When I kicked him out of the house, he didn't say, "Can we talk to our therapist?" or "I'm brokenhearted," or "What about the kids?"

He said, "This is my house." That's what he cared about.

The family had helped with the down payment, but I made every mortgage payment. I paid for all the repairs. He had some decor, and we had bought some furniture together, so there were items he visited from time to time. But it was not his house.

I was blown away that he didn't talk about the kids.

Kody said, on the show, that he was most worried about whether I would find a new boyfriend who would take his money. He wasn't hurt that I was leaving or concerned about Truely. He was worried that my imaginary boyfriend would break into his pots of gold.

There was no other guy and there wouldn't be for two years. But there was Truely, our funny, gorgeous, old-soul girl. She should have been first.

I felt shocked, but I also think he has always been greedy. His business deals always felt a bit questionable to me. I've watched him through the years at the family meetings, and he always decided where the money went. By the time we split up the family account, there was no money left—and we had been doing the show for fourteen years.

Dude, your kids don't have shoes and coats, but you have a new convertible.

That car made me mad—we were all driving crap cars and minivans. We just played along, like, "I guess we're new people now that we have this show." He said he needed it for some alone time.

Obviously, it was because he wanted to date—not to dad, and not to husband.

I learned recently, because Janelle talked about it on the show, that the family money hadn't been distributed evenly. My name was on the family account, so I could have looked at it, but it never occurred to me. But while I thought I was contributing to the family account by taking only what I needed, it turns out that money was simply being spent elsewhere.

I worked to be positive, but I also needed to work on my anger at myself. I felt embarrassed, especially when I realized my kids knew I was in a loveless marriage. My fans knew I was in a loveless marriage. My dad knew. It's humiliating. How could I allow it when I'm one of the most romantic people I know? Fair maidens? Yellow towels? Scottish lords?

What had I been thinking?

There had been some expert-level gaslighting. People gaslight because it works. People who don't gaslight don't expect it—they wouldn't think to do it. They take people at their word. Kody had a lot of words. We weren't loving enough, or attractive enough, or being nice enough sister wives. We weren't loyal enough or following his orders.

He wanted our independence, until he started to push us out, one by one. Then he used Janelle's independence against her to call her disloyal. He used Meri's undying loyalty against her when he convinced her to move to Flagstaff—so he could use the money from the sale of her house in Vegas to pay for Robyn's in Flagstaff—by telling her he wanted a reconciliation, before telling the camera he already considered himself divorced from her. He pushed me out initially by saying he didn't find me attractive because I wasn't kind to my sister wives, but ultimately by taking his love away from my children.

I realized my kids knew our marriage was broken, and I knew I was setting an example that it was okay to be in a loveless marriage and that it was okay to settle—that it was okay to be walked on and not have love and put yourself last.

No. I would not set that example for my kids.

I was frustrated with myself that I had let it go on for so long, but also that I just hadn't seen it. I hadn't been ready to see it. I tried to give myself some grace for that. You never leave until you're ready.

As I made my decision to leave, I realized some days needed to remain positive. Robyn's wedding day will always be a good memory. Valentine's Day, for the most part, was lovely. Robyn took over Passover, and those were good days. Meri's pajamas. Christmas at the cabin. Kody as a dad when the kids were little. The trip to Nauvoo. Cooking with my sister wives at Thanksgiving. The parties. The kids growing up together.

I didn't want to live my life moving forward feeling bitter or negative about the life I had led to that point. I wanted to be happy.

Chapter Thirty-Four

I HAD NO REGRETS

O ne morning, as I talked with Janelle over coffee, I told her I didn't much like polygamy.

No, no—stick with me here. I know this will be a surprise.

I think polygamy can cause a person to be too in her head, worried about too many relationships. *Do the wives like me? Do they like Kody? Do they like him too much? Does he like me? If he doesn't like me, will he just go to another wife?*

"Whoa," Janelle said, "polygamy is why you're strong, and it's why you're going to be able to leave. You are more independent than a lot of women because you've lived plural marriage."

What doesn't kill you and all that.

She had a point, though I would argue that women in monogamous marriages don't have to leave four people and all their children when they move to another state. The sister wives relationship complicated the breakup.

The more I thought about it, the more I realized I had no regrets. I'd made the best of it for me and my family, including my sister wives. I'd worked deeply on myself, from jealousy to fitness to mothering to self-care.

On the other hand, I don't think Kody ever worried about whether he was enough. He didn't have to work to be a better person. I think polygamy makes guys lazy and women work harder.

But I had built up strength and independence over the years. And no one would ever understand better than Janelle exactly what I was going through. I never would have predicted that having a sister wife would be a gift when it was time to go.

Kody would later claim on camera that he was a prisoner in his marriages, that he couldn't just say, "Hey bitch, I'm done with you."

Charming.

When I told him I was leaving, he immediately started talking about money. Not Truely. Not losing me.

"Well, we have to split everything fifty-fifty," he said.

"No," I said. "I made every house payment. I paid all the utility bills. I did all the repairs. If I paid for my house, it makes no sense to give you half."

Oh my gosh. He was so mad.

So here's a funny story: Originally, both our names were on the title to my house. But then he asked me to refinance the house so just my name was on the mortgage.

"Why?" I asked.

"This way, it will be an asset for you," he said.

Gosh.

That's altruistic and unexpected.

I was a bit bummed because I had been excited to have our names together on the house, like a real married couple. We didn't own much jointly, but it was nice of him to worry about me.

"Okay," I said.

About a week later, he told me he couldn't finance his house with Robyn—she hadn't yet found a place to buy—if his name was on my mortgage.

Oh. Right.

It felt like he was doing everything he could to disentangle himself from me and leave me as a single mom—and to further entangle himself with Robyn. It was demoralizing and embarrassing, and it hurt that something that important to me could be taken away so quickly.

But it may have worked out exactly as he'd said—as an asset for me.

He still continued to argue the fifty-fifty angle.

"All right, how about this," I said. "How about I keep the money from the sale of my house, and you keep the property at Coyote Pass?"

Looking back, I wish I had negotiated for Meri's and Janelle's names to be on that plot so it would be divided fairly, but instead, I said, "You're getting a better deal."

My piece would be worth more than what I would make on the house, but I needed to be done negotiating with Kody.

I took my name off the deed, which means I basically handed it to Kody and Robyn, rather than the family. Janelle and Meri would need to fight for their piece.

In a way, it was good that the conversation wasn't emotional—he didn't seem to care at all that I was leaving, which tracked. But I knew the family would take it harder.

I also needed to think about how our audience would take it. They had seen me tell Kody what I needed. They had seen me throw him out of my room. They had seen my tears, shock, and outrage.

I knew many of them were cheering for me, and it brought comfort. It has always been a little odd being a "character" on TV, but this time, it would be so personal. I needed to be authentic, maybe more than I had ever been, because I knew I would serve as an example for so many.

We needed to tell our producer, Tim, immediately. I know that sounds crazy, but he would need to know for the storyline for the season, but also because it would likely become noticeable that I was packing, and that Kody wasn't coming over.

I told Kody he needed to tell Tim with me.

"Why do I need to be there?" Kody wanted to know. "You're the one who's leaving."

Right, but we needed to figure out our strategy for the network. Also, you're the reason I'm leaving.

We met over Zoom, and Tim cried when we told him.

"I was afraid it was this," he said. By that time, we'd all spent so much time together that I think he genuinely cared about us. "This was not the show I wanted to film."

When we started the show, they told us that all reality television families break up. "Naw," we said, "that's not going to happen to us."

We used our phones to film during that season because of COVID, so we worked through how to film the divorce.

Tim stayed with us for another two years after that, and then he left in January 2024. I think it was too much to film our family falling apart, but I miss working with him. It was hard on the crew. They had to ask the same questions five times and relive it through everyone's paradigm and validate all of us and not take sides. And then they spent hours going over it again as they edited. It was as if they lived it as much as we did. The producer needed to tell a story, so he broke down everything we lived through and had us talk about it. Those sessions were hard for us, too.

From there, I started planning Ysabel's graduation. I wanted that to be a happy day for her, the kids, and the family. They wouldn't need to know I was leaving until after.

Robyn still didn't feel comfortable having family events inside, even with COVID testing, so we planned an outdoor event with an around-the-world theme. The wind blew hard that day, so everything kept falling over and blowing away. We had tables set up to represent where each of the moms was from, so mine featured German food and pictures.

We placed pictures of Ysabel everywhere, but the wind made it a disaster.

Ysabel wanted me to sing for her. I got together with Robyn's daughters, Aurora and Breanna, as well as Gabe, who has a great voice. We sang Natasha Bedingfield's "Unwritten," with everybody else learning the chorus and Aurora playing the guitar.

I remember knowing this was probably the last thing I would do with all the kids.

It was a good day, and I think Ysabel felt special and loved.

Chapter Thirty-Five

IT'S ABOUT TIME

I told Gwendlyn I was leaving Kody.

"Oh," she said, "it's about time."

"What?" I said, shocked. I had expected sadness, maybe even tears.

"You haven't been happy for years," she said.

Ouch.

When I told her I was also moving to Utah, she said, "Of course you're going to move to Utah."

So far, so good.

She was lovely. She made it easy, and she was incredibly supportive.

"Do you want to move with me?" I asked.

"No. College is free for me," she said. "I'm just going to stay here on my own."

Perfect. She had great grades, and she got a scholarship. She had hoped to move out when she turned eighteen, like the rest of my kids, but the pandemic killed that idea.

I told Maddie. Her daughter Evie needed surgery, and Janelle traveled to Maddie's new home in North Carolina to support her and love on Evie. Maddie had moved after her husband got a job there in 2016.

Truely, Ysabel, and I joined them. Hanging out with Maddie and Caleb, as well as Hunter, I loosened up a bit. I drank too much. For me, that meant three glasses of wine.

I needed to know that Maddie was okay with me leaving, as well as if I could still be her kids' Oma.

"Frankly, we're all surprised you stayed as long as you did," she said.

Oh my gosh, the relief. But also, you were?

We talked some more, and I wasn't being as careful as I should be because I'd had too much to drink. It was also nice to talk with someone who didn't blame me—who understood.

But I hadn't yet told Ysabel.

And she overheard.

Ysabel has always been daddy's girl, and she'd been broken-hearted by his response to her surgery. This hit her as another shock, another blow to the way she thought of her parents.

I thought back to how upset I had been when my mom left my dad—how I had blamed her—and I felt sick. Ysabel started to cry.

"When was the last time you saw your parents touch?" Maddie asked Ysabel, as she registered her heartbreak.

"And when was the last time you felt like they had a good marriage?" Hunter asked.

They were able to help her come to terms with it in a way I never would have been able to. They could be more objective about it—but also talk about their own frustrations with Kody.

In the end, Ysabel supported me fully and said she understood why I had to leave.

While I was still in North Carolina, I called Aspyn and Mykelti to let them know. They were also supportive—and not surprised.

I told Paedon over the phone, and then Janelle told the rest of her kids. Their support meant everything.

I knew it would be just Truely and me heading to Utah, and I still needed to tell her. I hoped to wait as long as possible, but I also needed to make plans—and Mykelti was a big part of that.

"I can't wait until we move to Utah!" I told Mykelti on the phone one day.

I heard Truely behind me.

"What?" she said. "Are we moving?"

Oh man.

"Yeah," I said. "We're moving."

I ended my call with Mykelti.

"When is everybody else coming?" Truely asked, obviously not understanding the all of it.

"It's just you and me, sweetie," I said.

"Are you divorcing Dad?"

Am I divorcing Dad. I didn't need a release. I wasn't legally married to him. I had already packed his stuff and moved him out seven months before—I did it while Truely was at school or sleeping because I wasn't ready for her to know yet because she was the one who it would impact the most.

It's an odd feeling to know that the thing that brought me the most joy—that I would be moving home to be closer to my family and I would bring my amazing baby girl with me—would be the thing that could cause her the most trauma.

I knew she had friends with divorced parents, and those parents had fought in front of their kids and gone to court to argue over houses and record albums and parental rights. I knew that those kids wondered, through the process of joint custody and adjusting households, if their parents would get back together.

My decision came in an instant.

"We're already divorced," I said. "Have you noticed anything different?"

"Well, how long have you been divorced?" she asked. I told her we had been divorced for several months. She said it hadn't been any different.

"Okay," I said. "Then nothing's going to change."

She said she didn't want us to fight in front of her, and I told her we never had, and we wouldn't start—and that she'd still see Kody.

"Am I finding out last?" she asked.

"Yeah," I said.

"But I'm the one it impacts the most."

She's so smart. She was crying hard, and I could see she needed time to process it. She went to her room. Ysabel asked if she could take Truely to a friend's home whose parents had recently divorced.

When Truely got to the house, she said, "Salutations, everyone," because she's that kind of kid. Someone asked her how she was.

"Well, I just found out that my mom and dad are divorced, and we're moving to Utah, so I'm not doing well," she said.

They spent the rest of the evening talking it through in a safe space.

I told Kody immediately that Truely knew, and by the time she saw him a couple of days later, she had already processed the news.

Preparing to tell the rest of the family I was leaving Kody would be one of the hardest steps.

I called my mom. She told me that it would be a hard conversation, and that was okay. She meant that when I have conversations, I tend to cave because I want everything and everyone to be fine.

"You're going to put both feet on the ground, and you're going to take a deep breath," she said. "And you're going to say what you need to say."

And so, I did. As I prepared, I figured Robyn knew I had kicked

Kody out because he'd brought his boxes back to her house. Janelle knew because we had been talking for months. Before I told the group all together, I called Meri off-camera. I didn't want to shock her in front of an audience.

"Really quick, I just want to tell you that I'm leaving Kody," I told her. "I don't think it's fair to tell you on camera."

She sounded shocked.

"Whoa!" she said. "I have so many questions!"

I told her to think on them, and that I would answer anything she had in person.

Then we filmed it as I told the group.

This would be the hardest meeting of my life. I didn't know if people would be understanding or if they would attack me—or if they'd try to persuade me to stay, which would be the hardest thing to handle.

I've been interested in color for a while, and on that day, I needed something that would help me feel strong and powerful. Red. Not just red, but scarlet red. Red sweater. Red sneakers. It felt necessary. There would be many days when I wore green to feel calm, but not that day.

I had everyone meet outside my house, and we set up our phones to record it.

And then I just blurted it out, which is how I do most things. I don't like major buildup—just say it.

I'm leaving Kody.

"I need to make a choice to have joy in my life, and peace," I told them. "There hasn't been a lot of hope at all until I decided to leave."

Meri didn't ask many questions, even though she said she planned to. She looked as if she was in shock, but she already knew.

"I'm just processing at this point," Meri said, on camera.

I told them I planned to move to Utah.

"I never said you could move to Utah," Kody said. "You never asked if you could move. You said you were moving."

Yes. Yes I did.

He said he wanted joint custody of Truely, but that objection quickly disappeared, probably with the realization that he rarely saw her and it would be a hard argument to make.

"I find it ironic that now that I'm leaving, now he wants to be involved in my kids' lives—now he wants fifty/fifty with them?" I said during an interview. "Well hell, he could have had fifty/fifty time with them the whole [bleeped] time we lived here."

I was furious.

"He doesn't get fifty/fifty. He hasn't been around enough for that."

Janelle, even though I had talked before about leaving Kody, cried. This made it real for her. I know she worried about how the split would affect our relationship and the relationship between our kids. "You've just been so much the fabric of everything," she said, and talked about how intertwined our memories were.

"I think this is still family," I said. "I think it's just going to look different."

There were several times when they were sad—when we were sad—and they asked whether I was sure, and Robyn got mad and made it about herself—not "Are you okay? I'm so sad for you," but "How does this affect me? This isn't what I signed up for, and you should stay in a crap marriage so I can have my fake version of polygamy." Or something.

This is hard, I thought. *But it's also so good to just be honest.*

Everyone knew I had been frustrated for years and figured I would continue to be frustrated. I had started talking about leaving after Truely got sick. They may have figured it would never happen.

All of a sudden, it was happening.

Gwendlyn started college online because of the pandemic, then started going to classes on campus. After Ysabel graduated from high school, I moved her to North Carolina to live with Maddie. I knew I would miss Ysabel, but I loved that she was being adventurous, and I knew she'd be safe with Maddie and Caleb. That was maybe step number eight in the move-to-Utah list.

Just before we took her to North Carolina, I put the house on the market—and told Kody I had done so.

Gwendlyn was incredible. While we were gone, she kept the Flagstaff house pristine for showings, and made sure her dog, Noël, was out when people came to see it. Within a week of us getting back from North Carolina, she found her own apartment and moved out.

The house sold almost immediately, and while the first buyer backed out, we had another within a week.

I met with the adults again to tell them Truely and I would be moving to Utah within two weeks. Kody lost his mind, even though I had told him in November that I was leaving him and that I was going to move to Utah.

He said, as we recorded, that I had always been mean to Robyn, and I had never tried to have a good relationship with my sister wives—and then he yelled, dramatically, "Man! Just the knife in the kidneys over all these years! The sacrifices that I made to love you! Wasted!"

That day may be one of the only times it was hard to read my face.

I can't believe he's saying this on camera, I was thinking. *He sounds like an absolute narcissist.*

And then I thought, *How insulting is this? It was a sacrifice for you?*

Here's what I remember about that day and the days that followed: Robyn misconstrued, I think intentionally, and controlled my words. She asked me if I wanted to work on my past relationships. Well, no. I don't want to live in the past, and that's why I'm leaving. I had tried to work on my relationship with Kody, but it was like shoveling mud—I'd work on it, and the outside problems continued to pour in. And the mud certainly wasn't trying to help.

I told her I needed some time.

She took that as I didn't want anything to do with her or her kids. That wasn't it—I just needed to recover, and to figure things out.

When Robyn turned my words against me, it felt like more of the same—a way to keep me and my children out of Kody's "big picture." None of the kids did anything wrong. If any of the kids had done anything seriously wrong, then you work it out. That's what parents are for. You reach out. You say "Let's chat." You say "I love you." That's not what happened. The greatest tragedy of all of this was what was happening with the kids. I love Robyn's kids. I love all our kids.

But I was so over Robyn that I thought, *Fine. If that's what she's going to do and that's what she's going to say, it means I won't have a relationship with those kids, and I think that's terrible—but they're her kids. I can't change that.*

They're not part of my life anymore, and that makes me sad.

Robyn later said that I would still be married to Kody until the church had approved the divorce—that I had to prove the marriage was broken—or I slept with someone else. That seemed inappropriate for a few reasons: First, I'd already left the church, so I didn't need a spiritual release. Second, I didn't believe in the church, so I wasn't worried about their definition of when I could quit Kody. And third, I wasn't going to have a family meeting and let everybody know when I'd made my big move.

I'll never kiss and tell.

(Well, I will. Probably within the next fifty pages.)

Our divorce was strictly between us and built on years' worth of problems, but Robyn expecting so much attention for herself and her kids to the detriment of the other wives, in combination with COVID, exposed our problems. Would we have made it if Robyn hadn't come into the family? I don't know. As our kids got older and we became a five-person house of empty nesters, our equilibrium might have tipped sideways. And I don't know that the family staying together was the best thing.

Chapter Thirty-Six

I HAVE COVID

I just divorced Kody Brown and . . . I'm going to Disneyland!

Janelle and I decided we needed to do something to cement our relationship. We knew I was moving and everything was going to change—though we couldn't know how much—and we both needed something fun.

We took Truely and Savanah and had an amazing trip.

That's when Kody got COVID. He called Janelle and asked her to come back to Flagstaff to get him medicine. Robyn was sick, too, and ended up going to the emergency room to get checked out. Kody was a mess—it hit him emotionally and he was severely depressed. The systemic inflammation caused by COVID can affect the way your brain works, so some people dealt with depression and even hallucinations during the pandemic.

Everyone in the house was sick except for Aurora, so I imagine she was doing all the cooking, setting meals by their doors. She slept in a different part of the house so she wouldn't get it, too.

"I'm in California," Janelle told Kody.

"Can you come home?" Kody asked.

When Janelle got COVID, I was shocked by how self-involved Kody was. He was worried because she messed up his schedule. He didn't do a thing for her—he was just mad that she got COVID because it proved her family wasn't following his rules. Garrison got it from a coworker who didn't tell anyone he was sick, and then everyone at Janelle's house got sick.

But Kody hoped Janelle would drive back from California so she could—what?—go to the drugstore for him? He could Instacart like everybody else.

"I feel so bad for him," Janelle said. Did I mention she's the nice one?

"No, you're not going," I said. "Girl, what would you do? Are you going to administer the medicine to him? No. Will you do anything more than drop it off at his door? No."

"I'm not coming back," Janelle told Kody. "You need to call somebody else to help you."

He called Janelle's son Gabe and asked if he could get him some things because he had COVID. Gabe said of course, but he was hurt that Kody didn't say "Happy birthday." Kody did call back later in the day to apologize for forgetting.

Later that week, he called Gwendlyn.

"Happy birthday," he said.

"Hi Dad," she said.

"I have COVID," he said.

I'm glad everyone recovered, and COVID sucks, but Janelle and I had a wonderful time. Without the pressure of having the same husband, our relationship changed. We still had the shared history, and we'd raised our children together, but the forced part was gone, as was the wondering part: Why does their relationship work, when ours doesn't?

Janelle and I went to Disney just after I moved to Utah. I had no idea leaving would be so simple. It was great to live my life for myself and my kids, and to focus on them. Every step felt good.

We moved almost a year after I told Kody I didn't want him in my room anymore. I think because everything was so methodical and logical, and because I had been heartbroken for so many years, I had already processed the sad by the time we left. I moved on to being happy—more excited with every step.

I hadn't seen our new place in person—Mykelti found it and FaceTimed me for a tour. I loved it. We went right upstairs, I let Truely pick her bedroom, and as soon as we put the mattresses down, it felt like home. I wanted a split level with the bedrooms on the same floor, and I didn't want a yard. I knew we'd be going back and forth to Flagstaff too often for that kind of maintenance. It was in a great area, but close to the freeway, which we'd be using often.

I bought new dishes while we were in Flagstaff, but I left them in the boxes, so I had fun coral plates with white flowers on them to unpack: cheerful. We surrounded ourselves with happy things. I didn't know what to do about family photos. Truely wanted them, so I made sure she had easy access, but I needed to feel like we had a fresh start. Putting up photos of everyone would have felt disingenuous.

"Let's just settle into it," I told Truely.

Aspyn lived in Salt Lake, and after I told Mykelti I was moving to Utah, they moved to Lehi so I could live close to both my girls. We got to be with each other all the time, and it was everything I had hoped for.

When I moved to Utah, I stopped everything for the kids, particularly since they didn't have a full-time dad, or even a part-time dad for the last few years. I had to be the best mom ever, just until we all got straightened out.

As I worked on that, Truely and I drove back and forth to Flagstaff constantly. I had to deal with the house, and we were still filming in Arizona.

We got doubles of everything, and then kept a suitcase packed all the time. We'd take a laundry bag, and when we got home, we'd wash everything and then repack the suitcase. We drove most of the time because it was less stressful than flying. Every time we came back to Salt Lake, we immediately restarted our everyday routine.

We needed that bit of adjustment because every single time we drove to Flagstaff, it was terrible, because I had to go back and live in the past. I couldn't move on. Every other week, I had to drive to Flagstaff and relive the hardest days of my life—and the set was three doors down from Kody and Robyn's house.

I couldn't simply leave the show. Our viewers had come this far on our journey. It didn't make sense not to show them what happy could look like.

But it meant my life was tumultuous. There's no way I could have dated that first year. Every time I came to town, it needed to be about my kids, about providing normalcy for Truely. But also, nobody needs to date someone so deeply engaged with the past.

The first couple of times we went back to Flagstaff, we stayed in our house because the sale hadn't closed yet. After that, we stayed in the same room of the same hotel every time because routine was everything.

The drive between took between eight and nine hours, and we would stop at restaurants or sightsee—several gorgeous national parks lay along the way. If I knew I needed to be in Flagstaff on Wednesday, I'd hang out with the kids on Monday and see my grandbaby, Mykelti's Avalon, who was born in April 2021. Then we'd travel on Tuesday.

Every single time we hit the road, I'd get sick.

"Tony wants to know why you're sick all the time," Mykelti said.

"I'm not sick all the time," I said.

"You're sick every time before you go to Flagstaff."

"Oh my gosh," I said. "I am sick before I go to Flagstaff."

I felt like I had the flu the whole way to Flagstaff every time until we got to the hotel. Then I'd think, *Oh, you're a baby. You need to get over this.* And then I'd be fine. But every single time we went to Flagstaff, I was a wreck—and it manifested as physical distress. I always knew even the simplest things could cause drama.

I had one last load to bring back to Utah, and I asked Kody for help.

I rented a trailer, and Garrison said he would help me. Kody said he wanted to see Truely while I was there, so he took her for a couple of hours, and then when he brought her back, I asked him if he would help me load the snowblower into the trailer, rather than having to wait for Garrison because then I could just start loading boxes. From there, Kody decided to manage my move. "Manage" is the wrong word. He tried to control my move, to control me.

I didn't pout. I didn't throw a fit.

"I need the snowblower loaded up, and I'd like it to be in the back of the trailer so I can pack around it," I said. I didn't say, "So I can pack the rest without you in my garage," but girl, I thought it.

Kody wanted to mastermind it. He believed the snowblower should go in last because of weight or something, but nothing about that made sense to me because the boxes weren't that heavy, so the heavy snowblower should be packed first. Also, it was my trailer, my garage, and my snowblower. I asked for help loading it—and that's all.

I kept saying, "You're going to help me load all of it, then?" because I didn't think he wanted to be there any more than I wanted him there. I figured he'd say, "You know what? We should put the snowblower in first." Then I could say, "Gosh. I think that's a swell idea."

Didn't work.

I told him I could fit the boxes in my car, but not the snowblower.

"I wouldn't . . ."

"I know you wouldn't," I said. "Thank you. I'm going to be in charge of this."

He moved things around and shouted, and then he started making fun of me, like, "Look who's big and strong now!" Right, I asked for your help to prove how big and strong I am.

Also, Truely was there. *Could you not do this in front of your daughter?*

Ultimately, he dragged the snowblower into the U-Haul.

"Okay," he said. "I would start packing boxes . . ."

Gosh. I think that's a swell idea.

It's a small thing, but it felt so good afterward. I did things by myself all the time. I can't tell you the number of times the sister wives rearranged furniture, packed U-Hauls, cleaned garages, or handled heavy loads of bulk groceries by ourselves. It felt good to say it: I got this. I appreciate your help. I don't need for you to mansplain how to load a trailer. I was proud of myself for staying calm and stating what I needed.

After I decided to leave Kody, I sometimes felt like I was on the sidelines of a game or watching a movie in a theater. I cared about the people I was watching, but the dramas that had felt so important before suddenly felt less so—except in the case of brokenhearted kids.

Truely grounded herself in the knowledge that she would see Gwendlyn, Janelle, and Janelle's kids. At first, she included her dad in that mix, but it only worked out that he could see her five times during that year, including an extra trip she made on her own for Christmas. He knew when we'd be in town—they sent everybody's filming schedule out to the whole group.

Truely has always had a strong voice, but that was rough. She struggled because she had only seen him a few times and she had never spent the night at Robyn's house. She finally stayed over one night when Mykelti stayed, too, and that was fine. On the next visit, Kody and Robyn put her in a room she could only get into from outside. That didn't seem safe—or like something you'd do to a little girl you love. Then they put her in Solomon's room, but it didn't feel homey—Solomon hadn't moved into his new room at Robyn's house yet, so Robyn and Kody had just set up the bed, and there were no curtains or anything, so she didn't sleep well. She didn't feel welcome.

On one trip down, I asked Truely about her plans in Flagstaff.

"I don't think I'm going to see Dad," she said. "I think he only wants to spend time with his kids."

"Well, you're one of his kids, Truely," I said.

"It's just not like that," she said. "He's going to spend his time with Ari and Sol."

Truely was twelve. It was devastating for me to hear. After a while, I stopped letting him know we were coming in because he never responded. Then, I started leaving her at home.

Kody and I met for lunch so I could talk with him about bringing Truely to town for Christmas.

"Gwendlyn's not going to be here for Christmas?" Kody asked as I, and the camera crew, joined him at the restaurant. "I was sick during her birthday, I was laid up with COVID."

I laughed, but not because he had COVID.

"You were also out of it, she was . . ." I started to say.

"Was she thinking that was funny, too?" he interrupted, not waiting for me to finish the story I tried to tell him, and laying me out for laughing at his distress. "I was out of my mind, but when I talked about getting anxiety, Christine, and depression?"

Right. Kody's COVID had caused great emotional distress. He had survived, but it was not in the past.

I tried to apologize.

"I'm sorry to even laugh about it, but Gwendlyn was like . . ."

"You're mean that way," Kody said. "It's okay."

I tried to explain that it was Gwendlyn's reaction that was funny, not his near-death experience, and that, now that Kody had lived through the experience, it was okay to laugh.

"I was in the fetal position on the floor sobbing," he said.

I figured I better save my Gwendlyn story for another day.

It's so nice to not be married to you, I thought. He kept talking about himself, and I just shut down. I didn't care. *I don't need to be here. This is the dumbest thing ever. There is nothing I can say that is going to make this conversation better.*

I sort of smiled.

"Mean." You never really knew me.

Maybe he didn't know any of us.

When I asked Janelle how she and Kody were, she kept it close. "Oh, we're figuring things out," she said. Despite Kody's belief that we spent all our time badmouthing him, Janelle was about as loyal as a person could get. For her, it made sense to stay with him. She's pragmatic. Their money was all tied together. She still had faith in an eternal bond.

About a year after I left, Janelle and Kody had a bad fight over Kody's rules and his relationship with the boys—you may know it as "The One Where Janelle Said 'F you' to Kody." We didn't see that scene until long after it happened, and Janelle keeps her laundry clean, so I didn't know how bad it was.

About six months after the fight, Janelle and I went to Idaho together to hike with my brothers. I don't know if it was the outdoors activity or the "I'm so over it" frustration, but she told me just how separate she and Kody had become.

"I had no idea that conversation had taken place," I said.

"We're over," she said. She later told me she didn't feel like she needed to tell him it was over, but I wanted her to feel what I had felt—that sense of empowerment, that it was my decision for it to be over. But Janelle had always been empowered in a way that was different from how I felt.

After I saw the episode with the fight, I better understood just how much she had said with those two words.

It's been good to see her happy since then. I can't wait for her to tell her story.

I learned so much that first year away from the family. The biggest change came from spending more time with the kids. That first Thanksgiving away from Kody? It was just the beginning.

Because of the lessons I learned from Maddie and Mykelti, I've relaxed. When the grandkids come over—we've added Maddie's Josephine and Emilia, and Mykelti's Ace and Archer—the breakables are gone, and I just enjoy the babies. My kids? They do exactly what they want to do in their own homes—without a committee.

As a family, we started to reclaim things I loved. We had stopped doing Shabbat when Robyn came into the family, and we no longer spent weekends as a group. My kids were sad to see it go, and I thought it would come back in Vegas, but nothing ever came back in Vegas.

When I moved out, I ditched the Jewish holidays, not because I didn't enjoy them, but because they didn't hold any personal or religious significance for me. It was too much, and I donated a bunch of stuff to a secondhand shop.

And I started to celebrate Easter.

Rebirth. New life. Spring. And chocolate bunnies.

Who doesn't love chocolate bunnies?

Chapter Thirty-Seven

I LOST MY BRAIN COMPLETELY

"You're an attractive woman," my son-in-law Tony said. "You should be getting laid."

"Hey!" Mykelti said, feeling my anguish. "That's my mom!"

"Right, but she's still an attractive woman," he said. "She should be getting laid."

Oh. My. Gosh.

From being the most chaste of the chaste to, well, sort of agreeing with Tony. I mean, not in those words, but good lord. I had been with a man who just wasn't into me for twenty-seven years. I didn't even know what a real kiss felt like. Worse, I felt like a fifteen-year-old girl worried that she couldn't do it right. Kiss, I mean.

Obviously.

I tried to ease Truely into the idea that I would start dating. As usual, that didn't go as planned.

"Would it be okay if I dated?" I asked my twelve-year-old daughter who still believed boys are kinda gross.

"I like us just how we are," she said.

Okay, I'll keep it quiet for a bit.

I hired a matchmaker, which feels incredibly modern and old-fashioned at the same time. There was no talk of a dowry, but we did talk about how to handle my past.

Plyg mom of six seeks understanding, hot, bald dad who has tattoos and likes motorcycles.

They vetted the guys and did a bit of a background check, so I felt safe. I had Truely at home, and I didn't need any nonsense. But it wasn't working. I couldn't get beyond the idea that Kody didn't find me attractive. If he didn't, why would anybody else? I needed to feel good about myself physically, which was different from loving myself as a mom and even as a woman. It's hard to date if you don't feel pretty or beautiful—certainly not sexy.

The matchmaker offered wonderful advice, but I didn't have a clue what I was doing. On the first date, I told the guy everything. That didn't last.

"You don't have to tell them everything all at once," the matchmaker said.

When I'd dated Kody, he already knew everything about me. Everyone in my community knew everything about me. Kody even knew everything about my parents and my grandparents.

"I don't?" I asked.

"Girl, no."

I worried about being recognized. If I had some cool, I might have said, "I have this big Instagram following where I cook with my daughter and go on great trips." But I had such a hard time not telling all my truth after being raised in a secretive community.

Do you have any kids?

"I do, and grandkids, too!" Yeah, I hadn't gotten there yet.

For whatever reason, I didn't click with any of the men I met through the matchmaker. As I listened to one of my favorite podcasts, an advertisement came on for an online site. It was a bit more general than, say, formerplygs.com. (Maybe that will be my next business . . .)

Going online was tough. I don't think single middle-aged men make up *Sister Wives'* main audience. But if someone—or the female friend helping with their profile—recognized me from an advertisement or magazine spread, the date would be weird. There would be no glamor shots, fudging my age, or waiting until later to talk about how many kids I had—or big decisions about how much to say about the divorce. Anyone who watched the show knew what I looked like when I sob, how hard I had worked to be healthy, and how I handled hard conversations.

Deep breath.

I worked on my profile at Mykelti's house.

"Oh no," she said. "You need new pictures. These are not sexy at all."

What is this thing, "sexy"?

My daughter started to read through the bio I had worked so hard on.

"Mom, just no. This is not sassy. This is not you."

Is it possible to feel both ground into nothing and built up in the same moment? It was like boot camp, with my daughter as the drill sergeant—resocialization.

There had been a gentle evolution toward less frumpy when I left the church. I remember being excited to buy capris that never would have covered those garments. Then I bought long shorts, and then short dresses—which I love. I think you can see some of the changes through the years on the show, but I still tried to stay modest out of respect for our community.

At home, I wore shorts and tank tops constantly. I put in my earrings. I bought a bunch of skorts. But I was still working on my self-esteem—being comfortable because it's hot and feeling attractive are different things. I needed to love my body more. It's fine to love who you are, all of who you are.

My girls had thoughts about my wardrobe.

"You need to dress differently," Mykelti said. "You have a great body, and you need to show it off."

She's blunt, that child, but she's empowering. I showed her, Ysabel, and Aspyn my outfits before I went out on dates.

"That's not going to work," they'd say when I showed them an outfit. "You can't wear things like that. Also, you need heels."

Or, "You need to show more skin."

When I was dating, my girls always knew exactly what to ask. They wanted to make sure I found the right guy and that he treated me well. Tony, of course, harassed me like crazy for all the particulars.

"You're not knowing the details," I'd say. I knew he wanted to make sure I was okay. He's a funny dude.

"Are you getting laid yet?" he said once. "We're not going to watch Truely anymore if you're not getting laid."

I think he liked to see me turn a deep shade of crepe myrtle.

As I scrolled one day through a sea of profile pics of men with fish (why do they think we want to see their fish?) on boats or in oddly lit basement shots obviously taken with their computers (or by a fellow axe-murderer), David hit me differently.

I messaged him, and I found out later that he had to pay $60 to get back into the site because he hadn't been active for three years.

I wish I had taken screenshots of it all—of my profile, of David's, of our messages back and forth. His pictures were perfect. His bio was perfect. He was even on his way to Disneyland.

As usual, before my first date with David, I sent my girls a picture of my outfit.

I had these leather pants and a blue off-the-shoulder blouse.

"Oh my God!" Mykelti texted back. "Yes, that's what you're wearing on your date!"

It was so out of my comfort zone—I even wore heels.

That was the first time I remember feeling sexy.

The first date was perfect. Flirty. Deep. Silly.

But on the second date, I laid everything out on the table.

"Oh, I know all about polygamy," he said. "My sisters lived it."

I mean, it's a small club—it was not the response I expected.

"You don't want to live it, right?" I asked.

"Oh God, no," he said.

"Then we're fine," I said. "I have a sister wife, Janelle. She's going to come with me everywhere I go, but your relationship with her will be platonic, of course."

"Done," he said.

We talked about the show a bit. I was telling him some little things and how it affected my life, and finally, he broke in with, "Kody's a dumbass."

I stared at him with my mouth hanging open.

"You watch my show?!" He did not look like a typical *Sister Wives* viewer. I don't picture you all as middle-aged bald dudes—no offense, because I think that's totally hot.

"Girl," he said, "I don't live under a rock. Yes, I've watched your show."

That's when he told me his favorite episode was the one where I went back to Flagstaff to get my snowblower.

True story:

David was watching an episode of *Sister Wives* when his sister, who had lived polygamy, walked in.

"What are you watching this crap for?" she asked. She hated the show because she hadn't enjoyed living polygamy.

As he watched, he realized I had left Kody.

He says he realized that day that out of all the guys in the world, he might be the only one who could understand my experience because his sisters had lived polygamy, and he paid attention. They talked to him about their heartache, and he listened. *I would be perfect for her*, he told me later that he'd been thinking. Still, he didn't expect to actually meet me.

He watched the show because he saw his sisters fight constantly with their sister wives, and he was hoping for drama.

"I tuned it out most of the time, to be honest with you, because you guys never fought," he told me. "You were boring."

Anyway, he also likes the episode where Janelle dropped the F bomb. And the one where Kody yells at me, "Just the knife in the kidneys!"

"You're really saying this on national television?" David told me he remembers saying, as he watched the kidney episode. He loved that I sat there quietly, saying all my words with my eyes.

David knew all of it. He knew about my kids and how I managed myself in a fight, how Kody had dragged down my self-esteem, and even how I had ended the relationship. I didn't have to tell David a thing about Kody. He had paid attention.

He was perfect.

Except for one tiny thing.

This time, I was ready for romance. I wanted to feel all the tingly, twitterpated, tickly feelings. My yellow-toweled self wanted her fairy tale.

We went to see *The Little Mermaid*. They played "Kiss the Girl."

Here it comes. I've been waiting years. Never gonna do a first kiss at the altar again.

This had better knock my socks off.

I puckered up, in my mind, in preparation. *This would be the perfect moment . . .*

Reader, he didn't kiss me.

He didn't hold my hand.

Huh, I thought. *This is weird.*

Right, based on my vast dating experience. But I *had* spent an awful lot of time in the bathtub with a novel.

A couple of days later, I had a terrible on-camera interview in my office for *Sister Wives*. Even as I was starting to date, I'd have to talk about my feelings about the past. I just wanted to move forward, but I kept getting dragged straight back to that last bedroom conversation with Kody.

"Today just sucked," I texted David. We texted each other all day, even without a kiss.

"Well, why don't you just come over and talk to me," he said.

What? Wasn't it a little early to visit his home? I was surprised he'd asked—and even more surprised I was considering it.

Shocked, even.

"Yeah, just come over," he said.

I dressed in my sweats because it was a set day and I needed, every time, my most comfortable clothes. My stomach was upset because I don't like talking about that stuff. It's yucky and stressful, and it makes me feel angry.

What if I just tell him everything, I thought, as I drove over. *What if I just told him how I feel?*

He already knew how many kids I have and that I was a plyg.

What if I tell him and he wants nothing to do with me? I thought. *He hasn't even kissed me. What if he's not attracted to me?*

When I got to his house, I said it straight:

"I'm going to tell you how my day went and how I'm feeling. But before I tell you all this, are you going to put me in the friend zone?"

"Wait," he said. "What?"

"Are you going to friend zone me if I tell you everything, and if I really open up to you, because I come with a lot," I said.

"No," he said.

I suppose I could have stopped there, but I was on a roll.

"Because you didn't kiss me on our date," I said.

"I know," he said. "I could tell you wanted to be kissed."

"But it was 'Kiss the Girl,'" I said. "I don't know what your deal is."

Sing with me now . . .

"I wasn't raised that way," he said. "I am a gentleman, and I don't kiss women on the second date."

Oh.

"I've lived my whole life being a gentleman," he said. "I'm just going to continue doing that."

But the song says . . .

"Okay, you'll have to show me you're attracted to me, because if you're not, and we're just going to be friends, then I need to know," I said.

"You," he said,

Don't be shy.

"are so damn sexy."

My heart settled down and sped up at the same time. Was this what I wanted? I felt like all my nerve endings had lost their anchors.

I told him all my stuff. All of my horrible, rotten stuff. And then I got up to leave.

Go on and . . .

He kissed me.

He knocked my flippers straight out of the water.

Besotted. Enchanted. Twitterpated.

He called me as I drove home, and he said exactly the perfect right things.

I lost my brain completely.

Chapter Thirty-Eight

YOU DRESSED REALLY WEIRD

*W*e talked about my insecurities about kissing and how I looked. We talked about everything.

"I don't care about all of that," he said. "I just think you're a damn good kisser."

"I think you are, too," I said.

Oh, I thought. *It's fine. It's great.*

And it was.

So fine.

We had all the hard conversations. I needed to know it would not be one-sided.

"Are we going to have sex?"

"Do you find me attractive?"

"Are we going to have an intimate marriage?"

All of it. I asked all of it. He might have said, "You know, you're cute, but I see this as just a fling."

Sweet. Moving on. Thanks for letting me know.

What's the worst that could have happened? I would have been sad for a bit, and then I would have moved on. Okay, really sad, but not three decades' worth of sad. We're all grown-ups. If it's not right, scram. And ask. If he's relationship-averse, don't you want to know early?

"I have to be blunt," David told me. "I'm not going to be like a Scottish romance novel."

He teases me that I'm the one who initiated that first kiss, but I was putting on my shoes.

As it turns out, our lives are so intertwined. His parents knew my grandpa. We both have memories of the colony in Mexico, where my mom's mom lived for a short time. We definitely went to the same wedding when I was fourteen: my mom's sister married David's best friend.

My grandpa Rulon taught David's dad how to deliver babies as he delivered two of David's sisters. When David was born with the umbilical cord wrapped around his neck, David's dad knew to loop in and unhook it before the baby is born because that's what my grandpa taught him to do, so some of Grandpa's love and knowledge was part of my husband's birth. I don't know that I believe in signs, but I do believe in connections and love.

The security that comes with knowing that I'm his person, and that he's going to come home every night because he wants to be around me, has changed every aspect of my world. We have intimate moments, all day long. Just goofing around is intimate—a shared joke, a shared moment. Hearing a song we both like on the radio is intimate. So many little conversations are intimate. It's lovely. Just— yeah, lovely.

I'm one hundred percent vulnerable and open and loved.

Which doesn't mean he doesn't tease me.

David always comments on people's outfits when he watches the news or a show, and I had a sudden realization.

"Oh my God," I said. "You were criticizing my outfits!"

"Oh yeah," he said. "You dressed really weird."

He especially loved my chaste wedding dress.

"That's sexy," he teases. "No wonder Kody had a thousand-yard stare."

My kids loved David pretty much at first sight. That doesn't mean they didn't struggle with the idea of their mom moving so quickly into a relationship after the divorce—they hadn't had the year to get used to it that I did.

Ysabel was the most reluctant. I think she was hoping for a dream, an ideal world where her dad and I would always be together. And she worried that David would somehow replace Kody.

"Kody will always be your dad," I told her. "David's just another person to love you."

After a few months, David said, "I think we should go jewelry shopping."

"Sure," I said. "I like jewelry."

"Well," he said, "ring shopping. For you."

Blink.

Right. Ring. Oh!

"Who's being an instigator now?" I said.

But first, we talked about moving in together, in a let's-start-looking-for-houses-in-the-meantime way.

Before I ever met David, I decided I would live with someone before I married them. I wanted the test drive. But when I met David, I just didn't want to be away from him, either.

We found a house that week.

It happened so fast it took my breath away. I figured I wasn't the only one.

The night before the move, I asked Truely how she was doing. She worried that our routines would change. We read together every night in my bed. We traveled. We learned so much about each other.

But David had been in from the first conversation he had with Truely.

"I was in the hospital," she told him. "And people always say, 'The way you healed is a miracle.'"

That's what I usually say. It was a miracle. Your life is a miracle.

"Oh my gosh," David said. "You must feel a lot of pressure from that."

Truely looked at him and her face changed completely.

"It's so stressful," she said.

They talked about the pressure Truely feels from living her entire life on the show—and how unnerving it can be when someone recognizes me when we're out in public. David listened, and it was almost a mind-meld—he could see beyond the girl in a beanie and baggie clothes, while still being able to engage in preteen humor.

She had blue hair at the time.

"You're a Smurf," David said.

"You're bald," Truely said.

David always says he'll be whatever my kids need him to be. All his kids are incredible with True. Everybody has extra aunts and uncles and brothers and sisters now. It's wonderful—our families meshed well together. Mykelti and David's daughter call each other "sister." They say they feel like the same person. Truely's the best aunt, and David's grandkids were heartbroken when Paedon moved away. His incredible kids have opened their hearts to me, and I love them. I didn't know how much my heart could grow.

Truely and I talked about what a good man and good dad David was, but Truely still seemed worried about the move.

I finally clued in.

"You know what, Truely? I've never lived with a man full-time before."

"Nope," she said. "Me neither."

"I don't know what to do," I said. "And I'm really nervous, too. What are we supposed to do with him every single night?"

"I don't know," Truely said.

It would be weird. We would all have so much to learn.

Truely and I decided we would make time for just the two of us as we made the transition. I love the one-on-one time I have with my shy, funny, smart girl.

We moved in with each other, and it *was* different. I felt like things were off. So, one morning, as David left for work, he said, "Are you okay?"

"Yeah," I said, in typical fashion. "I'm fine."

"Nope," he said. He shut the door, put his stuff down, sat next to me, and asked, "What's wrong?"

He stayed, and he talked with me. He reassured me that we would work on things as they come up, and I knew that we would keep talking until we found a solution. We decided we would do what was right for the two of us, no matter what.

After about half an hour, he said, "Are you okay?"

"Yeah," I said. "I'm fine." But I meant it this time.

"Not much has changed," he said.

"Nope," I said, "not much has changed."

But we talked it through, and I felt safe and loved.

That night, he came home.

Chapter Thirty-Nine

I WANTED JUST THE MAN FOR ME

*O*ne night David said he wanted to have a KISS-themed wedding. He meant that as a joke. But as we hung out on the couch, he said, "I want you to know that, if you agreed, we would drive to Vegas, and I would marry you right now."

Vegas.

Nope.

The day after Truely and I moved in with David, we all headed out for an off-road four-by-four RZR vacation because it was his friend Jason's birthday.

Truely, David, and I went for a ride in Moab. We walked up to one of the cliffs to take in the view.

David started talking.

"You know this is my favorite place in the world," he said. "And you're my favorite person, and I want to share this with you for the rest of our lives."

"Oh my gosh," I said, and I threw down all the crap I had been holding.

David got down on one knee.

"Will you marry me?" he asked.

Yes. Of course. Yes, yes, yes.

I could almost feel that yellow towel billowing out behind me. This was the story. This is where she always wanted me to go.

David was beginning to understand my world, and, being a smart man, knew the show would want to feature his proposal. So, they tricked me into filming it myself. "Hey," one of his friends said, "want me to get a picture of you two standing on the edge of a cliff?"

I handed him my phone. He hit record.

In March of 2023, David and I found our home, and then we moved in April. We headed down to Flagstaff for David's first time on camera, where we rented an Airbnb with all my kids. Janelle's kids came over, too, so he got to meet everyone—Gabe, Hunter, Garrison, and Savanah.

On camera. David had been sweet about filming—no one expects their Tinder date to turn into a reality show, and it's not his thing.

The kids, of course, teased him right away. He was wearing shorts and purple (he says they're cordovan) Uggs.

"Let's take a minute to talk about your Uggs," Hunter said.

Soon enough, David had them engaged in "real" conversation.

He'd been a single dad with eight kids working too many hours after he started his own business. His wife took her own life when their youngest was six. She was addicted to drugs, and she left a lot of heartache behind.

Ysabel got a little frustrated because David didn't know how to play cards, and then we talked about what he had been doing.

"Oh," she said. "He was being a real dad."

We all have some healing to do.

I stayed up late one night as I wrote this trying to decide whether to tell this story. Gwendlyn and Ben's engagement party was fabulous, they're perfect together, and Gwendlyn is the loveliest. They deserved an incredible night.

But Kody made me livid.

"Kody's going to be there, right?" David had asked me. Well, maybe. Kody had told Gwendlyn he wasn't going, and Gwendlyn started to cry. "But you're my dad," she said, or something along those lines. And he said something like, "Don't try to manipulate me with your tears."

Right.

Kody eventually decided to go, and our producer found out.

"If he goes, we'll have to film it," the producer told me.

"I don't want to film it," I said. "That's not fair." I don't think they need to have everything, every single bit of our lives.

"The first time they meet?" he said. "It needs to be filmed."

I told him it was up to Gwendlyn. Gwen decided she was fine with it.

Done.

At the party, Mykelti teased and tried to take the strain out of the situation.

"Mom, come over here so David can meet Dad," she said. She loves David.

We all stood in this awkward horseshoe formation being awkward so the crew could film the momentous moment.

"I hear you're hanging out with my grandkids," Kody said to David.

"Oh, no," Mykelti said. "He babysits them by himself sometimes."

Mykelti was trying to say, "We trust David. He's a great guy." She just wants the family to be all together.

Me being me, I put my head against David's shoulder—just gave him a little snuggle.

When we talked about it later, David said, "Kody went all red in the face when you put your head on my shoulder."

I might have smiled. He might have smiled, too. Everyone behaved.

But as Kody left the engagement party, he turned to Ben and said, "Welcome to the family—you've gotta watch out for this one," meaning Gwendlyn. "She's beautiful, but you have to watch out for Gwendlyn."

Not thanks for the great time.

Not I think you're wonderful together.

Not I love you.

It made me sad to the point of furious that he couldn't see Gwendlyn for the incredible, strong, dynamic person she is on the night of her engagement party.

I've worried about my kids, how they would regroup from the trauma of seeing their parents' divorce. I was a young adult when my mom left, and I know how it affected me. But they love seeing me happier than I've ever been.

With David, I can model what a good marriage can look like, and that's a serious level-up on my mom skills.

I hope that my kids see that a true partnership doesn't mean you have to sacrifice, and that it doesn't mean there's give-and-take. You both give. At times, one of you gives more than the other, but it always balances out.

Still.

As we began to plan our own wedding, I went full out. I remember saying to Aspyn, "I want all the bride stuff. I want it all."

David was there for every decision, from picking colors to figuring out we could have our guests sign wine barrels, rather than a reception book. We wanted his mom, Evelyn, who was ninety-three; my mom; Aspyn; David's daughter, Kati; my sister, Danielle;

and his sister, Tammy, to speak at the wedding. We didn't want a receiving line, we wanted a chaotic mess of grandkids.

Our daughters handled the shower and the engagement party—and threw me an incredible bachelorette.

Mykelti bought a penis-shaped wooden tray for one of her sister's bachelorettes—and she pulled it out for mine. I felt so honored!

They had asked how raunchy they could be, and I just shook my head. Piety raises its ugly head again . . . and they looked so sad.

"Okay," I said. "You can be a little naughty."

They were, but I won't tell you how. A woman has to have some secrets—even if she lives on TV.

I will tell you that they arranged for a fitness class led by some crazy in-shape moms, then we went shopping at Kendra Scott (where Aspyn was the store manager), and then . . .

Well. We blended their comfort level with mine.

The best part was how many of my friends and family came: daughters, friends, sisters, David's sisters.

It was perfect.

The wedding? It was everything I could have dreamed of. The girls—mine, David's—checked in on me all day. What I remember most was that they were present the whole time. I got to swing dance with Paedon. Truely was fully herself with purple hair and pure confidence.

I wore a gorgeous, low-cut beige dress with an overlay of white lace.

Did you see that David popped up his leg when he kissed me?

My parents were there. Siblings. The kids. Janelle.

I felt like a bride. Joy and laughter filled the day. And I finally had what I wanted.

I wanted just the man for me—and I wanted the family.

Chapter Forty

SHE STARTED TO CRY

Aspyn has one of Garrison's cats. His shelter cats, abandoned cats. He had three: Hunter has one, and Logan and Michelle have one. By the time Aspyn got hers, the cat had already passed through so many hands that she was self-grooming to the point of baldness. Several months and $1,000 later, the cat is doing okay.

Miss Abigail Buttons. She's gray and beautiful. Mitch calls her to bed to sleep with them at night, and he talks about her, too: "Oh, I have to tell you what she did today!"

Grief takes so many forms.

Garrison took his own life in March 2024, and it's the worst thing that's ever happened to any of us. Janelle and Kody's son. Our son. My son.

I'll always remember where I was when I got the call, Hunter on the other end, sobbing.

I called Paedon. Hunter had reached him first.

Our sons. His brothers.

"I don't know what to do," Paedon said.

"We're going to Mykelti's," I said. We all needed to be together immediately. I called Mykelti, as Hunter continued making phone calls. Aspyn knew, too. So many people to call. So many heartbroken people.

We gathered at Mykelti's, held each other while the little kids watched, confused.

"Why is everybody crying?" Mykelti's daughter Avalon asked.

In a haze, we made plans to go to Flagstaff.

Janelle. Oh my god.

I had Gwendlyn pulled out of class. David was in Park City that day, so it took him an hour and a half to meet us. He was my rock. I've been so independent, but I needed him. My kids needed him.

We've had several services for Garrison, where the entire family has gathered under tense circumstances. When we buried him, it was a beautiful service—another opportunity for some semblance of closure.

Closure, where I think everything is okay, until I remember something, even something silly, and then it's not. Then I'm sobbing. Random things. He was one of the first people I knew with food allergies—potatoes, pumpkin, and ginger. When he was little, he'd say, "That hurts my tummy," or "That hurts my mouth." I can't eat ginger without thinking of Garrison. He was the messiest kid I've met in my whole life. Outside all day long every day, and just as dirty as can be. Every day I'd help him wash his hands before he ate. I think about that gingerbread train we hot-glued together, or how we had to restrict the number of matches he lit on bonfire nights. He was the cutest little kid, and the orneriest.

That he understood Truely when she was tiny—that she liked him to be near her, watching cartoons, but didn't want to be held.

They would comment back and forth on whatever show they were watching.

"Wow," Garrison might say. "Twilight Sparkle is super shy."

"Yeah," Truely would say. "She's my favorite."

Deep wisdom about *My Little Pony*. She adored him.

He liked to scare his mom, even as an adult. She'd come around a corner and hear "MOM!" and drop the laundry. And then Garrison would say, "Happy Mother's Day," or whatever he was teasing about that day. It drove her mad, but she talked about his "jump scares" the other day, and she started to cry. Heartbreaking, and breaking, and breaking.

Maddie named our seventh granddaughter in his honor: Emilia Estelle, because "Estelle" means "star."

He shines on, and she's a bit of brightness. Mitch is building a Viking ship for Garrison, until Valhalla. Garrison's was not a battlefield fight, but it was a struggle we see far too often.

He did find satisfaction in being a soldier, which doesn't mean he loved every aspect of it. Some of his stories were tough. But he liked the people, and he liked his leaders. After he died, six fellow soldiers came to Flagstaff to tell us all about Garrison. He was a staff sergeant in the Army National Guard—a cavalry scout. They had great tales about him, and it was obvious they were hurting. They said he was always smiling and joking, masking his depression. We knew that, with such a big family, something would break our hearts, and I always felt that burying a child would be the worst thing. Anything I could have imagined feeling doesn't come close to the reality.

David took it hard, though he didn't know him well. Garrison was at our wedding, and he supported our marriage. His loss brought back memories of David's first wife's struggles and death, and the eternal mark it left on his family. Since Garrison died, David always seems to know ahead of the rest of us what we might need.

"You're never going to be the same," he's said.

We all understood we might lose Garrison, but we thought he might overdo it one night. Or he would crash his car. We don't talk about alcoholism in the young, or about death by suicide. He was so young.

In our family, alcoholism isn't a pattern. Mormons don't, generally, drink. My dad has never had a drink in his life, and my mom drinks an occasional glass of wine. I didn't know any alcoholics, and I wasn't around it much. It's shocking how much it changes people and their personalities until you barely recognize them: depressed, then angry, then sick all the time.

David has encouraged me to go to Al-Anon so I can watch for signs in our other kids, even if there isn't necessarily a way to stop it. You can't change people. But awareness opens a door for conversations, recognition, and safety. And healing.

Our beautiful, insightful son.

When I was taking oxy, I didn't drink because I knew you should never do that. Isn't that funny? I was aware enough to not mix substances, but not aware enough to understand that I was addicted. But as we filmed some of our worst episodes, I started up again with the nightly beer or glass of wine. Drinking is a funny thing: I never hit the point where I couldn't stop after one drink, or where it affected my life or my job, but I did hit the point where, either out of habit or chemistry, I felt I needed that evening cider to decompress. You might think, *I'm not going to drink tonight. I don't need it.* And then you find yourself with a glass in hand. That may be, in part, because one beer does not seem like a big deal. But in Vegas, I used it to cope. I drove my two minutes home from the set, and I walked in the door and opened a bottle of Michelob Ultra just so I could be a mom, and, for a long time, that felt nice. And I did it in Flagstaff. And I did it in Utah.

I still like an occasional glass of wine, but now I try to make sure it's an actual occasion rather than a habit. After my experience with oxycodone, I understand addiction—to anything—becomes a trap.

Janelle has spoken publicly recently about how substance abuse likely led to Garrison's death, and I feel like it's a slippery slope between that one beer and more—too much more. We know that alcohol can cause depression, and we know we make bad, impulsive decisions. Now I think, *Do I really need that?* I feel differently now about assuming you can bring a six-pack of beer to someone's house—I think you should ask. I also think this cultural norm that we need alcohol to relax and have a good conversation is just weird.

I treasure my conversations, my time, with Garrison.

Two weeks before he took his life, I asked if I could have some of his artwork for my home in Moab. His photography is beautiful.

"It's not good enough to frame," he said.

"Yes, it is," I told him.

The kids had one of his pieces framed for me for Christmas last year—a photo of the night sky. Sometimes, it almost feels as if I can find him there.

I would love to see him again.

EPILOGUE

*I*n real life—when I'm not writing a memoir—I don't want to talk about Kody anymore. I don't want to go down to our basement studio to film tell-alls that focus on how hard it was to leave my family. I don't want to drive to Flagstaff and see all the places where I lived in pain.

Writing this has been gut-wrenching—embarrassing. I'm telling people intimate things that I don't even want my kids to know. My friends are careful about what they say in front of me because they know some things will still hurt. I'm embarrassed that I stayed. I'm embarrassed that I allowed him to treat me the way I did. I'm embarrassed that I didn't love myself more. But I understand that I stayed until I realized tomorrow wasn't going to get better.

I believe my story has offered hope to people.

"Thank you for leaving him," women say to me when they encounter me out in public or in response to my social media posts. "Thank you for showing me that I could leave as well."

It goes further than a thank-you: these women understand how painful it was for me, and they have offered support and grace—some cheering on from the sidelines.

It means so much to me.

You've told me that your daughters left abusive marriages. You've told me that you learned you were married to narcissists or bullies. You've told me that you found peace when I started to plan my exit.

You've caused me to cry with you in bathrooms, in elevators, in conference center hallways. In a restaurant at Disneyland.

Costco. Bulk emotions.

"We see you," you've said. "We've been following you for years, and we hoped you would leave, and you left. And you found love."

It's humbling.

As I've shared my story with more people, mostly women, I've grown to understand that it's a good thing to talk about what happened. It's good to show the personal growth that happens after, about how independence allowed me to love myself, and that love of self allowed me to find David.

"I watch *Sister Wives* with my daughters," you've told me, "so they can see what a strong woman looks like."

It's sweet and kind—and mind-boggling.

Hope. That's ultimately what got me through, from hoping for a big family, to hoping for love, to hoping to gain back the magic of Wyoming, to hoping for another chance.

There's still a story to be told, and I'm one of many.

I recently told Janelle that I was working on this book.

"There's no gotchas, nothing you need to worry about," I told her. "If anything does come up in this book, you can fix it in your own."

I hope she'll write one.

I remember talking with her about how much I hated polygamy. But now I love the term "sister wife." Janelle will always be that for me. We became so close in Flagstaff—she was always the first person I would talk to.

Meri and I recently had a special moment, too, when I found out she was leaving Kody. I'm proud of her. She's so loyal, and I can't imagine the roller-coaster ride she's been on. When she left, I was excited for her. She deserves someone who loves her, too.

We still have hard days ahead. The kids are coming to terms with their relationships—or lack of them—with their dad.

My girls and I bought Savanah's claddagh ring in Ireland last year. I had asked Kody if he planned to buy Truely one, because he hadn't gotten her one when she turned thirteen, as he had done with our other girls.

"It's not on my radar," he said.

He hadn't gotten one for Savanah, either, so we got her the ring, and we got claddagh earrings for Truely because that's what she wanted.

We spend time with all the kids, except for Robyn's. Our kids miss them, but they don't have much to do with Robyn, either. Kody and Robyn even severed ties with Mykelti, who had once been so close to Robyn.

Perhaps that will change someday. Perhaps there will be a family reunion when we've all had time to recover.

There was a good ten-year stint where things had been magical, where Kody and I got along, and where Kody was a great dad. I still hope he'll step up. He has amazing kids.

And he now lives monogamy with his soulmate. I've learned there's nothing better than that.

All in all, Kody wasn't controlling. We had freedom to do what we wanted. I lived the life I wanted, and I created a great life for my kids.

I would do it all again.

Thank goodness I don't have to.

I still work to take care of myself. Before my wedding, I was five pounds away from my goal of 170 pounds because I counted calories and worked out daily. It was great—I felt so good.

Then I gained twenty back. When Garrison died, I was so sad. I just couldn't do it.

He would not want this life for me, I thought.

So I set aside one hour every day for me. I work out for at least twenty minutes with weights, walking, or my rowing machine. I break a sweat. (If I'm trying to lose weight, it's at least an hour.)

I spend at least twenty minutes in some kind of contemplative state, whether it's journaling or meditation.

And I spend at least twenty minutes in creation mode, where I bake or cook, organize a closet, or design a room.

If I hit that balance every day, it's a great day. An hour is the minimum that I give myself every day, even if I have to wake up earlier. That's happiness. That gets me through the rest of it.

Ultimately, I think the show helped our family. We all developed voices and learned to speak out. We learned to look back and think about all of it, rather than simply struggling through the day-to-day with no context.

Sometimes, I watch something now and I think, *Whoa. That was crazy.* And that helps me process.

I think *Sister Wives* has been a realistic representation of us. It has shown me at my best and my worst. You've seen me jealous, insecure, and sad, but also happy and excited. Motivated. Mediating.

The crew has been wonderful. When we left the hospital with Truely after she was born, one of the crew members rode with us. I think they think of themselves as her uncles because they've watched her grow up. We've watched them, too, as they've gone from young people to married people to people with kids. They've always done what they could to make our experience as positive as possible, even on those bad days.

But my kids are ready to be done with the show, for the most part.

"You know what?" Aspyn said. "I think I've lived your life long enough. I want to live my own life now."

Fair.

Truely was born on the show, and she has said she didn't feel like she had a choice. Now, I make room for her to decide what she'll be included in and I give her space when we film.

She was on the set once after I left Kody, and I thought, *We're not doing this.*

She's still in the background and part of activities, but she hasn't been on the set since. I don't need her to know about the show or all our stuff. I've never let her watch it, especially the last few years. Most of the other kids don't watch it, either.

I admit that I was surprised when we learned there would be another season. *How can there be anything after all that?* I thought. *What are they going to film?*

It would have been incredible to simply live my life with David.

Instead, I'm working with the producers on storylines. Maybe the starting over is the story? That hopeful bit?

So much of my life now is figuring out retirement, taking care of our vacation rental and looking for another one, and spending time with all the grandkids. Janelle and I still do things together, and we'll film that. She has her flower farm, which feels like a dream come true. I'll visit her there.

I have loved doing the show. I loved it being a part of our life. I love all the opportunities we've had. But most of all, I love the change that has come for me as a person—I love who I am today. That came from the show, and living polygamy, and all the people I've met along the way.

"I'm waiting for my David," you've told me. Thinking about the day you'll find him brings tears to my eyes.

So does thinking about the day you'll find you.

CHOCOLATE PIE HEAVEN

⅔ cup white sugar
¼ cup cornstarch
½ tsp salt
½ cup Hershey's cocoa powder
2¾ cups half & half
4 egg yolks, beaten
1 tbsp unsalted butter
2 tsp vanilla
Pie crust of choice
Whipped cream

Bake pie crust according to directions if using pastry pie crust. If using graham cracker, no need to bake. Put sugar, cornstarch, salt, and cocoa powder in a pot and whisk together. In a separate bowl, blend half & half and egg yolks, add to pot and turn burner to medium heat. Stir constantly for 6 to 8 minutes until mixture starts to boil. Slice butter into small chunks and add, stir until melted and thickened a bit. Remove from heat, add vanilla. Pour into pie crust of choice. (FYI: If you try it at this point, you will burn your mouth!) Cover pie with plastic wrap and cool in fridge until set. Serve with fresh whipped cream.

ACKNOWLEDGMENTS

I couldn't have done any of this without my family, and I'm thankful to be surrounded by people I love and who teach me daily to be better.

Janelle, thank you for your generosity in sharing your children with me. I am so grateful to be a mom to your kids. Aspyn, your exceptional balance of grace and determination inspires me. Mykelti, you are truly the strongest and most resilient person I know. Paedon, you have the biggest and kindest heart, loving everyone. Gwendlyn, you strive for justness while maintaining your wonderful humor. Ysabel, you listen and care—but refuse to let people walk over you. Truely, you are a brilliant advocate for everyone, an old soul who blesses all of us. Logan, your sense of purpose and ambition astound me. Maddie, you're determined and won't take crap from anyone. Hunter, you are a just, kind, and sincere gentleman. Garrison, I miss your jokes, hugs, humor, understanding—just you, always. Gabe, you have a brilliant mind, dissecting everything yet wanting to help people be whole. Savanah, you are the stalwart champion of the underdog. Leon, you always seek a true self-love while also loving the true essence of people. To David's children: thank you for welcoming me into your lives and letting me be an Oma to your children. Colton, you have overcome so much and still manage to be there for everyone. Kati, you're so full of laughter and love, and you're a strong, fierce mamma bear. Rae, your wisdom, thoughtfulness, and accomplishments are way beyond your years. Payton, thank you for giving me the awesome advice to stand up for myself and tell people, "I am Christine Mother &*#* Woolley . . ."—and for being so incredibly insightful with Truely.

For these couples who showed me what true love looks like (until I found mine with David): Maddie and Caleb, Mykelti and Tony, Aspyn and Mitch, Logan and Michelle, Leon and Audrey, and Gwendlyn and Benjamin.

To our grandchildren—I'm so lucky to be their Oma: Axel, Evie, Joey and Emilia, Avalon, Archer and Ace, Alice and Emma, Hudson and Paisley, Charlie, Henry, and Louis. There are more in the grandchild list, and more coming, but, hey, I gotta respect their privacy!

My family, especially my siblings, who have supported me the entire time I've been on *Sister Wives*, even when they thought it was a crazy idea: Phil, Wendy (her husband, KC, is also amazing), Steve, Danielle, Mary, Levi, Bethany, Erin, Brittany, and Breanne. My other family has also supported me in the best of ways: Beth Elaine, Wynter, Lorilyn, Genielle, Tammy, Tricia, and David's mom, Evelyn, who is an inspirational example of a lady, filled with kindness and goodness—and who doesn't put up with crap from others.

To David Tenzer, our first manager/agent, who I consider one of my truest friends: you showed me that the outside world has awesome people in it who truly have my back.

To our production team: Christopher Poole Productions (formerly Puddle Monkey) and executive producer Tim Gibbons (our first producer, who was with *Sister Wives* until two years ago—we owe the idea of the show to you and your incredible wife, Megan), executive producer Christopher Poole, and Sven Nilsson (the new producer who started after our wedding in the middle of family chaos), and the editors: Stephanie Colemere, Erin Williams, Jake Sorensen, and Jonathan Greene.

Special thanks to Figure 8 Films and TLC. I have appreciated our partnership, even though spilling my heart is ten kinds of painful. Special thanks to Laurie Goldberg, Meaghan Werner, Cassie Bryan, and Nicole Vanderploeg. At Figure 8 Films, thank you to executive producers Bill Hayes, Kirk Streb, Deanie Wilcher, and Sven Nilsson; EVP of production management Kami Winningham; supervising producers Jen Stocks and Mary Wilcher; senior producer Scott Wildfong; coordinating producer Maggie Kay; director of photography Doug Monroe: camera person Alex Walkling; audio person Keith Highley; associate producer Elijah Stordeur; and production accountant Shannon James. At Trailblazer Studios, thank you to post-production supervisor Christine Mallia and post-production coordinator Corin Warinner.

Thank you to my friends from Vegas: Deirdre, Ashli, Becky (Hayden Mae, her daughter, still calls me Mom), Connie, Alice, Michelle and Ronda, and Tina and Kimberly—the first friends I made outside my church. Thank you to my awesome girlfriends in Flagstaff; most had never even seen *Sister Wives*, and it was so refreshing to have such a supportive group of friends during an immensely hard transition in my life: Krista (her daughter, Talei, is still one of my daughters, too), Connie, Christie, and Becky.

Thank you to the members of Principal Voices for helping me understand I could live without fear. Thank you to Anne Wilde, the first feminist I ever met. And thank you to Joe Darger and his family for being cool polygamists.

Thanks to Kelly Kennedy, who helped me organize my thoughts and put them into words like she could read my mind, my heart, and my soul. Thanks to James Leonard, who first believed in my book. Thanks to Simon and Schuster—my editor, James Melia, has been incredible to work with, so easygoing and patient. And thank you to James's assistant, Matt Attanasio, editorial director Aimée Bell, publisher Jennifer Bergstrom, marketing and publicity vice president Sally Marvin, senior publicity manager Sydney Morris, marketing coordinator Fallon McKnight, senior managing editor Caroline Pallotta, senior production editor Alysha Bullock, and head of interior design Jaime Putorti. It's incredible how many people had a hand in this!

A very, very special THANK YOU to the fans of *Sister Wives*. I have been humbled so many times by the vulnerable, comforting, heartfelt messages you've shared with me. When people say they've watched the whole season—especially those of you who have watched it many times—I am overwhelmed by all the time you've spent with my family, watching our children grow up into the most wonderful humans I have ever known, all the way to the present where we are all apart and a bit broken. Thank you for looking beyond your comfort into our lives.

I'm so blessed by so many incredible people in my life. THANK YOU!